D1117814

RELIGION IN THE LIBERAL POLITY

RELIGION

IN THE

LIBERAL POLITY

TERENCE CUNEO
editor

University of Notre Dame Press

Notre Dame, Indiana

Copyright © 2005 by University of Notre Dame
Notre Dame, Indiana 46556
www.undpress.nd.edu
All Rights Reserved

Manufactured in the United States of America

Library of Congress Cataloging-in-Publication Data

Religion in the liberal polity / edited by Terence Cuneo.
p.   cm.
Includes bibliographical references and index.
ISBN 0-268-02288-7 (cloth : alk. paper)
ISBN 0-268-02289-5 (pbk. : alk. paper)
1. Human rights—Religious aspects—Christianity.
2. Christianity and politics.   I. Cuneo, Terence, 1969–
BT738.15.R55   2004
201'.723—dc22
2004023682

∞ *This book is printed on acid-free paper.*

For Nicholas Wolterstorff

With esteem, affection, and gratitude

CONTENTS

CONTRIBUTORS

Terence Cuneo is Assistant Professor of Philosophy at Calvin College. He is the co-editor of *The Cambridge Companion to Thomas Reid* (Cambridge University Press, 2004) and the author of a number of articles in ethical theory and early modern philosophy.

Christopher J. Eberle is Assistant Professor of Philosophy at the U.S. Naval Academy. Eberle is the author of numerous articles in political philosophy and religion, as well as *Religious Convictions in Liberal Politics* (Cambridge University Press, 2002).

Kent Greenawalt is Professor of Law at Columbia Law School. His books include *Religious Convictions and Political Choice* (Oxford University Press, 1988), *Conflicts of Law and Morality* (Oxford University Press, 1989), *Private Consciences and Public Reasons* (Oxford University Press, 1995), *Law and Objectivity* (Oxford University Press, 1995), and *Fighting Words* (Princeton University Press, 1996).

John Hare is Noah Porter Professor of Philosophical Theology at Yale University. He is the author of *Ethics and International Affairs* (Macmillan, 1982), *The Moral Gap* (Oxford University Press, 1998), *God's Call* (Eerdmans, 2001), and *Why Bother Being Good?* (Intervarsity Press, 2002).

Timothy P. Jackson is Associate Professor of Christian Ethics in the Candler School of Theology, Emory University. He is the author of *Love Disconsoled* (Cambridge University Press, 1999) and *The Priority of Love: Christian Charity and Social Justice* (Princeton University Press, 2003).

Richard J. Mouw is president of Fuller Theological Seminary. He is the author of *The God Who Commands* (University of Notre Dame Press, 1990), *Uncommon Decency* (Intervarsity Press, 1992), and *He Shines in All That's Fair: Culture and Common Grace* (Eerdmans, 2001).

Mark C. Murphy is Associate Professor of Philosophy at Georgetown University. He is the author of numerous articles in political philosophy and ethics. His books include *Natural Law and Practical Rationality* (Cambridge University Press, 2001) and *Divine Authority* (Cornell University Press, 2002).

Jeffrey Stout is Professor of Religious Studies at Princeton University. His books include *The Flight from Authority* (University of Notre Dame Press, 1981), *Ethics after Babel* (Princeton University Press, 2001), and *Democracy and Tradition* (Princeton University Press, 2003).

Paul Weithman is Associate Professor of Philosophy at the University of Notre Dame. In addition to many articles on political philosophy and ethics, he is the author of *Religion and the Obligations of Citizenship* (Cambridge University Press, 2002) and editor of *Religion and Contemporary Liberalism* (University of Notre Dame Press, 1997) and (with Henry Richardson) *The Philosophy of John Rawls* (5 volumes, Garland, 1999).

Merold Westphal is Distinguished Professor of Philosophy, Fordham University. His numerous books include *Kierkegaard's Critique of Reason and Society* (Penn State University Press, 1991), *Hegel, Freedom and Modernity* (State University of New York Press, 1992), *Becoming a Self: A Reading of Kierkegaard's Concluding Unscientific Postscript* (Purdue University Press, 1996), and *Overcoming Onto-Theology* (Fordham University Press, 2001).

Nicholas Wolterstorff is Noah Porter Professor of Philosophical Theology, emeritus, Yale University. He is the author of many articles and books on philosophy of religion, epistemology, history of modern philosophy, aesthetics, and political philosophy. His books on political philosophy include *Until Justice and Peace Embrace* (Eerdmans, 1983), *Religion in the Public Square* (with Robert Audi) (Rowman and Littlefield, 1997), and a work in progress entitled *Justice: Human and Divine*.

INTRODUCTION

TERENCE CUNEO

Forty years ago philosophy of religion was nearly given up for dead. Strange things happen in the academy, however, and the last thirty years have witnessed a remarkable revival of the discipline. Indeed, not since the high medieval period have we seen such a flowering of creative and incisive work on, among other things, the existence and nature of God, the problem of evil, and the rationality of religious belief. Nevertheless, the revival has had its limitations. In particular, there has been relatively little recent philosophical work done on the relations between politics and religion. The aim of this book is to help fill this gap.

That there has been comparatively little recent philosophical work done on the relations between politics and religion is surprising, for political philosophy itself has undergone a renaissance of sorts in the last thirty years. Since the publication of John Rawls's *A Theory of Justice* in 1971, *liberalism* in particular has been developed and defended with considerable sophistication and care. Why, then, has there not been a more extensive interchange between these two recently revived disciplines? The answer to this question is not entirely clear. Perhaps, however, one clue is this: although the revivals of philosophy of religion and political philosophy share a similar recent history, they have been marked by rather different aims and philosophical visions. Contemporary philosophy of religion has been largely a reclamation project. The task has been primarily to rediscover

1

and develop lines of thought originally developed in the period running from the ancients through the Reformation. Contemporary political philosophy, by contrast, has not looked backward in the same fashion. Indeed, a striking feature of a prominent strain of contemporary liberal theory—a broadly pragmatist strain that includes the work of otherwise diverse figures such as John Rawls and Richard Rorty—is a deep-seated reluctance to engage in what we might call "traditional" political philosophy. Whereas Plato, Aristotle, Aquinas, Locke, Mill, and Marx viewed political philosophy as a branch of ethics, philosophers such as Rawls and Rorty do not. To the contrary, these philosophers endeavor to avoid saying anything in defense of certain core liberal ideas that appeal to what Rawls calls a "comprehensive doctrine"—roughly, a contested, substantive view about the nature of the just, the human good, or God.[1]

But if the task of the political philosopher is not the traditional one of offering defenses of particular conceptions of the just and the human good grounded in particular comprehensive doctrines, what is it? The primary task of the political philosopher, suggests Rawls, is to excavate the "political culture": to mine the fund of ideas about the just and the human good that is implicit in the shared political culture of a liberal democracy so as to arrive at a conception of what Rawls calls "political justice."[2] To this Rawls and others add an exhortation: when engaging in public discourse on constitutional essentials and matters of basic justice, citizens of a liberal polity should avoid appealing exclusively to comprehensive doctrines as well. Rather, when engaging in such discourse, what citizens of a liberal democracy ought to do is appeal to a fund of ideas about the just and the human good that is implicit in the shared political culture of that liberal democracy.

But why this rejection of the aims of traditional political philosophy? Why this reluctance to appeal to comprehensive doctrines when engaging in political theorizing or public political discussion concerning certain types of issues? In Rorty's case the answer is clear: the project of doing traditional moral philosophy and theology is dead. And in its train comes the death of traditional political philosophy. Rorty thus recommends that we simply abandon traditional justifications for core liberal doctrines such as the existence of universal human rights in favor of the idea that denizens of twenty-first-century liberal democracies make themselves more powerful and persuasive to others—even if it means "manipulating [the] sentiments" of others.[3] In Rawls's case, the answer to these questions is less iconoclastic: we live, says Rawls, in a pluralist culture characterized by deep and ineliminable doctrinal conflict—*reasonable* deep and ineliminable doctrinal conflict. Accordingly, the hope of coming to any sort of stable consensus on matters of the human good and basic justice by appeal to any of these doctrines is at best highly unlikely. Better, then, suggests Rawls, to appeal to ideas implicit in our shared political culture to forge a common conception of political justice. And better to appeal to such ideas when engaging in public political discussion on constitutional essentials and matters of basic justice. Only then does a citizen of a liberal democracy guarantee that her views are intelligible to her fellow citizens. And only then does she express toward them the sort of respect necessary for any liberal democracy to flourish.

Thus understood, liberal theory has provoked three types of response from philosophers and theologians with religious concerns. Some have attempted to accommodate important features of the Rawlsian program by endorsing the idea that, when engaging in public dialogue on coercive law or public policy, religious persons ought to appeal to nonreligious reasons accessible and intelligible to any reasonable person.[4] Others with more radical sensibilities have claimed that religious folk should reject liberalism outright.[5] Finally, there are still others who wish to embrace liberalism, but reject the idea that when theorizing or engaging in political dialogue of certain kinds, we ought not to appeal to comprehensive religious perspectives.[6] Definitive of the latter two responses is the conviction that there is no shared political culture, no "public reason" extensive and rich enough to undergird the basic principles of justice in a liberal democracy. The case, instead, is this: when defending and developing core liberal claims such as the centrality of human rights or engaging in public political discourse, we have no choice but to appeal to particular comprehensive doctrines on the nature of the just and the human good.

Appealing to comprehensive perspective when theorizing and debating in the public square is, according to these thinkers, not only unavoidable but salutary. For example, it is frequently pointed out that core liberal doctrines such as the universality and inalienability of certain human rights have had their roots in religious soil. Sever the root, it is claimed, and the sap that has nourished liberalism dries up.[7] Granted, it doesn't immediately follow from this that the core liberal doctrines have no other kind of justification. But three questions arise for anyone who is at once both a liberal and religious: are there, within secular comprehensive doctrines, accounts of human rights, the nature of justice, and the like that can justify core liberal practices and doctrines in the way that religious accounts traditionally have? And how should persons who espouse both liberalism and traditional theism develop theistic strategies of supporting these core liberal doctrines? Finally, is it appropriate for a religious believer to appeal to these religious reasons when debating matters of coercive law in the liberal polity? These are the questions that the essays in this volume are concerned to answer.

I. Foundations: Rights and Authority

Common to liberal theory of all sorts is the thesis that human beings have rights of various sorts, and that the possession of these rights accounts for the fact that we have obligations of certain types. It is precisely this claim, however, on which many of liberalism's critics focus their attack. Alasdair MacIntyre, for example, goes so far as to claim that "human rights are fictions" akin to witches and unicorns.[8] Likewise, the theologian Joan Lockwood O'Donovan maintains that Christians should dispense with the concept of a right.[9] Finally, Annette Baier argues that, although rights are real enough, they are not deep in the moral universe. Rather "rights are only the tip of the moral iceberg, supported by the responsibilities that we cooperatively discharge and by the individual responsibilities that we recognize. . . ."[10]

In the opening essay, "God, Justice, and Duty," Nicholas Wolterstorff disputes all of these claims. Wolterstorff argues not only that rights exist, but also that moral duties are determined by rights. In some cases, the rights in question are those possessed by individual human beings. In other cases, the rights in question are those possessed only by God. But what reason does a theist have to believe that rights are ontologically more fundamental than duties? Wolterstorff's strategy is to make his case by engaging the divine command theory, central to which are two claims: first, that moral obligations are grounded solely in God's commands and, second, that moral obligations are ontologically more fundamental than rights. In response, Wolterstorff points out that not just anyone's commands are authoritative for us. So what makes it the case that God's commands are authoritative? God's commands are authoritative for us, contends Wolterstorff, only if God has certain "standing rights." It is these standing rights that give God a claim to our obedience and, hence, put us under obligation to obey God's commands. God's standing rights, though, are not themselves grounded in God's commands; it is not as if a certain range of God's commands have authority simply because God issues some further command to obey that range of commands. We could, after all, ask of this command: why is it authoritative? And so on for each additional command. The consequence is that there is at least one obligation that is not simply the product of God's command, namely, the obligation to obey what God commands. If this is true, however, a theist ought not to believe that rights are at the "tip of the moral iceberg." Rather, they are what lie deepest in moral reality.

In "The Image of God and the Soul of Humanity: Reflections on Dignity, Sanctity, and Democracy," Timothy P. Jackson raises the issue of how a Christian should think about the *imago dei* and how it might ground human rights. Central to Jackson's discussion is the distinction between a person's sanctity and her dignity. Although both concepts have been used interchangeably in recent theological and philosophical discussion, Jackson argues that they are not identical. A person's sanctity, Jackson contends, is her need to receive love and the potential to give it, while a person's dignity is the worth grounded in the actual extension of her love to others and herself. Thus understood, a person's sanctity is more fundamental than her dignity: it is the ground of human rights and, according to Jackson, the image of God in human beings. In so arguing, Jackson rejects two major tendencies in philosophy and theology. In the first place, by restoring the concept of sanctity to our moral lexicon, Jackson wishes to offer a corrective to secular theorists such as Ronald Dworkin and Peter Singer, who have more or less ignored the concept in favor of that of dignity. Second, by identifying the *imago dei* with sanctity, Jackson rejects a major strain of Western Christian thought in which the image of God is identified with a person's intellect or will. The essay closes by contending that although the very young, old, challenged, and guilty may not possess dignity, they do possess sanctity. Accordingly, such persons enjoy "sanctity" rights and are due the provisions and protections of a liberal democracy.

John Hare's "Evolutionary Naturalism and Reducing the Demand of Justice" picks up the theme, sounded in Jackson's essay, about whether there is a plausible secular account of natural right and justice that can support a liberal democracy. Hare proposes that we consider two naturalistic, evolutionary accounts of natural right and justice: those developed by Larry Arnhart and Michael Ruse, respectively. Arnhart's "Aristotelian" view attempts to ground justice in a natural desire for "reciprocity." However, Hare contends that Arnhart's position is open to several objections, among which is that, in Arnhart's view, our natural desire for reciprocity is simply a desire for what has utility of a certain kind. But the useful and the just often come apart. So we cannot ground the demands of justice in a desire for reciprocity. In contrast to Arnhart, Michael Ruse contends that the objectivity of the demands of justice is a projective illusion. Nonetheless, Ruse says belief in the objective demands of justice is *adaptive* for us. In response, Hare argues that, on the assumption that Ruse's view is correct, anyone who sees it as correct has an epistemic reason to believe that justice does not make objective demands of us. Thus, Ruse's view has the untoward consequence that these people both ought and ought not to believe in the objectivity of the demands of justice. They ought to believe in the objectivity of the demands of justice insofar as so believing is adaptive and ought not to so believe because it is false that the demands of justice are objective. Hare closes with the speculation that empirical evidence supports the view that, if ordinary persons were to believe Ruse's view, they would tend not to act in ways that are just.

Paul Weithman's contribution, "Why Should Christians Endorse Human Rights?" is also concerned with rights, but primarily with what we call "civil liberties"—such as rights to speak freely, rights to assemble peaceably for legitimate purposes, and rights of association. Weithman contends that individuals who have rights are simultaneously protected and liberated by the possession of those rights: on the one hand, they are protected from harms of certain kinds and, on the other, left free to engage in conduct of certain types. As it happens, Christian theorists such as Wolterstorff and Michael Perry have primarily stressed the protective function of the possession of rights. But while the possession of rights does serve a protective function, Weithman argues that Christians have excellent reason to emphasize its liberating function. In particular, Christians should value people's ability to assure themselves that their most fundamental commitments are authentically their own. This can be done, however, only if people enjoy considerable freedom to assess and critically scrutinize these commitments. But people are able to assure themselves that their most fundamental commitments are authentically their own only if these rights are honored by the government and other powerful entities and individuals. So Christians should endorse the claim that people have rights or civil liberties of certain kinds.

My own essay, "Can a Natural Law Theorist Justify Religious Civil Liberties?" extends some of the themes in Weithman's contribution. My aim is twofold: I argue, in the first place, that recent attempts by natural law theorists to ground religious civil liberties in the so-called basic good of religion are unpersuasive. Contrary to what Robert George, John Finnis, Germain Grisez, Mark Murphy, and other natural law theorists claim, I argue that there is no basic good of religion. I contend, in the second place, that natural theorists can nevertheless offer a multipronged justification for the provision and protection of religious civil liberties. In short, my claim is that participating in religious traditions of certain kinds can be a manner by which we participate in other basic goods. Moreover, I argue that participation in religious traditions of certain kinds is crucially important for the formation and sustenance of what I call "effective identities"—identities that allow us to discern salient features of situations, formulate sufficiently clear priorities among ends, implement action plans that have a reasonable chance of realizing ends, and so on. As such, the formation and sustenance of effective identities is something the state should have a great interest in. Accordingly, all other things being equal, the state ought to provide and protect religious civil liberties.

These essays by Wolterstorff, Jackson, Hare, Weithman, and Cuneo all emphasize that an agent's possessing rights of certain kinds puts some limitations on the way the state and other powerful groups and individuals can treat that agent. In the final essay in this section, "The Renunciation of Conscience," Mark Murphy considers the flip side of this issue. Rather than ask what sorts of rights individual agents have vis-à-vis the state and other agents, Murphy considers the nature of the demands that the state can make on individual agents. Using Nicholas Wolterstorff's Stone Lectures, *Dual Citizenship, Dual Nationality,* as a springboard, Murphy asks how Christians ought to negotiate the sometimes conflicting demands of divine and political authority. The position defended by most traditional theists is that, if an agent reasonably believes that the demands of divine authority conflict with those of the state, she ought to accede to what she takes to be the demands of divine authority. But not all Christians have thought as much. Thomas Hobbes, for example, argued at length that, if an agent reasonably believes that the demands of God and the state conflict, that agent ought to capitulate to what she takes to be the demands of the state. Hobbes's arguments for this claim, contends Murphy, are surprisingly powerful and require us to think much harder about why a Christian is sometimes entitled to refuse to do what the state demands. Murphy concludes that, despite its power, Hobbes's view is unacceptable to a Christian, for if one were to accept it, one would be cut off from friendship with God.

II. Religious Reasons and Virtuous Conduct in the Liberal Polity

If the essays in the first part of this volume are a response to the reticence on the part of some prominent liberal theorists to engage in traditional political philosophy, those in the second part are a response to another type of reticence that characterizes much of contemporary liberal thought. This second sort of reticence is a general tendency on the part of many liberal theorists to avoid treating substantive epistemological issues in any detail. Of course, avoiding substantive epistemological issues is perfectly appropriate if they have little bearing on one's philosophical project. But this is manifestly not the case with respect to many liberal theorists, for central to numerous forms of liberalism is an important epistemological claim that we can call the "public justification thesis." This thesis tells us that respecting our fellow citizens requires that, when we support coercive laws of certain kinds in the public arena, we offer them reasons that they can accept. In particular, the reasons we offer must be "intelligible" or "accessible" to other "reasonable" agents or persons who are "adequately informed and fully rational."[11] Since religious reasons fail to satisfy these criteria, they are not to be used (or used exclusively) in public discourse of certain kinds.

The central thesis of Jeffrey Stout's "Religious Reasons in Political Argument" is that, insofar as liberals have offered any account of substantive epistemic concepts to buttress the public justification thesis, their accounts have been overly restrictive. Take, for example, what Rawls says about the "reasonable." Rawls glosses "reasonable people" as such: ". . . knowing that people are reasonable where others are concerned, we know that they are willing to govern their conduct by a principle from which they and others can reason in common."[12] Apparently for Rawls, being reasonable means appealing to certain kinds of principles that are implicit in the shared political culture of a liberal democracy. However, Stout contends, surely one can be entitled to reject this account of the reasonable and its implications. Consider in this regard some of our best examples of civic discourse such as Lincoln's Second Inaugural speech, which appear to touch upon matters of basic justice and weigh in favor of certain coercive policies.[13] Civic discourse of this sort appears not to conform to the Rawlsian account of the reasonable. Rather, speeches such as Lincoln's clearly express the speaker's religious convictions and engage in immanent critique of opponents' religious and moral views by appealing to considerations that do not comprise "public reason." Since appealing to religious reasons and engaging in immanent critique are important ways of respectfully engaging in public discourse with the views of others—especially when they are themselves religious—any account of the public justification thesis that rules them out is flawed.

Christopher Eberle's essay, "What Does Respect Require?" grapples with Gerald Gaus's recent attempt to defend the public justification thesis. As Eberle notes, Gaus is one of the few liberal theorists who explicitly recognizes that the public justification thesis relies on substantive epistemological views about what "good reasons" are in public political discourse. Gaus's view is also noteworthy insofar as it is a sophisticated attempt to motivate and defend these views. In defending the public justification thesis, Gaus attempts to avoid two extremes: on the one hand, he attempts to avoid a "populist" view according to which good reasons are those that everyone agrees to, and, on the other hand, a "God's-eye" view according to which good reasons are those that fully idealized agents in fully idealized conditions would accept. Gaus's proposal attempts to strike a median between these two extremes. In Gaus's view, a good reason is a claim an agent is justified in accepting given her system of beliefs as corrected by evidence she regards as having evidential force. Eberle counters by arguing that Gaus's middling proposal is arbitrary: it offers us no cogent reason to idealize away from some of our actual beliefs (as Gaus would have it) rather than all of them. Eberle argues, furthermore, that liberals who wish to claim that there is something inappropriate about appealing only to religious reasons in public political discourse of certain kinds face a general problem. Neither the appeal to populist views, God's-eye views, nor positions that combine elements of both views provide good reasons to accept the public justification thesis.

In his contribution, "Religious Convictions and Public Discourse," Richard Mouw explores issues of public justification as they arise in a somewhat different context. Mouw considers the ways in which Roman Catholic theologians and Reformed thinkers have taken very different approaches to the propriety of appealing to religious reasons in public discourse. Interestingly enough, Catholic thinkers such as John Courtney Murray have arrived at something like the public justification thesis by appealing to natural law principles that have their home in a religious context. According to these thinkers, the principles of natural law dictate that when the church speaks on certain issues in the public domain, it should use nonreligious language that the state can comprehend. The natural law approach, however, has come under fire by other Catholic thinkers such as Michael Baxter, who contend that not only is it permissible, but it is also important that Christians use religious discourse in the public arena—even if the content of this discourse is not fully intelligible to others. Mouw presents Nicholas Wolterstorff's broadly Calvinist view as striking a middle position between those of Murray and Baxter. Mouw urges, however, that Wolterstorff's broadly Calvinist view is in need of supplementation. In particular, suggests Mouw, the concept of common grace that figures so prominently in certain strains of Reformed thought can be a rich resource for Christian thinkers who wish to avoid the excesses of both Murray's and Baxter's approaches.

Stout, Eberle, and Mouw, then, reject the public justification thesis in favor of the claim that it is sometimes appropriate to appeal simply to religious reasons when supporting coercive law in the public domain. Kent Greenawalt's essay, "Religion and the Public School Teacher," raises the question of whether public school teachers ought to adhere to something like the public justification thesis when in the classroom. As his point of departure, Greenawalt considers Nicholas Wolterstorff's suggestion that public schools should be impartial with respect to religion insofar as they ought not to have as their purpose the approval or disapproval of any citizen's religion or irreligion. This formulation of impartiality leaves open the question of whether public school teachers should, as employees of the public school, aspire to be impartial in this same sense when in the classroom. Greenawalt contends that this question is an especially difficult one that fully exploits a tension between a teacher being an employee of the public school and the difficulty—or psychological impossibility—of not allowing one's "control beliefs" regarding religion to bear upon one's own teaching and scholarship. After canvassing several ways of attempting to address the tension, Greenawalt closes by suggesting that, given her power and role as employee of the public school, the school teacher should aspire to restrain the expression of her own religious views when in the classroom.

Of all the civic virtues the possession of which is necessary for the good functioning of a liberal democracy, liberal theorists tend to emphasize *civility* as being especially important. Indeed, one might view the liberal's attraction to the public justification thesis as being motivated by the concern that, when debating in the public square, we conduct ourselves in a civil fashion.[14] Merold Westphal's essay, "Shame as a Political Virtue," aims to correct what he views as an over-emphasis on the virtue of civility in contemporary liberal theory and the neglect of the political virtue of shame in both the liberal tradition and the history of philosophy more generally. In contrast to the Confucian tradition, Western philosophers have failed nearly unanimously to appreciate the virtue of shame. As Westphal argues, neither Aristotle, Spinoza, Nietzsche, nor Sartre succeeds in seeing shame's importance; to the contrary, they offer us inadequate accounts of it. An exception to this general trend, suggests Westphal, is Emmanuel Levinas, who offers us a nuanced account of shame as a political virtue—an account, it should be noted, that refuses to separate comprehensive moral doctrines from political philosophy. It is an account, Westphal concludes, that Christian political theorists would do well to heed.

III. Acknowledgments

This book has its origin in the seminar "Political Philosophy after Liberalism," led by Nicholas Wolterstorff at Calvin College in the summer of 1998 and sponsored by the PEW Charitable Trusts. Four of the essays included in this volume (those by Cuneo, Eberle, Murphy, and Wolterstorff) are the result of work done in that seminar.

For the various types of support they provided, I would like to thank the PEW Charitable Trusts and Susan Felch, former Director of the Calvin Summer Seminars in Christian Scholarship at Calvin College. And while work on this book was completed at Calvin, I should like to express my thanks to the two institutions at which most of the work on this project took place, the Vrije Universiteit, Amsterdam, and Seattle Pacific University. Seattle Pacific University, in particular, provided a Faculty Research Grant that supported work done on this project during its latter stages.

I have already mentioned that Nick Wolterstorff's seminar in the summer of 1998 was the seed from which this book grew. In fact, however, Nick's influence on this project extends far beyond this. In some cases, as in the essays by Murphy, Stout, Mouw, and Greenawalt, this influence is explicit. In all cases, however, it is at least implicit, for all of the contributors to this volume (with the exception of Nick himself!) have either been colleagues, students, or discussion partners with Nick on matters of politics and religion. As one of the few philosophers working in mainstream contemporary philosophy of religion who has turned his attention to issues of political philosophy, Nick has taught us all how to think about how the religious person should conduct herself in, and conceive of, the liberal polity.

A theme deep in Nick's work is that if the religious person is to discern how she ought to conduct herself in, and conceive of, the liberal polity, then she will need to pay close attention to what justice is and how it should be implemented in society.[15] However, Nick has not only written about this subject profoundly, he has also lived out his views in the connections he has made with South Africa and the Palestinians as well as closer to home in the institutions where he has worked. He embodies the conviction that philosophy and the intellectual life matter and that this importance is plain and does not require any special defense.[16] Since Nick's life and work have been responsible in so many ways for this book's publication, I dedicate it to him.

NOTES

I thank Chris Eberle, Steve Layman, and Luke Reinsma for comments on an earlier draft of this introduction.

1. Although, admittedly, the extent to which Rawls rejects the aims and methods of traditional political philosophy is a matter of some controversy. Paul Weithman's essay "Liberalism and the Political Character of Political Philosophy," in *Liberalism and the Good*, ed. R. Bruce Douglass, Gerald M. Mara, and Henry S. Richardson (New York: Routledge, 1990), contends that the rejection is only partial. Jean Hampton's essay in the same volume, "Should Political Philosophy Be Done without Metaphysics?" argues otherwise.

2. For Rawls, "political justice" is a term of art. In an essay published after *Political Liberalism* (New York: Columbia University Press, 1993), Rawls writes that political conceptions of justice have three features: "First, their principles apply to basic political and social institutions (the basic structure of society); second, they can be presented independently from comprehensive doctrines of any kind (although they may, of course, be supported by a reasonable overlapping consensus of such doctrines); and finally, they can be worked out from fundamental ideas seen as implicit in the public political culture of a constitutional regime, such as the conceptions of citizens as free and equal persons, and of society as a fair system of cooperation" (John Rawls, "The Idea of Public Reason Revisited," *The University of Chicago Law Review* 63 [1997]: 767).

3. "Human Rights, Rationality, and Sentimentality," in *On Human Rights: The 1993 Oxford Amnesty Lectures,* ed. Susan Hurley and Stephen Shute (New York: Basic Books, 1993), 122.

4. See especially Robert Audi's contribution to *Religion in the Public Square: The Place of Religious Convictions in Political Debate* (Lanham, Md.: Rowman and Littlefield, 1997) and his *Religious Commitment and Secular Reason* (Cambridge: Cambridge University Press, 2000). In *Love and Power* (Oxford: Oxford University Press, 1988), Michael Perry also endorses this view—although Perry has since changed his mind. Paul Weithman, in his introduction to *Religion and Contemporary Liberalism* (Notre Dame, Ind.: University of Notre Dame Press, 1997), also expresses some sympathy with the Rawlsian approach, as does Phil Quinn in "Religious Citizens within the Limits of Public Reason," *Modern Schoolman* 78 (January/March 2001).

5. See Stanley Hauerwas and William Willimon, *Resident Aliens* (Nashville, Tenn.: Abingdon Press, 1989); Oliver O'Donovan, *The Desire of the Nations* (Cambridge: Cambridge University Press, 1996); John Milbank, *Theology and Social Theory* (Oxford: Blackwell, 1993); and Alasdair MacIntyre, *Whose Justice? Which Rationality?* (Notre Dame, Ind.: University of Notre Dame Press, 1988).

6. See Nicholas Wolterstorff's contribution to *Religion in the Public Square;* Christopher Eberle, *Religious Conviction in Liberal Politics* (Cambridge: Cambridge University Press, 2002); Timothy Jackson, "The Return of the Prodigal? Liberal Theory and Religious Pluralism," in *Religion and Contemporary Liberalism;* Philip Quinn, "Political Liberalisms and Their Exclusions of the Religious," also in *Religion and Contemporary Liberalism;* and, Stephen Carter, *The Culture of Disbelief* (New York: Basic Books, 1993).

7. See Glenn Tinder, *The Political Meaning of Christianity* (San Francisco: Harper Collins, 1991).

8. *After Virtue,* 2d ed. (Notre Dame, Ind: University of Notre Dame Press, 1984), 70.

9. "The Concept of Rights in Christian Moral Discourse," in *Preserving Grace,* ed. Michael Cromartie (Grand Rapids, Mich.: Eerdmans, 1997).

10. "Claims, Rights, Responsibilities," in *Prospects for a Common Morality,* ed. Gene Outka and John P. Reeder (Princeton: Princeton University Press, 1993), 168.

11. The latter quotation is from Robert Audi, "The Place of Religious Argument in a Free and Democratic Society," *San Diego Law Review* 30 (1993): 689.

12. *Political Liberalism,* 49, n. 1.

13. As Stout notes, Rawls denies this claim.

14. This motivation for adhering to the public justification thesis comes out most explicitly in Paul Weithman's introduction to *Religion and Contemporary Liberalism.*

15. For Wolterstorff's work on justice, see especially *Until Justice and Peace Embrace* (Grand Rapids, Mich.: Eerdmans, 1983); *Educating for Life: Reflections on Christian Teaching and Learning,* ed. Gloria Stronks and Clarence W. Joldersma (Grand Rapids, Mich.: Baker Book House, 2002); "Christianity and Social Justice," *Christian Scholar's Review* 16 (March 1987); "Justice as a Condition of Authentic Liturgy," *Theology Today* 48 (April 1991); "The Contours of Justice: An Ancient Call for *Shalom,*" in *God and the Victim,* ed. Lisa Barnes Lampman (Grand Rapids, Mich.: Eerdmans, 1999), and the articles cited in the bibliography to this book.

16. I thank John Hare for these words.

PART I

FOUNDATIONS:
RIGHTS AND AUTHORITY

GOD, JUSTICE, AND DUTY

NICHOLAS WOLTERSTORFF

I

My project in this essay is to probe one aspect of the connections among justice, duty, and God—one aspect of how justice and obligation relate to each other and fit into a theistic framework. Before I can explain what aspect that is, I must explain what I have in mind, here in this inquiry, by justice; different people have different things in mind when they speak of justice.

I have in mind not justice as a virtue but justice as an attribute of social relationships. Which attribute? That which consists in the persons who stand in that relationship possessing or experiencing what is theirs—to use the language of the ancient Roman jurists (*suum cuique*). In other words, possessing or experiencing what belongs to them, what is due them. In the case of retributive justice, that which is due them is some "evil"; in the other cases—call the other cases *positive* justice—that which is due them is some life-good. If it is a life-good that is due them, then what is due them is what they have a right to, what they are entitled to. If it is an "evil," what is due them is that which is their desert. My discussion will assume that some rights are natural, that is, not conferred by law, custom, or anything else of the sort; I recognize that this assumption is controversial.

It will prove helpful to bring one additional concept into the picture. When a person fails to do what he ought to do, he is guilty; guilt is the dark side of obligation. What is the dark side of rights? When someone does not possess or experience those life-goods to which she has a right, what is her condition? She is *wronged. Being wronged* is the dark side of rights, the dark side of positive justice.

This identifies the sort of justice that I will be talking about. It does not tell us what justice is, thus understood; it does not explain it or illuminate it. My own view, which here I must express in near-epigrammatic form, is that (positive) justice is what respect for the worth of persons requires; one treats a person unjustly when one fails to treat him or her in the way that respect for the worth of one and another aspect of the person requires. Other writers have offered essentially the same account. Here, for example, is a passage from Jean Hampton: "*A person wrongs another if and only if (while acting as a responsible agent) she treats him in a way that is objectively demeaning . . . that is, disrespectful of [that individual's] worth.*"[1]

My project is to offer an answer to the most fundamental question concerning the connections among justice, thus understood, and obligation, that is, *moral* obligation: which is deeper in the moral universe, justice or obligation? Are moral rights ultimately grounded in moral duties or moral duties in moral rights? Or is neither grounded in the other? Are justice and obligation two equally fundamental dimensions of the moral universe, interrelated, of course, but distinct in such a way that neither is grounded in the other? And, assuming that one of the two ultimately grounds the other, how is God related to that which is deepest? Does bringing God into the picture have implications for which of the two, justice or obligation, must be regarded as deepest?

People disagree more even about God than about justice. My own understanding of God is a Christian understanding. But the facet of the Christian understanding of God that will be pivotal in my discussion is a facet common to the Judaic, Christian, and Muslim understandings of God. God, as understood by all the Abrahamic religions, is a God who speaks; specifically, God is one who issues commands and injunctions to us human beings, who makes promises to us and covenants with us. If God does indeed speak in this manner, what are the implications for our understanding of how justice and obligation are related to each other and to God?

II

As preparation for our discussion, we must consider to what extent duties and rights are the correlatives of each other. Begin with this question: if one person has a right against another to some life-good, is it then the case that the latter has a duty to try to bring it about that the former possesses or experiences that good? Is there, in that way, a duty correlative to every right?

It all depends on whether it is subjective or objective duty that we have in mind. Suppose that a person in prison is innocent; justice has miscarried. Suppose also that though he is innocent, nobody in the criminal justice system has acted culpably. All the evidence available at the time pointed to his guilt; his innocence is not established until twenty years later by a DNA test unavailable at the time of his conviction. People not guilty of a crime have a right to the liberty of freedom of movement. Yet it is not the case that those who imprisoned this person have violated their obligations. Quite to the contrary: they have done what they ought to have done. So this is a case in which a person has a right to the life-good of moving about freely whereas his jailers, by keeping him imprisoned, are not only not violating their obligation but are in fact fulfilling their obligation. Had they not imprisoned him, they would have been culpable.

Only if we have our eye on what is customarily called "subjective" duty is that true, however. The objective fact of the matter, unknown to the criminal justice system when it convicted him, is that he should not be in prison. Since he is innocent, he ought not to be imprisoned. Objectively speaking, it is the obligation of the system, as is the case with all innocent people, to grant him his right to freedom of movement. And in general, it appears to me to be the case that if one person has a right against another person to some good, then, though that latter person may not have a *subjective* duty to play his part in bringing it about that the person possesses or experiences that good, *objectively* speaking that is his duty.

The converse is not the case; a person may have an objective duty to try to bring it about that someone possesses or experiences some life-good without that latter person having a right against the first to that good. There are duties without corresponding rights—*being guilty* on account of treating a person a certain way without that person *being wronged* by one's treating them that way.

Begin with the point made by Joel Feinberg in the following passage:

> When a traffic signal directs me to stop, it is difficult to find an assignable person who can plausibly claim my stopping as his own due. The original legislators may be long dead, and if vision is clear and no other motorists are in sight, there is no other person to whose right of way I owe respect. In short, I have a legal duty of obedience that is correlated with no other person's right against me.[2]

I find the claim made here either not relevant to our purposes or not convincing. Let us assume that, in this case, one's legal duty of obedience is also one's moral duty. It's true that no individual person's right is violated if I proceed cautiously through a red traffic signal at three o'clock in the morning when "vision is clear and no other motorists are in sight." But rights attach not only to persons but to groups of persons and institutions. The state has a right to the good of drivers obeying its traffic laws. That is the right I violate in proceeding through the red light; I am guilty on account of having violated that right of the state. Perhaps Feinberg quite intentionally meant to make a claim only about persons; if so, what he said is correct but not relevant to my project here, since I want to speak about rights in general, not only about those attached to persons. On the other hand, perhaps he meant to be talking about rights in general, even though he happened to mention only persons. Then what he says is not correct.

Consider an example of a different sort. Suppose that you are a lifeguard at the beach on a windy day and you see two people, at some distance from each other but equidistant from you, struggling for their lives in the surf. It is obvious to you that you cannot save both; there is a fighting chance that you can save one if you plunge in immediately and head for one. Neither of these two swimmers, call them Rick and Rich, has a right to your trying to save him. If you try to save Rick but not Rich, it cannot be claimed that you have violated Rich's right to your trying to save him; if you try to save Rich but not Rick, it cannot be claimed that you have violated Rick's right to your trying to save him. Yet if you do nothing, you are guilty—guilty of not having tried to save either Rick or Rich.

But perhaps the correct analysis is not that this is an example of a duty without a correlative right but that the correlative right is of a different sort from that which we just now took it to be. It's true that neither Rick nor Rich has the right to your trying to save him. But what about this different, conditional, right: the right to your trying to save him if you do not try to save the other? It would appear that both Rick and Rich have this conditional right. If you make no attempt to save either, then each has been deprived of that right; each has been wronged.[3] Your duty as lifeguard can be seen as grounded in those rights.

Third-party promises offer clear counterexamples to the principle we are considering, that if someone has an objective duty to try to bring it about that someone possesses or experiences some life-good, then the latter person has a right against the first to that good. For suppose that X promises Y to try to bring it about that Z possesses or experiences good G. If the only thing relevant to the situation is X's promise, Z does not have a right against X to G; indeed, Z does not have a right against anybody to that good. The right in the situation belongs to Y: Y has a right against X to the good of X's doing what X promised Y that he would do.

X, on the other hand, has a duty not only with respect to Y but also with respect to Z: his duty to Y is to keep the promise he made to Y; his duty to Z is to try to secure to him the good G.

A natural response to counterexamples of this sort is that, yes, they do constitute counterexamples, but not very interesting ones. When making third-party promises, one acquires a duty with respect to each of two people; one's duty splits in two, as it were. And though one's duty to one of those persons has no correlative right, one's duty to the other person does. It would be more interesting if there were two-party situations in which one party has a duty to try to secure to the other some good, but the other party has no right to that good, nor to the first party's trying to secure it to him. Call such duties, if there are any, *right-free* duties.

Duties of charity are the clearest examples of such duties.[4] Recall the following well-known parable of Jesus.

> Then Peter came up and said to [Jesus], "Lord, how often shall my brother sin against me, and I forgive him? As many as seven times?" Jesus said to him, "I do not say to you seven times, but seventy times seven."
>
> "Therefore the kingdom of heaven may be compared to a king who wished to settle accounts with his servants. When he began the reckoning, one was brought to him who owed him ten thousand talents; and as he could not pay, his lord ordered him to be sold with his wife and children and all that he had, and payment to be made. So the servant fell on his knees, imploring him, 'Lord, have patience with me, and I will pay you everything.' And out of pity for him the lord of that servant released him and forgave him the debt. But that same servant, as he went out, came upon one of his fellow servants who owed him a hundred denarii; and seizing him by the throat, he said, 'Pay what you owe.' So his fellow servant fell down and besought him, 'Have patience with me, and I will pay you.' He refused and went and put him in prison till he should pay the debt. When his fellow servants saw what had taken place, they were greatly distressed and they went and reported to their lord all that had taken place. When his lord summoned him and said to him, 'You wicked servant! I forgave you all that debt because you besought me; and should not you have had mercy on your fellow servant, as I had mercy on you?' And in anger his lord delivered him to the jailers, till he should pay all his debts. So also my heavenly Father will do to every one of you, if you do not forgive your brother from your heart." (Matt. 18:21–35)

Peter, playing the philosopher, thinks he has discovered a reductio ad absurdum in Jesus' teaching about forgiveness. Surely if my brother wrongs me seven times, I am not required to forgive him seven times! Jesus, by his hyperbolic answer, indicates that he meant exactly what he said.

What had he said? Jesus uses the forgiveness of financial debts to clarify his point about treatment of the person who has wronged one—the person who has "sinned against" one. It is assumed in the parable that though repayment of the debt was due in each of the two cases, neither creditor was able to pay. In that society the king was then within his rights—his retributive rights—to sell the creditor, along with his family and possessions, to recover the principal of the loan and whatever interest might be due. But in response to the creditor's plea for mercy the king, "out of pity," forgives all that is still due. So too, says Jesus, you are to forgive out of mercy or pity those who have wronged you.

When is mercy an appropriate attitude toward a person who has wronged one? Jesus does not say—not as reported here, anyway; he lets his hearers and readers figure that out for themselves. His point is that when mercy is appropriate, they are to forgive. Someone has wronged another person. The wronged party now has certain retributive rights. Out of mercy he is to forego those; he is to forgive. The one who wronged him does not have a right to this foregoing; if he did, the foregoing would not be forgiveness. Instead, the one wronged has a right to the wrongdoer's being punished. But he foregoes claiming that right. That's what you ought to do, says Jesus; that's your obligation. Who ought to do that? Peter and the other disciples. Who else? That too is something Jesus does not make clear in the parable.

I interpret Jesus as saying that they *ought* to forgive; it's their duty, their obligation, to do so. Might he instead have been issuing a conditional threat: if you do not forgive your brother out of mercy, "from your heart," then God will not forgive you? I doubt it. It seems to me much more plausible to interpret Jesus as saying that refusal to forgive one's brother out of mercy or pity, when he is in a pitiable condition, is refusal to do what one ought to do, and that God will deal with one accordingly.[5]

I will eventually propose that, though duties of charity are right-free duties in the sense explained, nonetheless they too are grounded in rights. Though the person whom one ought to forgive does not have a right to one's forgiving him, thereby making the duty here a right-free duty, God has that right; duties of charity are in that way structurally similar to third-party promises. But that will be for later.

III

We are ready to begin exploring the grounding connections that are the focus of my interest in this essay. Suppose that X tortures Y solely for the pleasure X finds in doing so—the delicious sense of power it gives him to have Y wholly at his mercy, to be able to extract screams from Y whenever he pleases. In thus torturing Y, X has flagrantly violated his obligations; he is, accordingly, guilty. Guilty *of* what, guilty *on account of* what? One cannot just be guilty, period; guilt is not a basic state. One is guilty by virtue of something; something brings it about that one is guilty. And that which brings it about that one is guilty, that which accounts for one's guilt, is something that was done—specifically, something that was done by oneself, not by another.[6] One is guilty on account of something one did.

Something of what sort? X was guilty on account of his torturing Y. But there are all sorts of things we do that don't make us guilty on account of doing them. I am presently drinking a cup of tea; I am not guilty on account of doing that. So what was it about X's torturing Y that made X guilty on account of so doing?

Well, in torturing Y, X was accountable, responsible, for depriving Y of some life-good. Yes indeed. But there are all sorts of actual and potential goods in Y's life such that, had X deprived Y of them, X would not on that account be guilty. X is not guilty on account of his failure to extend to Y the gift of a CD of Frans Brüggen's recording of Bach's *Mass in B minor*, though that might well have been a good for Y—in better days, when he was not being tortured.

X is guilty on account of *wronging* Y, on account of being responsible (accountable) for depriving Y of a good to which Y had a *right*. What accounts for the guilt of the one is his wronging of the other. The wronging grounds the guilt; the right grounds the duty. X has the duty to not torture Y solely for the sake of X's pleasure because Y has the right to not be tortured by anyone at all solely for the sake of the torturer's pleasure.

In turn, wronging a person is grounded in the showing of disrespect for what is of worth about the person—in this case, an utterly appalling showing of disrespect.

I hold that the pattern of grounding which I have just presented—duty grounded in rights and rights constituted by what respect requires—is paradigmatic of the pattern of grounding in general. I think the best way to argue my case is with a reductio ad absurdum line of thought. Let us see why, within a theistic framework, the attempt to ground rights in duties, justice in obligation, ultimately does not work out.

Consider the line of thought that moves in the opposite direction from the one just presented—the line of thought that starts with wronging and asks what accounts for it rather than starting from guilt and arguing that wronging is what accounts for that. There are, of course, a good many people nowadays, by no means all of them moral theorists, who find this alternative line of thought far more attractive than the one that I presented and will be defending. We live in a culture of rights, so it is said; the deleterious consequences thereof are all around us. What we need is a culture of responsibility.

What accounts for Y's being wronged by X's torturing him? There are all sorts of things X can do to Y that would not amount to Y's being wronged by X. So what is it that accounts for the fact that, in this case, Y is wronged? What accounts for it—so this line of thought would have it—is that in torturing Y as he did, X did to Y what X ought not to have done to Y. Y's being wronged by X is grounded in X's being *guilty* for having done to Y what he did. Wronging is grounded in guilt. Or with the distinction in mind between subjective and objective obligation, the more precise thing to say is that objective duty grounds right.

And what accounts, in turn, for the fact that in torturing Y as he did, X was violating his duty—his objective duty, and in this case, no doubt, his subjective duty as well? What accounts for the fact that he is subjectively guilty, culpable, blameworthy? The violation of rights, so I suggested, consists in the failure to show due respect; that is where the preceding line of thought wound up. Where does this alternative line of thought wind up?

Attempts to answer this question fall, for the most part, into two types. Theories belonging to the one type hold that moral obligation is ultimately grounded in rules of a certain sort; moral guilt consists of doing something that violates the moral rules. The attempt to justify these rules, or to show that they are justified, typically takes either a utilitarian or a contractarian form. Theories of the other type hold that moral obligation is ultimately grounded in the demands of some authority; moral guilt consists in violating the demands of the moral authority.

Either way, at bottom it is not the right *of a person* to my treating him or her a certain way that puts me under moral obligation, but something more abstract: the applicability to me of certain *rules* or of certain *demands*. Guilt is not to be tracked to violating what is required for respecting the worth of persons but to what is required by the moral rules or the moral demands. Where persons and their worth are central in the picture that I will be defending, rules or demands are central in this alternative picture.

On this occasion, I must set rule-theories of moral obligation off to the side so as to concentrate on a certain demand theory, specifically, the divine demand theory, the only one with any currency among theists.[7] I am myself of the view that rule-theories of moral obligation, be they utilitarian or contractarian, fit poorly— to put it mildly—within a theistic framework; and that, even if they did not fit poorly, the rules proposed by those who attempt to ground moral obligation in rules either do not in fact yield obligation (typical of utilitarian theories), or do so by tacitly presupposing the prior existence of rights, usually the right of each person to have his or her interests given fair consideration (typical of contractarian theories). But on this occasion I must refrain from offering a defense of those claims so as to give the divine demand theory the critical scrutiny that it deserves. What I shall attempt to show is that though God's demands do indeed generate moral obligations on our part, their doing so presupposes a moral obligation on our part prior to, and not generated by, those demands.

The divine demand theory comes in two main versions, differentiated by where in God's life the theory locates the relevant demands. Some hold that God's *will* generates obligations, others that God's *commands* do so. The line of argument that I will develop pertains, with suitable adaptations, to both versions. Continually mentioning both will prove exceedingly cumbersome, however. Accordingly, I will develop my argument by reference to the much more common of the two versions, specifically, the command version, leaving it to the reader to apply the argument, with appropriate adaptations, to the volition version.[8] (I might add that I myself find the command version of the theory more plausible, on the face of it, than the volition version.) My discussion will pass over all the ins and outs of the divine command theory to focus exclusively on what is directly relevant to our purposes here.[9]

IV

The divine command theory of moral obligation gets its initial plausibility from two facts. First, the Hebrew, Christian, and Muslim scriptures pervasively present God as issuing commands to human beings. And, second, by our own issuing of commands, we human beings often generate in our fellow human beings obligations to do certain things that previously they were not obligated to do. By commanding his troops to start the bombardment, the officer places them under obligation to do so. Before he issued the command, they were not obligated to do that; his command generated the obligation. It is these two facts that the divine command theory of moral obligation takes and runs with. Let it be added that there are other ways in which we generate obligations than by commanding; acts of charity typically generate duties of gratitude in the recipients.[10]

Evident as it is that obligations are generated by the issuing of commands, it is equally evident that some commandings do not generate obligations. An imposter officer does not generate in a body of troops the obligation to perform some military maneuver by commanding them to perform it, nor do I generate in you the obligation to surrender the desirable seat that you found on the train by commanding you to surrender it.

What accounts for the difference? Well, an act of commanding can be defective in one way or another—malformed, not properly formed, not well formed. Worse yet, the conditions for the performance even of a malformed act of commanding can be absent, so that, though imperative language was used, no act of commanding occurred. A condition of some illocutionary act being a well-formed act of commanding is that it generate an obligation in the addressee to do what is commanded.

So the imposter officer did not, by what he said, perform a well-formed act of commanding, a decisive sign thereof being that he did not generate in his troops the obligation to perform the military maneuvers that he commanded. Why not? What was lacking on his part, making his act of commanding—if he even performed such an act—malformed?

The imposter officer lacked the *authority* to issue military commands to this body of persons. Let me use the word "power" in that not-very-common sense according to which it is the synonym of "authority." The imposter officer lacked the *power* to issue such commands to these people; that's why the command he issued was malformed in such a way that he generated in them no obligation to do what he commanded. The legitimate officer possesses that power.

As a corollary of the legitimate officer's having the power to issue certain military commands to these troops, the troops have the obligation to obey such commands of that sort as he may issue to them, by doing what he commands; and as the corollary, in turn, of that obligation, the officer has the right to his troops' obedience, by doing what he commands them to do—when the commands that he issues are of the sort that he has the power to issue.

Let me call this power on the part of the officer a *standing* power; let me likewise call the obligation to obedience that the troops have, and the correlative right to obedience that the officer has a *standing* obligation and a *standing* right. This standing power, obligation, and right are not generated by the officer's commands; they were already there. It is because they were already there that the officer, by commanding his troops to do A, can now generate in them the obligation to do A—assuming that A is an example of the type of action that the officer has the power (authority) to command. The standing power, obligation, and right are the indispensable normative context for the officer to generate obligations in his troops by issuing commands to them. It is because the imposter officer lacks that power, with the consequence that the troops lack that obligation and he lacks that right, that he cannot generate in them the obligation to perform some military maneuver by commanding them to perform it.

The fact that the legitimate officer has this power is of course not a coincidence; having that power is an intrinsic component of his office, his position, as officer of these troops. It comes along with the office.

The phenomenon of an *office*, or a *position*, with powers intrinsic to it, is an important element of human affairs in general.[11] There is the office of umpire in professional baseball, the office of judge in a court system, the office of president of a country, and so forth.

Having a certain office gives one the authority to do things that otherwise one would not have the authority to do; for example, holding the office of President of the United States gives one authority to move into the White House. Of course, if one had enough power at one's disposal, one could move into the White House even if one did not have the authority to do so. But rather often, that which one has the authority to do, by virtue of having a certain office, is something that cannot even be done except by one having that office—and then only when one is actually functioning in that office, acting in that capacity. The authority carries the power along with it. In professional baseball, only someone who has the office of umpire has the ability, the power, to call a player "out." Spectators in the stands can shout "out"; often they do. But only the umpire can *call* a player out; only the umpire has the power to *declare* him out. And not even someone whose profession is that of umpire has the power to declare a player out when off duty and himself a spectator in the stands; he can do so only when acting in the office, the position, the capacity, of umpire. Furthermore, a person has the office of umpire with respect to certain players and not with respect to others; offices are typically *with respect to* specific groups of people. Only a person who has the office of judge has the power to declare a person legally guilty; he has that power only when functioning in his office, in his capacity; and he has that office and, hence, that power, only with respect to certain people.

To have the authority to do certain things is to have the *right* to do those things. Intrinsic to all offices is the possession of various rights—and likewise of various responsibilities: the person who occupies the office of President of the United States not only has the right to occupy the White House but also the duty to present a budget annually to Congress. What we have seen is that among the rights intrinsic to an office will often be the right (authority, power) to issue commands of a certain sort to a certain group of people.

The power of a person to issue commands of a certain sort to a certain group of people is so familiar that we overlook how extraordinary it is. Given the connection noted between commands, on the one hand, and obligations and rights, on the other, the power to issue commands implies the power to generate in certain people the obligation to obey by performing actions of a certain sort, the corollary of which is the right on one's own part to their obedience by doing that. Such power is extraordinary.

It will be crucial for our subsequent discussion to keep in mind the distinction I have introduced and employed, between the *standing* powers, obligations, and rights which make it possible to generate obligations in others and rights in oneself by issuing commands, and the *new* obligations and rights thus *generated.* The issuing of commands does indeed generate in people obligations to do specific things that previously they were not obligated to do — or generate additional grounds for the obligatoriness of things they were already obligated to do. But commands do not generate these obligations ex nihilo. For the generation to occur, the one who commands must already have the standing power to place these people under obligation to do a thing of this sort by issuing to them a command to do a thing of this sort, and they must have the standing obligation to obey him by doing such things as he commands them to do — provided he has the authority to command them to do things of that sort. The issuing of commands is not the sort of thing that can generate obligations outside the context of powers, obligations, and rights already there.

V

Enough has been said about the nature and import of human commanding; let us now, using what we have learned, reflect on the divine command theory of moral obligation. The Hebrew, Christian, and Muslim scriptures all present God as issuing commands to human beings to do certain things, thereby generating in human beings the obligation to obey God by doing those things. The divine command theory extrapolates from this biblical presentation to claim that all moral obligations are generated in this fashion. Every moral obligation, so the theory claims, is the content of a command of God; every moral obligation is what obedience to some command of God requires.

When we approach the theory with the previous discussion in mind, two substantial objections come to the fore. In the first place, the theory proposes to illuminate how God generates moral obligations by pointing to an analogous phenomenon in human affairs: we human beings generate obligations by, among other things, issuing commands. Now some of the obligations that we human beings generate by issuing commands are moral obligations. Hence it is not the case that all moral obligations are generated by God's commands; some are generated by human commands. The very phenomenon in human affairs that the theory uses to illuminate God's generation of moral obligation is incompatible with the theory itself.

How might the divine command theorist respond to this first objection? One response he might try is to claim that the obligations we human beings generate by the issuing of commands are never moral obligations; they are military obligations, legal obligations, game obligations, or whatever, but not moral obligations.

This response to the objection strikes me as having no plausibility. Up to this point in my discussion I have deliberately refrained from saying anything at all about the sort of obligations generated by our well-formed commands; in particular, I have not said that they are moral obligations. But surely many of them are. When a parent commands (requests, asks) his child to clean up his room, he generates in the child the obligation to obey him by cleaning up his room— plus, if it was not already obligatory, the obligation to clean up his room. Surely the first of these, at least, is a moral obligation, though perhaps only a prima facie one. Shortly I will consider whether all obligations of obedience generated by well-formed commands are prima facie moral obligations; all we need here is the concession that some are.

Another response to our first objection that the divine command theorist might consider is to concede that sometimes, by commanding someone to do something, we generate in him the prima facie moral obligation to obey the command by doing that; but then go on to claim that the reason you and I are sometimes morally obligated to obey the commands of our fellow human beings is that God has commanded us to obey those commands, thereby generating in us the moral obligation to obey God by obeying our fellow human beings. Absent that divine command and the moral obligation generated thereby, we would never be morally obligated to do what our fellow human beings command us to do. So yes, it's true that a human being, by commanding S that he do X, can generate in S the moral obligation to obey him by doing X; but such obligation-generation by a human being is entirely parasitic on, and derivative from, God's having generated in us the moral obligation to obey God by obeying our fellows.

I leave it to the reader to decide whether, on this analysis of the situation, our human generation of obligations by the issuing of commands really does any longer illuminate *God's* generation of moral obligations by the issuing of commands; reasoning by analogy would seem to suggest that we are morally obligated to do as God commands because there is someone else commanding us to do so; and so on, ad infinitum. Apart from that, the response assumes that it is not of the *essence* of well-formed commands to generate obligations; the obligation to obedience gets attached to commands by God's action of commanding us to be obedient. That seems incorrect to me.

The second objection to the divine command theory that comes to the fore when one approaches it with the preceding discussion in mind is more important for my purposes here. The theory holds that all moral obligations are generated by God's commands. It holds, thus, that God generates moral obligations where there were no such obligations before, none at all. By legislating and commanding, God generates moral obligations ex nihilo. Our previous discussion makes this claim seem questionable.

Suppose that God has commanded me to do X and that I now ask what makes it morally obligatory for me to do this thing, X, that God commanded? After all, it is by no means the case that everything everybody commands me to do is something that I am on that account morally obligated to do. So why in this case? What is it about God's having commanded me to do X that makes it morally obligatory for me to do X?

The only answer, so far as I can see, is that, by virtue of God's "office" or "position" with respect to us, God has the standing power to place me and my fellow human beings under moral obligation to do something by commanding us to do it; as the corollary of that power, we have the standing moral obligation to obey God by doing such things as God may command, and God has the standing moral right to our obedience. But obviously we cannot now say that that standing obligation of ours was in turn generated by some command of God—specifically, by God's command to obey God's commands. That would set us off on an infinite regress. God's generation of moral obligations on our part, by issuing commands to us, *presupposes* the existence of a moral obligation on our part *not thus generated.*

How might the divine command theorist respond to this point? One response he or she might consider is to deny that there is that standing obligation. There is no obligation on our part to obey God by performing such actions as God may command, nor any right on God's part to our obeying God by doing what God commands. There are only the specific obligations generated in us by God's actual commands, along with the specific rights generated in God to our obedience to those actual commands.

How shall we reply to this response? Well, notice that it leaves the divine command theorist without anything to point to that would account for why it is that God generates moral obligations in us by issuing commands to us. On this view, if God commands me to do X, then it's just a brute fact that thereby God has generated in me the moral obligation to obey God by doing X; if God commands me to do Y, then it's just a brute fact that thereby God has generated in me the moral obligation to obey God by doing Y; and in general, for any act that God commands me to perform, it's a brute fact that I am morally obligated to obey God by performing that act. Nothing explains this. That's just how it is.

Instead of regarding this appeal to brute fact as a deficiency of his view, the person considering this line of response might go on the attack and insist that, rather than being a deficiency in the view, it's a virtue of it; all attempts to offer an account here are misguided. Human beings can issue commands which do not generate obligations; accordingly, when a human being does generate an obligation in someone by commanding that something be done, there will always be something which accounts for that. Let it be conceded that what accounts for it is the speaker's standing power to issue such a command to this person, along with the standing obligation and the standing right which that standing power implies. But God could not possibly issue commands that do not impose obligations, since God could not possibly issue anything other than well-formed commands; so there's nothing to account for.

Two replies to this response are in order. If one is willing to rest with brute fact at this point, why not take the next step of simply eliminating reference to divine commands and holding that God creates moral obligations by fiat? Why not be a divine fiat theorist rather than a divine command theorist? Why not hold that God's bringing about of moral obligations is a basic act on God's part? God does not generate my moral obligation to do X by performing some other action, namely, commanding me to do X, thereby generating my obligation to obey him by doing X, and thus my obligation to do X; God brings about my obligation to do X simply by deciding to do so. God says, *Let S be morally obligated to do X,* whereupon S is so obligated.

In short, the response to our second objection, that there simply is no standing obligation on our part to obey such commands as God may issue, effectively undercuts the divine command theory rather than supporting it,[12] doing so in such a way as to pay a price that the divine command theorist wished not to pay. The divine command theorist assumed that, by pointing to the nature and effects of human commands, he could illuminate the nature and source of moral obligation; just as we human beings generate obligations by commanding, so too God generates obligations. But there is nothing in human affairs that is anything like the generation of moral obligations by fiat.[13]

Furthermore, the argument that there is nothing to account for here since God could not issue malformed commands is not valid. Let it be agreed that God's office or position with respect to us, combined with God's nature, do imply that it is impossible for God to issue malformed commands to us; nonetheless, the fact that, by virtue of his position or office, God has the *power* to issue commands to us of a certain sort, explains how it is that, by actually issuing a command to us to do so-and-so, God generates in us the new obligation to obey him by doing that.

Be all this as it may, however, the response—that there is no standing obligation on our part to obey God by doing such things as God may command—is untenable for any theist of an Abrahamic sort. We human beings *do* have that obligation, and God has the corresponding right. Some of our obligations are obligations to do some specific thing: to help *this* blind person across *this* street at *this* time. Other obligations of ours are obligations to perform actions of a certain type when an instance of the type becomes possible or relevant. The obligation in question is of this latter sort: we have the obligation to obey God by doing such things as God may command.

The only other response that I can think of, by the divine command theorist to our second objection, is to agree that there is indeed the standing obligation on our part to obey God by performing such actions as he may command, but to insist that this is not a *moral* obligation. Though the obligations generated by God's actual commands are moral, the standing obligation is not. This, if I interpret him correctly, is the solution Robert Adams is proposing in the following paragraph from his discussion of the divine command theory in his book *Finite and Infinite Goods:*

> One central feature of the human practice of commanding is that persons to whom commands are issued have some obligation to obey them. If their relationships to the commander are not such as to sustain obligations, the command is not valid; perhaps it is not "really" a command. This feature of the practice is surely part of what is taken into the content of God's intentions in commanding. That might be thought to create a problem of circularity for the theory that the nature of obligation is to be understood in terms of divine commands. The solution to this problem is that the kind of obligation whose nature is to be understood in terms of divine commands is fully valid moral (and religious) obligations, whereas the obligation that is presupposed as involved in the practice of commanding is a premoral social or institutional obligation that may or may not have full moral validity.[14]

Let me expand a bit on what I take Adams's thought here to be. The root notion of obligation is *requirement*. Requirements come from many sources: from the laws of the land in which one lives, from the rules of the game one is playing, from the rules of politeness in one's society, from the rules of etiquette for a person of one's status, from one or another social role that one fills—and, as we have seen, from some command issued to one. One of the tasks of the moral theorist is to determine where, in this panoply of requirements, moral requirements are to be found.

We can state in declarative sentences what is required of a person by one or another of these sources of requirement: "The rules of etiquette require that you place the fork to the left of the plate"—alternatively, "According to the rules of etiquette, the fork is to be placed to the left of the plate." But we can also express such requirements in imperative sentences using the language of "should," "ought," and "must": "You should (ought to, must) place the fork to the left of the plate." Such imperative sentences, all by themselves, leave obscure the source of the requirement expressed; sometimes the context makes that source clear, sometimes not.

Adams's suggestion is that there is another source of requirement, distinct from any of those that I have just now mentioned; namely, the social-linguistic practice of giving and receiving commands. One of the rules governing that practice is that the addressee of a well-formed command (in Adams's parlance, a "valid" command) is to obey that command by doing what is commanded. If you and I are now engaged in that social-linguistic practice, you as the one issuing a command and I as the addressee thereof, then I am required by the rules of the practice to obey you by doing what you command—assuming that the command you issued is well formed. I ought to do it, I should do it, I must do it, by virtue of the rules of the social-linguistic practice. I would be violating the rules of the practice if I did not obey you.

In the course of my discussion I have said, many times over and in several different ways, that it belongs to the *nature* of a well-formed command to place its addressee under obligation to obey by doing what is commanded. To say that it is a rule of the social-linguistic practice of giving and receiving commands, that one is to obey such well-formed commands as are issued to one by doing what is commanded, is to get at the same point from a different angle—with this addition: to make the point in the second way is to specify the source of the requirement, while to make it in the first way is to leave the source unspecified. Here is an analogy: one can say that the queen in chess is that piece which moves in such-and-such a way, or one can say that the rules for the movement of the queen in chess are such-and-such. The point is the same.

The application Adams makes of his general point goes like this: there is indeed the standing obligation on our part to obey God by performing such actions as God may command. But that is not a moral obligation; it is, instead, a requirement of that social-linguistic practice of giving and receiving commands in which God participates along with us. Moral obligations, by contrast, are what obedience to God's actual commands requires of us: the requirements of the social-linguistic practice versus the requirements of God's commands. So it's true that moral obligations are not generated by God ex nihilo, that is, in the absence of all obligations whatsoever; but they are generated in the absence of all moral obligations.

How shall we appraise this response to the second of my objections to the divine command theory? Well, let us suppose that God has commanded me to perform action X. Then I have the following obligations:

1. the standing obligation to obey God by performing such actions as God may command me to perform, and
2. the generated obligation to obey God by performing the action X that God commanded me to perform.

The first of these is an obligation to perform actions of a certain type; the second is an obligation to perform an action of that type. So if I violate (2), then perforce I also violate (1); conversely, there is no other way to violate (1) than by violating either (2) or some other specific obligation which is like (2) in being an example of the type specified in (1). Now, on the analysis under consideration, every violation of (2) is a violation of a moral obligation, thus an act of moral wrongdoing. Hence all violations of (1) are perforce acts of moral wrongdoing. Yet (1) is said not to be a moral obligation.

I find this implausible. Let it be conceded that (1) is a requirement of the social-linguistic practice of giving and receiving commands; that does not prevent its *also* being a moral obligation. (See the final words in the passage from Adams: "a premoral social or institutional obligation that may or may not have full moral validity.") What else is needed to make it a moral obligation? If the fact that all examples of the type are moral obligations is not sufficient, and if it is not sufficient that there could not possibly be a violation of (1) that is not a case of moral wrongdoing, then what would be sufficient to make (1) a moral obligation? What is lacking?

Suppose that something which I am legally required to do is also something that I am morally required to do—whether because it is morally required or not. Then every violation of the legal requirement is perforce also a case of moral wrongdoing—even though it was and remains a legal requirement. Nothing mysterious in that. It looks analogous; but there's a crucial difference.

In the case just imagined, one and the same act is a violation of two distinct sets of standing requirements, moral and legal; there is, indeed, nothing mysterious about that. The relation between (1) and (2) is different. Here there is only one standing requirement, namely, (1). It is the requirement, the obligation, to perform actions of a certain type whenever that becomes a live possibility. That type is: obedience to a command of God issued to us. We are obligated to bring about an instance of that type whenever there is open to us the possibility of doing so; and there is that possibility whenever God issues a command to us—and only when God does so. So suppose that God issues to me the command to do X. Then there is open to me the possibility of performing an instance of the type, specifically, this instance: obedience to *this* command of God to me, that I do X. So given that I have the standing obligation to perform any instance of the type when the live possibility of so doing is opened up to me, I am obligated to perform *this* instance of the type.

I do not see how my obligation to perform this instance of the type can be a *moral* obligation when my obligation, which it is conceded that I have, to perform *any* instance of the type which becomes possible for me, is *not* a moral obligation.

My own view concerning the general relation between, on the one hand, the requirements of the social-linguistic practice of giving and receiving commands and, on the other hand, our moral obligations, runs along the following lines. Certain things are required of us by the laws of the land, others by the social roles we play, yet others by the rules of politeness in American society, and so forth; none of these, as such, is a moral requirement. Well-formed commands are like laws, roles, and rules in that, just as certain things are required of us by law, roles, and rules, so also certain things are required of us by commands. At the same time, however, commands are unlike laws, roles, and rules in a fundamental way. Commands introduce *persons* into the situation; for every command, there is a person issuing the command. More specifically, commands introduce the possibility of *obedience or disobedience* to a person into the situation. What is enjoined on me by a command may be something that I was already required to do by law, role, or rule; alternatively, it may not have been required of me by anything at all. Either way, the command, if it is well formed, introduces this new factor: if I do not do what is enjoined on me by this command, be that independently required of me or not, I perforce treat the person issuing the command in a certain way; I disobey her. That way of treating a person seems to me always a case, prima facie, of moral wrongdoing—perhaps trivial moral wrongdoing, but moral wrongdoing nonetheless. It is a case of morally wronging a person. To disobey a well-formed command is perforce to show a certain degree of disrespect for the person issuing the command.

So I agree that it is a rule of the social-linguistic practice of giving and receiving commands that one is to obey such well-formed commands as are addressed to one; the rule simply unfolds the nature, the essence, of a command. But I hold that obedience to well-formed commands is not only required by the rules of our social-linguistic practice; it is required by morality as well. When the fork is placed to the right of the plate, neither fork nor plate has been wronged; but when someone asks me, with a well-formed request, to place the fork to the left of the plate, and I, for no good reason, refuse to do so, then that person has been morally wronged and I, who have done it, am on that account morally guilty. In short, my view is that not only is that standing obligation to obey God by performing such acts as he may command a moral obligation; the much more general obligation, to obey persons in general by performing such acts as they may enjoin on us with well-formed commands, is a moral obligation.

Before I move on, let me take note of one more feature of the divine command theory highlighted by our discussion of commands in general—a feature which is not a flaw in the theory as such, but which does pose a difficulty to anyone who wishes to use the theory to argue that rights are ultimately grounded in obligations. Consider that power, that right of God to issue commands to us. This right is not the corollary of any specific obligation that God generated in us by issuing some command to us; nor is it the corollary of some requirement of the social-linguistic practice of giving and receiving commands.

VI

The major question emerging from our discussion of commands in general, and of God's commands in particular, is this: how are we to account for that standing moral obligation on our part to obey such commands as God may issue to us, by doing what God commands, along with its correlative, the standing moral right on God's part to our obedience to his commands? Whatever the success of the divine command theory in accounting for other moral obligations, it cannot account for this one. How, then, do I account for it?

Another aspect of how God is presented in the Hebrew, Christian, and Muslim scriptures is that God makes promises to us and covenants with us. The answer that we offer to the question above will have to be framed in the light of the implications of this additional aspect of the biblical and Koranic presentation of God. Accordingly, let me postpone my answer until those implications have been brought to light.

Promises and covenants work in just the opposite way from commands. Whereas the one who issues a well-formed command generates in the addressee the obligation to obey, by doing the thing commanded, and generates in himself the right to the addressee's doing that, the one who makes a well-formed promise generates in himself the obligation to keep his promise, by doing the thing promised, and generates in the addressee the right to his doing that.

In my discussion of commands I observed that commands do not always generate in their addressees the obligation to obey; sometimes they do, sometimes they do not. What accounts for the difference? I asked. It seems right to think of the command which does not generate the obligation to obedience as defective in some way; the well-formed command, the properly formed command, does generate that obligation. The defect that I pointed to in certain commands was that the one issuing the command lacked the power to issue a command of that sort to these people—that is to say, he lacked the power to generate in them the obligation to do a thing of that sort by commanding that they do it. I called this a *standing* power, on the ground that the person must already have that power if he is actually to generate those obligations in those people. And I observed that a corollary of his having this standing power is that the addressees have the standing obligation to obey such commands of this sort (which are in all other ways well formed) as he may issue to them—the corollary of that, in turn, being that he has the standing right to that obedience.

All the same things, mutatis mutandis, are to be said for promises and covenants. It is typically the case that there are things which the head of an organization, functioning in her capacity as head, can generate in herself or the organization the obligation to do, by contracting to do them, which the other members of the organization cannot thus generate in themselves or the organization the obligation to do; they lack the power to do that. Likewise, there are certain actions that the officer of a body of troops can obligate himself to perform, by promising his troops to perform them, which an imposter officer cannot thus obligate himself to perform. Of course, the head of the organization has that power only when functioning in her capacity as head; and the officer of the troops has that power only when functioning in his capacity as officer.

I further observed that it is usually not coincidental that only the person in a certain office or position has the standing power to issue commands of such-and-such a sort to such-and-such persons. Such a standing power is typically an intrinsic component of the office or position in question; the standing power comes along with the office. The same thing holds, mutatis mutandis, for promises and covenants. The power to make certain contracts comes along with the position of head of the company; the power to make certain promises comes along with the position of officer of these troops.

It would be tedious to elaborate these points of similarity in more detail; let us move to the application. An implication of the biblical and Koranic presentation of God as making promises to us and covenants with us is that God has the power, the *standing* power, to generate in himself the obligation to perform some action by promising or covenanting with us to perform that action. A corollary of God's having that standing power is that God has the standing obligation to keep such promises and covenants as he may make, by doing what he promised or covenanted; a corollary of this, in turn, is that we have the standing right to God's keeping such promises as he may make.

That standing obligation on God's part is a moral obligation, as is that standing right on our part. The obligation, let it be said, is also a requirement of the social-linguistic practice of offering and receiving promises and covenants. But promises and covenants are engagements between or among persons; when, for no good reason, I break a promise, I wrong a person, show him or her disrespect. The obligation to keep one's promises is both a requirement of the social-linguistic practice of making and receiving promises and a prima facie moral requirement.

Presupposed by the biblical presentation of God as issuing commands to us, thereby generating in us the moral obligation to obey by doing the thing commanded, is the standing moral obligation on our part to obey such commands as God may issue, by doing the thing commanded, and the standing moral right on God's part to our obeying such commands as he may issue. Presupposed by the biblical presentation of God as making promises to us, thereby generating in himself the moral obligation to keep his promise by doing the thing promised, is the standing moral obligation on God's part to keep such promises as he may make, by doing the thing promised, and the standing moral right on our part to God's keeping such promises as he may make. Just as we have moral obligations toward God and God has moral rights against us prior to God's issuing of commands, so too God has moral obligations to us and we have moral rights against God prior to God's making promises to us and covenants with us.

I am well aware that most members of the Christian tradition, past and present, would or will find the latter suggestion abhorrent. Quite a few would be willing to concede that we have standing moral obligations toward God and that God, correlatively, has standing moral rights against us; but almost all would resist the view that God has standing moral obligations toward us and that we have standing moral rights against God. Some would deny that God has any moral obligations at all toward us; most of the others would hold that such moral obligations as God has toward us have been freely assumed by God by his promising and covenanting. My argument has been that if one reflects on the necessary conditions of promising and covenanting, one sees that that cannot be. If God has no standing obligations toward us and we have no standing rights against God, then the biblical and Koranic presentation of God as making promises to us and covenants with us is not true, that is, not literally true; it is, at best, a picture.

Why do most members of the Christian tradition find it abhorrent to think of God as having standing moral obligations toward us and of us as having standing moral rights against God? My guess is that it is because of the tendency, lodged deep in the tradition, to think of morality as grounded in laws, rules, or demands. How could God be "subjected" to those? My suggestion is that it is a mistake to think of morality that way.

VII

My argument has been somewhat complex, so let me take a moment to review. My question was how, within a theistic framework, we should think of the grounding relation between justice and obligation, rights and duties. Are moral rights grounded ultimately in moral duties or moral duties ultimately in moral rights? Or is neither grounded ultimately in the other? The answer that seems to me correct is that duties are grounded ultimately in rights. To defend that conclusion, I presented a reductio argument against the opposite view, that is, against the view that rights are grounded ultimately in duties.

If every right is grounded ultimately in some correlative duty, how are we to understand duty? What grounds or constitutes obligation if not the requirements of justice? The great majority of answers to this question fall, so I suggested, into one of two types. The answers of one type hold that moral obligation is what is required if one is to conform to laws or rules of some sort—call them the laws or rules of morality. The answers of the other type hold that moral obligation consists in what is required for obedience to the demands of some authority—call it the moral authority, far and away the most plausible candidate for the moral authority being God. A complete discussion of the issue would obviously require that we scrutinize answers of both types; on this occasion, that was impossible. I have confined myself to an analysis of the divine command theory of moral obligation. What we have seen is that there is at least one moral obligation that cannot be generated by God's commands, namely, the standing moral obligation on our part to obey such commands as God may issue. That standing moral obligation is part of the normative context within which God exercises his power to generate obligations in us by issuing commands. Just now, by our analysis of the conditions of promises and covenants, we have discovered that God's promises to us and covenants with us also presuppose a prior normative context; they presuppose the standing obligation on God's part to keep such promises as he may make to us, and the correlative standing right on our part to God's keeping his promises to us.

Might the standing obligation presupposed by God's promises be an obligation generated by God's commands, with its correlative right then grounded in that obligation? Certainly not. The obligation presupposed by God's promises is an obligation on God's part; the obligations generated by God's commands are obligations on our part. Might the reverse then be the case? Might the standing obligation presupposed by God's commands be an obligation generated by a promise of God, with its correlative right then grounded in that obligation? Certainly not. The obligation presupposed by God's commands is an obligation on our part; the obligations generated by God's promises are obligations on God's part. The standing obligations that are a condition of God's speech-acts of commanding and promising cannot be generated by those speech-acts themselves— nor, so far as I can see, by any other speech-acts of God.

The solution is to recognize that the explanatory order runs in the reverse direction. Our standing obligation to obey such commands as God may issue to us is grounded in God's right to our obedience to his commands. To fail to obey God is to violate a right of God, to deprive God of what is due him. It is to wrong God. And that right, in turn, consists in the fact that obedience to God's commands is what is required of us if we are not to show disrespect for something about God that is of worth, of excellence. Not obeying God's commands is incompatible with due recognition of God's excellence.

And what about that other standing obligation, God's obligation to keep such promises as he may make to us? This obligation is to be understood as grounded in our right to God's keeping his promises to us. Were God, *per impossibile,* not to keep his promises to us, that would violate a right of ours, deprive us of what is due us. It would wrong us. And that right consists in the fact that keeping the promises one makes is what is required of one if one is not to show disrespect for something about the addressee that is of worth, of excellence. Not keeping one's promise to someone (in the absence of extenuating circumstances) is incompatible with due recognition of that person's excellence.

Once one has recognized that our standing obligation to obey such commands as God may issue to us is grounded in God's right to our obedience, it would be arbitrary not to regard our other obligations to God as grounded in the same way, namely, in God's rights. And once one has recognized that God's standing obligation to keep such promises as he may make to us is grounded in our right to his keeping his promises to us, it would likewise be arbitrary not to regard obligations to human beings in general, be they obligations on God's part or our part, as grounded in our rights.

God is worthy of honor and respect. So are we; we are not worthless. God's rights are that which the due honoring of God's worth, God's excellence, requires; our rights are that which the due honoring of our worth, our excellence, requires.

It is time to bring back into the picture the distinction that we made early in our discussion between right-bound duties and right-free duties. The existence of right-free duties requires a qualification in the principle just enunciated, that obligations to human beings are grounded in the rights of human beings.[15] My duty of charity to some human being is not grounded in the right of that person against me to that charity—nor in the right of any other human being against me to that act of charity. The best way to account for such duties within a theistic framework of the Abrahamic sort is now quite evident, however. Duties of charity are grounded entirely in the commands of God, not in the rights of human beings; they are generated by God's commands. It is on account of God's command to forgive the one who has wronged me that I am obligated to forgive him, not on account of his right to be forgiven, since he has no such right, nor on account of the right of any third party to my forgiving the first.

In short, what accounts for the difference between right-bound duties and right-free duties is that right-bound duties are grounded in correlative rights. I am obligated not to assault my neighbor because he has a right to my not assaulting him; and he has a right to my not assaulting him because there is some excellence in him such that due honoring thereof requires that I not assault him. Right-free duties have no correlative rights in which to be grounded. They are, nonetheless, grounded in rights, specifically, in God's rights to our obedience. Though the party who wronged me is not wronged should I refuse to forgive him, nonetheless there is *someone* who is wronged, namely, God.

Of course, God may command things that respect for my neighbor already requires; in the Torah, God does in fact command some such things. Due respect for my neighbor requires that I not bear false witness against him; in the Torah, God commands of me that very thing. Not bearing false witness is thus doubly obligatory. Should I bear false witness against my neighbor, I would both wrong him and disobey God. And in disobeying God, I would wrong God—deprive God of his right to my obedience. I wrong both neighbor and God. When violating one's right-free duties, one wrongs only God; when violating one's right-bound duties, one wrongs one's neighbor, and sometimes, if not always, God as well. Therein lies the distinction.

VIII

There is nothing deeper in the moral universe than the fact that God and we alike have rights and can be wronged—nothing deeper than the fact that we can both be shown less than due respect for that about us which is of worth. God and we are alike in that regard. Deeper than guilt on account of violating some rule or demand is guilt on account of wronging someone. Persons are deeper than rules and demands in the moral universe; wronging persons is deeper than violating moral law.

If one shows disrespect to someone, be it God or fellow human being, for that about them which is of worth, then a disorder, disparity, discrepancy, dissonance, intrudes into one's relationship. There is nothing deeper than that dissonance in the relation among persons, divine and human. If someone is unmoved by the fact that he is showing disrespect to a person, be it God or human, for something about the person that is of worth, then there is nothing more to say to him. One has gone as deep as one can.

God did not have to create us. But in creating us, God created creatures with a particular contour of excellence, creatures of such a sort that there is about us that which is worthy of respect and unworthy of disrespect; we are thereby inherently capable of being wronged, also in principle by God. One's confidence in the goodness of God incorporates confidence that God does not wrong us. One of God's excellences consists in God's respect for his own excellences and for those of his creatures. Of course, the particular form that God's respect for us takes will perforce be unimaginably different from the form that our respect for each other takes.

In creating us, God created creatures capable of wronging their creator; God made himself vulnerable to being wronged by us. God made us vulnerable as well—vulnerable, in our case, not just to being wronged by the other but to the impulse to wrong the other. In good measure it was by making us vulnerable to the impulse to wrong the other that God made himself vulnerable to being wronged.

Along the way I have pointed to a number of important issues that could not be considered on this occasion, even though they were directly related to my argument. There are also a number of important issues *raised* by my argument that I have not been able to consider. Among the most important of these is this: by virtue of which of the offices or positions that God has with respect to us is God authorized to issue commands to us, and to make promises to us and covenants with us?

NOTES

I have benefited very much from incisive comments made on an earlier draft of the essay by Terence Cuneo, Mark C. Murphy, and the members of the Graduate Students' Philosophy of Religion Discussion Group at Yale. My thanks to all of them.

1. The passage is to be found in her chapter "Forgiveness, Resentment and Hatred," in Jeffrie G. Murphy and Jean Hampton, *Forgiveness and Mercy* (Cambridge: Cambridge University Press, 1988), 52.

2. Joel Feinberg, *Social Philosophy* (Englewood Cliffs, N.J.: Prentice-Hall, 1973), 63.

3. This solution to the puzzle was suggested to me by Robert Adams. Kelly Sorenson mentioned an alternative solution: the *pair* has the right to one member of the pair being saved. I find this solution less plausible, for the reason that I find it dubious that pairs (and sets in general) have rights. I do hold that certain kinds of groups have rights—nations (peoples), for example.

4. What about duties to works of art, and duties to the earth and its nonhuman inhabitants? Are these not cases of one's having a duty to secure some good to something without that entity's having a right against one to the good in question? Whether these are examples depends very much on one's analysis of them, and the analyses are highly controversial. Do we really have duties to works of art, or is the precise way to put the matter, rather, that we have duties to our fellow human beings *with respect to* works of art? So also, do we really have duties to the earth and its inhabitants, or is the precise way to put the matter, rather, that we have duties to our fellow human beings, or to God, *with respect to* the earth and its nonhuman inhabitants? Or what about going in the other direction? May it be that works of art do have rights, and likewise the earth and its nonhuman inhabitants? In each of these analyses, the person or other entity to which one has a duty has a right against one to one's performance of that duty.

5. To the best of my knowledge, I am following the entire Christian tradition in interpreting the point of the parable as a command or instruction rather than a threat. Mark C. Murphy has suggested to me another interpretation: may it be that, rather than issuing either a command or a threat, Jesus is sketching out a way of life involving certain social relationships and inviting us into this way of life on the ground of its excellence? I doubt it. This interpretation seems to me not to account for the imperative sternness of Jesus' language—namely, that very feature of the language in which the other interpretation hears a threat.

6. It may be that the way in which one did that of which one is guilty is by someone else acting on one's behalf. It was this concept of representative action that lay behind that strand of the Christian tradition which taught that "In Adam's fall, we sinned all."

7. In fact, the *divine* demand theory seems to me the only version of the demand theory of obligation with any plausibility whatsoever. All other proposed candidates for the moral authority have deficiencies that obviously undercut their candidacy. Durkheim proposed one's society as the moral authority; the demands of a society on its members generate their obligations. It is hard to view this proposal as anything more than the product of theoretical desperation.

8. The best critical analysis, in my judgment, of divine demand theories is by Mark C. Murphy. See his "Divine Command, Divine Will, and Moral Obligation," in *Faith and*

Philosophy 15 (January 1998): 3–27, and his "Theological Voluntarism" in *The Stanford Encyclopedia of Philosophy* (Fall 2002 Edition), ed. Edward N. Zalta, http://plato.stanford.edu/archives/fall2002entries/voluntarism-theological/. The best defenses of the theory, I would say, are by Robert Adams and Philip Quinn. See Adams, "A Modified Divine Command Theory of Ethical Wrongness," in his collection *The Virtue of Faith and Other Essays in Philosophical Theology* (Oxford: Oxford University Press, 1987), and his more recent discussion in chapter 11, "Divine Commands," of his *Finite and Infinite Goods* (Oxford: Oxford University Press, 1999). For Quinn, see his early *Divine Commands and Moral Requirements* (Oxford: Oxford University Press, 1978), and his more recent essays, "An Argument for Divine Command Ethics," in *Christian Theism and the Problems of Philosophy*, ed. Michael Beaty (Notre Dame, Ind.: University of Notre Dame Press, 1990), "The Primacy of God's Will in Christian Ethics," in *Philosophical Perspectives* 6, *Ethics*, ed. James Tomberlin (Atascadero, Calif.: Ridgeview Publishing Company, 1992): 493–513, and "Divine Command Theory," in *The Blackwell Guide to Ethical Theory*, ed. Hugh LaFollette (Oxford: Blackwell, 1999).

9. In chapter 6 of my *Divine Discourse* (Cambridge: Cambridge University Press, 1995), I discussed aspects of the theory different from those that I will be discussing here.

10. This fact has led to the quixotic claim by Derrida and other participants in the interminable flurry of discussions about "the gift" that one can never give a true gift, since always some return is required (and, if one knows what one is doing, expected). See Jacques Derrida, *The Gift of Death*, trans. David Wills (Chicago: University of Chicago Press, 1995). My own view is that, rather than treating this argument as revealing the astonishing, hitherto unnoticed, truth that there are no true gifts, one should treat it in the opposite way, as a reductio ad absurdum argument against the assumption that something is not a true gift if gratitude is (morally) required.

11. What I am here calling an *office* I called in chapter 5 of my *Divine Discourse* a *standing*. I have changed terminology so that here I could highlight the distinction between an office and its attendant powers, obligations, and rights, and have the word "standing" available for the latter.

12. Philip Quinn has presented this view in some of his essays. For references, and for critique, see Mark C. Murphy, "Theological Voluntarism."

13. The person who holds that God generates obligations in human beings by sheer fiat would presumably not want to say that this is true for all our obligations; God does generate some obligations by the issuing of explicit commands. So one way of fitting things together would be to say that God generates by sheer fiat our standing obligation to obey such commands as God may issue and generates all other obligations by the issuing of commands.

14. *Finite and Infinite Goods*, 266–67.

15. Earlier I noted that in the case of third-party promises, one has a duty to try to bring it about that someone possesses or experiences some good even though that person does not have a right against one to one's doing that. However, the person to whom one made the promise does have a right to your doing your duty to the third party.

2

THE IMAGE OF GOD AND
THE SOUL OF HUMANITY

Reflections on Dignity, Sanctity,
and Democracy

TIMOTHY P. JACKSON

If we start with the idea of man as an animal endowed with reason, we are
not led by any necessary inference to God, and therefore not to man as a being
essentially related to God.

—Karl Barth, *Church Dogmatics*

Upon arrival in heaven . . . leave your dog outside. Heaven goes by favor.
   If it went by merit, you would stay out and the dog would go in.

—Mark Twain, *The Autobiography of Mark Twain*

I. Introduction: Cultural Diagnoses

Thomas Jefferson's original draft of the Declaration of Independence held the
equality of all men to be a "sacred and undeniable" truth. It was Benjamin Franklin

who changed the wording to characterize human (or at least male) equality as simply "self-evident," in order to emphasize that the disgruntled colonists were forming a new nation based on shared reason rather than revealed religion.[1] Neither Franklin nor Jefferson was an atheist, but this shift from sanctity to self-evidence announced (and reinforced) a profound tension between traditional Christianity and the emergent American democracy. For more than two and a quarter centuries, the American polity has wrestled with the meaning of this tension. Is the affirmation of human equality—together with rights to life, liberty, and the pursuit of happiness—a matter of secular philosophy alone, or can/must biblical faith still play a crucial part in our public discourse? Quite generally, are Christianity and democracy fruitfully interrelated, must they be forcefully severed, or is there some third alternative?

I propose to approach these and related questions by examining what Christian political thinkers frequently hold to be the ground of human equality: the image of God. Within the Western Christian tradition, that image has often been identified with humanity's intellect and will—with what Thomas Aquinas, for example, calls "reason" and "rational appetite."[2] Intellect and (free) will, in turn, frequently are held to be the foundation of personal dignity. Our selves, our identities as unique persons, are due respect because of our capacities for independent thought and action. Because we can formulate and achieve self-conscious ends, we ourselves are to be treated as ends and not as means only. Just how profound the thought and how ethical the action must be to count as dignified is much debated—must my ideas be brilliant and my deeds heroic, or is it enough to be capable of *any* self-conscious thought and action?—but the key point is that one must *achieve* dignity in time. Minimally, one must reach "the age of reason," or, maximally, one must exercise rational control in some remarkable way.

Whatever the details, the general commitment to dignity is not to be undervalued. As the engine that drives concern for individual conscience and defense of democratic freedom, it is one of our chief cultural successes. We in the West have not always practiced respect for dignity, of course—blacks, women, and gays, among others, can attest to this—but the ideal of respect is part of the creed of a faithful church as well as a liberal polity. Too much blood has been lost in this connection, by both Christian martyr and American patriot, to belittle the relevant virtue.

Nonetheless, I maintain in this essay that the praise of rational dignity has grown myopic and amnesiac. Franklin's "enlightened" editing has effaced too completely Jefferson's intuition about the sacred. In our insistence on dignity, we have become largely blind to and forgetful of its origin in sanctity. We have become increasingly unmindful, that is, of the fact that persons with interest-based rights—i.e., rights that turn on autonomous agency—only emerge out of impersonal needs and potentials that are communally produced and must be graciously addressed. The self has forgotten the soul, if you will, and the result is an impoverished view of both God's image and liberal democracy. To counteract this decline, I aim, first, to clarify the meaning of "dignity" and "sanctity," "self" and "soul," in light of the *Imago Dei;* second, to argue that liberal democracy cannot survive when rights are based exclusively on the self and its dignity; then, third, to conclude by gesturing toward some of the practical implications of the views I defend.

To anticipate in more detail, my theological diagnosis, shared by many concerned to rehabilitate Christianity, is that the *Imago Dei* has been far too intimately associated with intellect and will. My political diagnosis, shared by many concerned to rehabilitate liberalism, is that the democratic citizen has been far too intimately associated with freedom and dignity. These two excesses are not unrelated, of course, given (especially Protestant) Christianity's historical contributions to democratic culture. And the two excesses together suggest a potent prescription: to reconstrue political theology such that both the image of God and the citizen of a democracy are understood with primary reference to sanctity rather than dignity. I propose that we substantially disassociate the image of God from reason and volition and reconnect it with a particular human need and potential: to give and/or receive agapic love. In turn, I suggest that bearing the image of God is a sufficient condition for full and equal citizenship in a democratic state and thus for the provisions and protections due a citizen. In many circumstances, the need for agapic love constitutes the right to receive it; even as, in many circumstances, the capacity for agapic love constitutes the duty to give it. To care for the needy and vulnerable—the young, the poor, the retarded, the sick, the senile, the guilty—is to acknowledge fully the *demos* from which democracy gets its name. It is also to imitate the *Christos* from which Christianity gets its name.

II. Dignity and Sanctity

Definitions

The Latin term *dignitas* literally means "a being worthy, worth, worthiness, merit, desert," while *sanctitas* means "inviolability, sacredness, sanctity."[3] Though both Latin words and their English cognates have subsequently been used in theological contexts, sometimes interchangeably,[4] *dignitas* seems initially to have been at home in political and economic spheres, referring to the grandeur and authority of a particular office or station, while *sanctitas* originally had ethico-religious overtones, referring to moral purity or holiness, especially when these were seen as divine gifts.[5] The more our English-speaking literature accents rational agency as the *singular* human station, the more the very idea of sanctity may seem quaint or absurd and so the more it will wither in relation to dignity. When this occurs, dignity cannot help but be identified with social elites, those with power and prestige, and those outside of these elites will, in turn, seem worthless or burdensome.

Harkening back to the Latin, I define "dignity" as achieved merit based on personal performance. Dignity is won by individuals in self-consciously embodying the good, freely choosing the right, and/or effectively maximizing social utility. Whether referring to a virtue of character or a principle of action, dignity is accomplished in time and inspires or ought to inspire respect and admiration in others. As such, dignity is closely allied with social justice, construed as giving persons what they merit. A dignified party is given her due when she is respected, and she is often respected for being willing and able to give others their due (*suum cuique*). More broadly, dignity underlies the calculation of rewards and punishments. Insofar as dignity entails the self-conscious exercise of autonomy, it is the necessary and sufficient condition for moral responsibility. According to Immanuel Kant, for instance, to be able to give oneself imperatives and to act on them for the sake of duty is to be a dignified agent. Such an agent, in turn, is a member of the kingdom of ends and can be held accountable for her personal choices.[6]

I define "sanctity," on the other hand, as gifted inviolability based on impersonal essence. Sanctity inheres in the species by virtue of its typical needs and given potentials: the basic need for food, drink, company, clothing, health, and freedom, for example, together with the passive potential for rational thought, bodily growth, emotional pleasure, and religious faith.[7] Whether understood as a creation of God or a contingency of evolution, sanctity presupposes no particular action in time and induces or ought to induce awe and wonder in others. As such, sanctity is closely allied with agapic love, construed as willing the good for someone independently of merit. A sanctified party is not approached from within economies of exchange, but rather is treated with awe precisely to indicate that he is beyond price. More broadly, sanctity underlies the extension of compassion and self-sacrifice. Insofar as sanctity entails unself-conscious grace, unfulfilled promise, or unmet need, it invites charitable service. For Jesus, for instance, the innocence and fragility of children make them especially sacred.[8] Children are the paradigmatic members of the kingdom of God (Matt. 19:14); together with the hungry, the thirsty, the stranger, the naked, the sick, and those in prison, they are "the least of these" that are intimately identified with Christ himself (Matt. 25:44–46).[9]

The word "sanctification" connotes growth in holiness and thus may seem to imply achieved merit, but this is misleading. The lead definition of "sanctification" in *The Oxford English Dictionary* is: "The action of the Holy Spirit in sanctifying or making holy the believer, by the implanting in him of the Christian graces and the destruction of sinful affections."[10] The key points are: (1) that the believer is largely passive in this process—he or she is "*made* holy" by the Spirit; and (2) that what is bestowed is sanctity, not dignity—he or she is "made *holy*" by the Spirit. Admittedly, a saint is called "sanctified," and we sometimes equate "saintliness" either with regularly doing one's duty or with going beyond the limits of duty.[11] But here the "duties" in question are duties of justice—honesty, fair dealing, promise-keeping, and the like—while the distinctly religious connotation to "saintliness" refers to performing the duties of love—forgiveness, compassion, self-sacrifice, and the like. On the whole, it seems better not to conflate holiness with moral merit, at least not the merit associated with doing justice. Holiness and moral merit are distinct, given that the former is a gifted grace beyond the calculation of worth or attribution of cardinal virtue, while the latter implies a positive appraisal of worth or celebration of cardinal virtue.

The holy is "consecrated" or "set apart,"[12] an upshot of one or more of the theological virtues (faith, hope, love); the morally meritorious is useful or admirable, an upshot of one or more of the cardinal virtues (prudence, temperance, courage, justice).[13] In addition, holiness is sometimes ascribed to those who especially need to receive or have the potential to give the fruits of theological virtue, as well as to those who currently possess such virtue. Think of the need for loving care of children or the physically impaired—we may call them "sacred" or "angelic"—and think of the manifestation of care in Christian saints. Similarly, moral merit is sometimes ascribed to those who especially need to be treated with or have the potential to show cardinal virtue, as well as to those who actively exercise it. Think of the need for justice of an assault victim or a slave—we may call them "deserving" or "righteous"—and think of the manifestation of justice in nineteenth-century abolitionists.

If keeping one's own counsels, as well as one's promises to and contracts with others, is the quintessence of doing justice today, then blessing the young, the weak, the needy, and the guilty is the quintessence of incarnating love. Kantian dignity would ignore or overcome bodily requirements and emotional inclinations, while Christian sanctity is partially composed of such requirements and inclinations. Kant offers a categorical imperative to persons capable of self-control ("act only in accordance with that maxim through which you can at the same time will that it become a universal law"), while Christ offers concrete beatitudes to "nonpersons" out of control ("Blessed are you who are poor . . . you who are hungry . . . you who weep . . . when they exclude you, revile you, and defame you").[14] It is far from my intention to ridicule Kant's account of personal dignity; it is one of the most insightfully conceived and powerfully written visions of (part of) the moral life we have. Kant preserves the distinction between the personal and the narcissistic,[15] and defending sanctity does not entail vilifying dignity. My aim, rather, is to highlight the distinctive differences between dignity and sanctity, then to show their interdependence. A proper understanding of both is necessary for a full understanding of God's image.

Dignity and Sanctity Related

For all their contrasts of meaning, there is an internal relation between dignity and sanctity. The recognition of sanctity is a precondition of the achievement of dignity, so one cannot seek to respect the latter without also honoring the former. If the young, the weak, the needy, and the guilty are not cared for, they will never grow (or grow back) into persons capable of giving or receiving justice. Even though rationality and autonomy are very great goods, sanctity is the prior value: a function, in fine, of the body and its passions. The needs and potentials that make us human are located first, chronologically and causally, in the nonrational flesh. Moreover, the animated body—the unfolding unity that is uniquely oneself—is bequeathed sexually. (Whether or not original sin is transmitted sexually, à la Augustine, original sanctity clearly is.) Through the unitive and procreative goods of sex, we acknowledge basic needs and vulnerabilities, as well as express deep affections and engender new lives. By and large, male needs female, and female needs male, not simply to perpetuate the species but also to find romantic complementarity.[16] (A schooled *eros* can be the vehicle of *agape*, also known as unconditional care.) The needs and vulnerabilities are not to be lamented, for they make the affections and the lives possible.[17]

Sanctity and dignity are not mutually exclusive, I want to emphasize, nor are they essentially antagonistic. One does not grow out of sanctity once one becomes a self-conscious agent, and truly self-conscious agents appreciate their ongoing physical limits and passional aspirations. When sanctity is defined in terms of impersonal needs and potentials, it is prior to dignity, to repeat, but even dignified persons remain needy and characterized by unfulfilled promise. Even rational individuals making autonomous choices are not without profound dependencies on one another and on God. And no finite person is pure act, with an identity that is so fully realized that there is no room for growth, no potential for improvement. Changes and challenges still come, often in unplanned and unexpected ways.

Putting the point more forcefully, dignity and sanctity need each other. Attending to each provides an important check on both. If a Western accent on personal dignity has tended to make us blind to the underlying dynamics of the human body and the human community, a too-exclusive focus on sanctity can become paternalistic and oppressive. The codependent family, the cultish church, and the welfare state may try too vigorously to orchestrate our lives. Personal autonomy protects us from such intrusive or patronizing collectives by upholding individual power and responsibility.

Reason and will also provide needed governance of the emotions. Even a defender, like myself, of the importance of bodily passions must admit that they can, at times, be disruptive of sound perception and wise action. Emotions are not simply unwelcome losses of control or erroneous judgments of fact; as many have pointed out, emotions, though fallible, give spice to life and are indispensable to proper connectedness to the world and other people.[18] An autonomy capable only of calculation is a lonely, inhuman thing; nevertheless, emotions must be schooled and disciplined by rational insight and intention. That said, reason and will must not overreach themselves.

Dignity Becomes Self-Defeating

When rational dignity becomes prideful, it neglects or even despises the exigencies of the flesh — the need for food and drink, the drive for sex, vulnerability to pain and injury, the fear of death — since these remind us of the narrow confines of our personal freedom. Only so much of our lives is under our self-conscious control. A prideful dignity also tends to neglect or despise those human beings who live mostly in the body and its passions: fetuses, babies, the mentally impaired, and the senile. These classes of individuals are literally "nonpersons," inasmuch as they are not self-aware agents capable of independent thought and action. If only rational agents ("autonomous persons") have a right to life, then there will be no substantive moral objection to abortion, infanticide, and involuntary active euthanasia for the irrational or nonrational.[19] Moreover, it has not been too large a leap in the past for an ethic of pure dignity to treat the poor, the illiterate, the criminal, the crazy, the gay, and the female as also outside the bounds of the moral community. These groups also live uncomfortably emotional, even "animal," existences, according to some zealots of "reason" and "will" (see Aristotle and Nietzsche on slaves and women, Social Darwinists and old-line Stalinists on weaklings and peasants).

Neglect of human sanctity leads to the loss of personal dignity itself. Dignity withers not merely because without care for the young and needy there can be no future generations, but also because persons who do not honor their own neediness and finitude will tend to lapse into either a comic self-importance or a paralyzing despair. A foolish egotism or a degrading pessimism readily besets both groups and individuals who worship exclusively at the shrine of *Dignitas*. At the first extreme, a culture that embraces scientism and technical reason to the denial of humane values will believe it can pollute the environment, practice eugenics, and build nuclear weapons with impunity. Similarly, a man who embraces self-assertion and self-sufficiency to the denial of embodied limits will believe he can mortify the flesh, dominate women and children, and reject civil society with impunity. At the second extreme, a civilization that dwells on past glories compared to present impotencies will believe it has nothing more to lose in indulging resentment, dogmatism, and the terrorist's disregard for innocent human life. Similarly, a woman who holds that raw power is all and that human sanctity, her own and others', is but a myth will have no grounds to protest abortion for sex-selection, the hegemony of dominant males, and the gendered inequalities of unbridled capitalism.

Any ethical system that cannot recognize and preserve the necessary conditions for the emergence and/or continuance of its own highest good is, on its face, inconsistent. Kant argued that a noumenal agent ought not to take his own life—suicide is literally self-contradictory[20]—but the crucial issue is not whether to respect dignity once it is achieved but how and why to bring it about in the first place. (We must say "yes" to life before we say "yes, indeed" to reason.) An ethic of pure dignity that values only extant autonomy, cedes rights only to the already autonomous, and constrains the autonomous solely with appeals to rational self-interest is building castles in the air. Respecting only achieved dignity cannot be willed as a universal law, for the two reasons adumbrated above: (1) without unearned care being given to the "merely" sacred (those who are not yet autonomous agents), no dignified persons ever emerge, and (2) any dignity that already exists is itself eroded when the agent believes, narcissistically, that there is no other value than her freedom or when the society believes, equally narcissistically, that there is no reason to choose one course over another other than that it is collectively chosen. It may be that only dignity, one's own and others', ought to be respected, but respect is not the only necessary moral attitude, even politically; reverence for sanctity is the antecedent virtue by which we continue to live, one which informs and constrains individual and corporate liberty.

I call the opinion that rational dignity alone has rights the "we have no king but Caesar" view, because it takes the collective good of autonomy and makes it the *solum bonum*. An ethic of pure dignity would read Western history as the saga of Rome without Jerusalem, of works without grace, of justice without love— i.e., of Caesar without Christ. But this tack is self-deceptive, especially for democracies and even when it claims to be limited to politics, as I try to demonstrate at more length in section 5.[21]

III. Selves and Souls

Definitions

Like "dignity" and "sanctity," "self" and "soul" are sometimes treated as synonyms, each meaning roughly "an individual" or "a person." In my lexicon, however, "self" and "soul" denote different aspects of a human being. Taken narrowly, the former term ("self") points to the contingent and idiosyncratic dimension of humanity, whereas the latter ("soul") denotes the necessary and universal. The thesis that there is a universal human nature with identifiable lacks and capacities, beneath or behind what is historically attained or self-consciously constructed, is out of fashion in some quarters these days, but it still has its defenders.[22] My own commitment to this thesis can only be judged by the plausibility of my lexicon and the work I attempt to make it do.

By "self" I mean the subject of the constellation of words and deeds, traits and talents, that flows from and then back into our higher cognitive and volitional faculties. We are defined by our personal virtues and vices, our particular turns of mind and efforts of will. The self is conditioned by time and chance, to be sure, but it is most distinctively associated with conscious reflection and free choice. As *The Oxford English Dictionary* observes, combining "self-" with another word often means "expressing reflexive action, automatic or independent action."[23] The self both thinks and acts, both in relation to others and reflexively. With respect to another, a range of questions must be answerable if we are to claim to know his or her self. How smart is she? How loyal is he? What have been his triumphs and transgressions? To what does she give her attention and energy? More specifically, does he like modern art or classical literature? Does she like me? Similarly, the self asks reflexively: "Who am I now and who might I become in the future? If I study hard, might I become a lawyer? If I pray hard, might I become a saint? And why did I decline to ask my best friend Helen to marry me, but then turn around and elope with Ursula, whom I just met?" The self is also the part of us that answers the latter questions via inward address or outward action. We often don't know our selves until we overhear our own interior monologue or observe our own exterior behavior.

So regarded, the self is both a state and an activity. It is a state inasmuch as it is constituted by whatever mental and moral habits have been cultivated in the past. At any given time, one has an identity composed of a myriad of dispositions and demeanors shaped by experiment and experience. But the self is also an activity inasmuch as it is the ongoing process of relating one's past identity to the future via the present. "Given who I have been, what can I do now to become who I want to be?" This process requires imagination and determination to be done well, but it is performed by every sentient person to a greater or lesser degree.[24]

By "soul" I mean those shared vulnerabilities and inchoate powers that come along with being human. Unlike what might be called "self-ish" factors—the things that consciously individuate us—"soul-ish" realities are the common phenomena of our finitude: the ability to feel pain and/or joy, the need to be loved and/or to love, the potential for bodily and/or psychic growth, etc. If "dignity" is identified with the achieved merit of mature selves, then "sanctity" refers to a gratuitous legacy owned equally by all souls. Selves are to desert and prudence as souls are to grace and providence. Selves are intentionally made and making, governed from within—as in "self-made man"—but souls are given and taken, gifted from without. All human selves have souls, but not all human souls have selves. Treating "personhood" as synonymous with "selfhood," all human persons (you and I) have souls, but so do pre-persons (fetuses and babies), post-persons (the senile and the aenile), and nonpersons (the mentally retarded and unconceived future generations).

Emotion and the Body

If intellect and will are the primary seats of the self and its dignity, then emotion and the body are the primary seats of the soul and its sanctity. Rather than associating the soul with some impassive and immaterial part of the person, I associate it with the passionate and material flesh. "The human body is the best picture of the human soul," as Ludwig Wittgenstein says.[25] With its multiple orifices of sense perception, food consumption, waste elimination, affect expression, and sexual union, the body is sacred. If to be a dignified self is to be hard and angular, to be a sanctified soul is to be permeable. Love and hate, joy and fear, humor and anger, cynicism and piety flow into and/or out of our bodies as surely as do air and water, bread and wine, blood and semen, urine and feces. Equally certainly, these "soul-ish" exchanges have little to do with our higher cognitive and volitional faculties. They are not merely autonomic, but neither are they autonomous choices. On the contrary, they often work better when we stop thinking and let go. Mental aptitude and will power are undeniably important, and their loss is normally tragic, but there is a world of noncognitive well-being[26] and emotional engagement with others that is not reducible to "reason" or "rational appetite."

I learned about the limits of reason, and the potency of charity, while working one summer in the locked Alzheimer's ward of a California nursing home and hospital. There I spoke every day with a lovely woman whose words made absolutely no sense, and there I watched every day as a former ballerina giggled like a five-year-old girl as she pirouetted down the hall strapped to her wheelchair. One must never romanticize the affliction that is Alzheimer's disease, but my sadness over the diminishment experienced by these two elderly women was tempered by a sense that they were still present to me and to God, still capable of receiving and even giving love. In the final stages of dementia, all a patient can do is take, but so long as human caring can get through the ears and eyes, nose and mouth, to touch the soul, so long is that soul sacred. A patient who is beyond all care, giving it and receiving it, is already dead and may be removed from "life support," even if vestigial biological processes remain. But a patient still able to receive care remains alive and one of us, even if independent personality has waned.

The body is influenced by individual choices in time and space, of course—one has the physique at forty that one deserves—but the innate potencies and involuntary systems of the body do not vary much across borders or time zones. Here is no Cartesian dualism, I emphasize, since I do not equate the self with a separate metaphysical substance distinct from the soul and the matter in which it inheres. Again, the self and the soul are dimensions of the maturing human being, typically inseparable in reality if separated all too often in thought. To consider either the self or the soul to be ethereal or ghostly is more Hellenistic/Greek than Hebraic/Christian. Each human life is an evolving yet indivisible unity of mental and physical properties, volitional and emotional attributes, though at the margins (such as in the very young and the very old) the mental/volitional may be minimal and the physical/emotional maximal.[27]

The ancient Greek word *psyche* is usually translated "soul" and then contrasted with *soma*, which is usually translated "body." When construed in this way, "soul" is often connected with "mind" (*nous*) and "volition" (*thelema*), as quite distinct from (even opposed to) "passion" (*thumos*) and "flesh" (*sarx*).[28] My account departs from this complex and venerable tradition precisely because it aims to be truer to Moses and the prophets than to Plato and the philosophers. In the

King James Version of the Bible, Genesis 2:7 describes how "man became a living soul," the word translated as "soul" here being the Hebrew term *nephesh,* which usually is rendered as "a breathing creature," but it can also connote the broader notion of "vitality" as such. A breathing creature or the embodiment of vitality is much closer to what I mean by "soul" than is a detached or immaterial Greek psyche as described above. (Interestingly, the Greek word for passion, *thumos,* can literally mean "breathing hard.") When God breathes into Adam, He is animating dust, making it/him "a living soul"; but Adam has not yet had the experiences, has not yet made the intentional choices, that will constitute him a unique person/persona/self. Adam's self emerges only with reflection and decision—only after he is made aware of the tree of knowledge and perhaps, I am tempted to say, only after he has eaten from it and thus become "self-conscious." Prior to God's prohibition in the Garden, if not Adam's violation of that prohibition, Adam is a living human being but only potentially a responsible moral agent. Prior to God's "Thou shalt not," as Søren Kierkegaard reminds us, "[t]he spirit in man is dreaming."[29]

Autonomy and Holiness

The ancient Greek word *autos* is usually translated "self," either alone as the reflexive pronoun or in combination with other personal pronouns, as in "himself" (*heautou*) and "yourself" (*seautou*). In turn, *nomos* is rendered as "law" or "regulation." Thus something or someone is "autonomous" if it/he/she is literally "self-lawed"—meaning self-regulated or self-governing. The Greek idea was originally at home in the context of relations between city-states, with a polis claiming "autonomy" when it deemed itself neither client, colony, dependent, nor slave of another polis—Athens or Sparta, say—but rather an independent political body entitled to pass its own laws and generally capable of self-rule. As Jerome Schneewind, citing R. Pohlmann, has written,

> Initially standing for a political conception in Greek thought, the term ["autonomy"] came to be used in religious controversies during the Reformation; but its main use in early modern times was in political discussions. Kant seems to have been the first to assign broader significance to it, using it in his theoretical as well as his practical philosophy.[30]

If the Isle of Milos would claim political autonomy from Athens, Kant would claim personal autonomy from God. Kant was no more motivated by a tendency to licentiousness, of course, than Milos by a desire for anarchy. Rather, Kant "invented" the contemporary conception of "morality as self-governance," to borrow Schneewind's terms, because he believed in "the dignity and worth of the individual."[31]

Kant turned a collective political notion into a matter of individual conscience by insisting that "the true vocation of reason must be to produce a will that is good"[32] and that the good will acts neither for private advantage nor for the common good "but from the idea of the *dignity* of a rational being."[33] For Kant, "*[a]utonomy* is ... the ground of the dignity of human nature and of every rational nature," and an autonomous being "obeys no other law than that which he himself at the same time gives."[34] An autonomous will is, literally, "a law to itself."[35] Thus Kantian morality is not a matter of obedience to the commands of the Deity (much less of other people) but of the reflexive activity of our inmost selves. We must freely *choose* to act on rational principles that we ourselves authenticate, and the capacity "of doing ... actions not from inclination but *from duty*"[36] is the ground of our distinctively moral value as noumenal agents.

In contrast to Kant's frequent use of the German word *Autonomie,* the word "autonomy" appears nowhere in the major English translations of the Bible (e.g., the King James Version and the New Revised Standard Version). Instead of "autonomy," we hear much of "holiness" (*qodesh* in Hebrew, *hagiosune* in Greek). Holiness is a function of being inspired by or reflective of God and God's perfection; a holy human being or person is one "[s]pecially belonging to, commissioned by, or devoted to God."[37] In Scripture, to be holy is to possess sanctity, even as, in Kant, to be autonomous is to possess dignity. The difference is that biblical sanctity is seen as a gift from above, something passive, while Kantian dignity is judged an achievement from within, something active. In English, we speak of a person as "exercising autonomy" and as capable of "self-governance," but it would sound odd to say that she "exercises holiness" and is capable of "soul-governance." In declaring that the only thing that is unqualifiedly good, "good without limitation," is "a good will,"[38] Kant helped foster invidious contrasts between personal dignity—something rational—and impersonal sanctity—something religious.

Admittedly, Kant did discuss the idea of "a holy will," but such a will was inhuman. "Complete conformity of the will with the moral law is ... *holiness,* a perfection of which no rational being of the sensible world is capable at any moment of his existence."[39] The best we humans can hope for is "endless progress" toward perfection in a "postulated" afterlife,[40] on Kant's view, while a truly holy will is outside of the bounds of moral obligation and bodily drive altogether.[41] The two decidedly unchristian presumptions here are: (1) that holiness is located in the will alone, and (2) that holiness and humanity are incompatible. In Christianity, "holy communion" is equated preeminently with a social and very bodily act of eating and drinking—indeed, the elements consumed are body and blood—rather than with any noumenal free choice, however dutiful. Whatever his merits, and they are considerable, in leaving behind embodied sanctity as a part of the good life (the goodness of life), Kant left behind much of the image of God.

Let me now explore the biblical meaning of the image of God, asking how it might be unrationalized and thereby retrieved for purposes pious and democratic. Discussion of the *Imago* will allow me to pull together the foregoing distinctions between dignity and sanctity, selves and souls. To anticipate a possible misreading, this is no childish exercise in misology: to note the limits of reason is not to be irrational. As a corrective to Kant's allowing reason to criticize itself, I try to overhear the critique of reason by God and the flesh. Reason, like autonomy, has its proper place. As above, I offer not irrationalism but what might be called a "critique of pure dignity." This will set the stage for a discussion of the place of sanctity and its accompanying rights in a liberal society.

IV. The Image of God

Definitions

In Genesis 1:26, God resolves to create "humankind" (*adam*) "in our image" (*tselem*). The Hebrew word *tselem* can mean either an illusory shade/phantom or an accurate representation/figure. Given that God is the artisan, one inclines to the latter reading, but one ought not to gloss over the ambiguity here too quickly. The "shady" or "unfinished" nature of humanity is nicely captured by the Hebrew term. In Genesis 1:27, at any rate, we are given a further unpacking of *tselem*. There the image of God is equated with sexual differentiation and perhaps gender complementarity: "male and female he created them," and "God blessed them and God said to them, 'Be fruitful and multiply. . . .'"[42] This accent on bodily difference within the first couple makes it unmistakably clear that the *Imago Dei* denotes more than individual mind and will. The image of God may be said, loosely, to inhere in each individual, but, properly speaking, Adam and Eve together constitute the *Imago*. Their love for and cooperation with each other highlight the fact that, from the outset, the image of God is social and bodily, not inward and abstract. Adam and Eve need each other, and their union—which will later be called their "one flesh" (Gen. 2:24)—has the potential for procreation.[43]

The second creation story (Gen. 2:4b–25) contains a different chronology from that of the first (Gen. 1:1–2:3), with man being made first, then the animals, then woman. Some commentators construe this account as more patriarchal than the initial story in which male and female are created simultaneously and together constitute the image of God. They point out that Eve's being made from Adam's rib reverses the natural order of biological birth, in which man comes out of woman, and apparently gives priority and authority to Adam that Eve lacks. Other commentators have disputed this construal, noting that Eve is called a "helper" (literally a "partner") fit for Adam. Her being made from his rib connotes equality and relatedness, they maintain, not subordination. Eve alone is bone of Adam's bone and flesh of Adam's flesh, and the order of her appearance makes her the culmination of creation rather than an afterthought. Indeed, rather than being brought in as a mere prop to please Adam, Eve is arguably more active and intelligent than her "husband."[44] I favor the more egalitarian reading of Genesis 2:4b–25, especially when it is paired with Genesis 1:1–23, but one need not deny the ambiguity involved to draw several important conclusions about the meaning of the *Imago Dei*.[45]

In what, specifically, does the image of God consist? The answer lies in the biblical affirmation that "God is love" (1 John 4:8) and that "those who abide in love abide in God, and God abides in them" (1 John 4:16). In terms borrowed from my previous discussion, to be made in God's image is to embody an impersonal sanctity that ought to be honored and protected, as well as to have the potential for a personal dignity that ought to be respected and admired. We are made, in short, first to be loved and then to love. Adam and Eve clearly want and need each other, and this interdependence characterizes them before they fall into sin and shame. The need to receive love and/or the potential to give it I equate with the core of human sanctity, while the actual extension of love to others (and oneself) I equate with the highest human dignity, so high, in fact, as finally to outstrip dignity as a matter of giving and receiving only what is reciprocally due.[46] Both sanctity and dignity stem from the God who is love, however (see 1 John 4:7–12), and for this reason the first parents and all their progeny are said to be in God's image.

The above equations make two points, the first anthropological and the second theological. First, they highlight the fact that all human lives, male and female, share equally in the divine.[47] (This is an important corrective if rationality and autonomy are thought of as peculiarly masculine ideals.) The young and the old, the masculine and the feminine, the weak and the wicked, all need agapic love and can receive it with profit—usually but not exclusively in the context of family life; hence they must be counted as bearers of God's image. We were not created self-sufficient but rather soul-dependent. Second, the equations represent a truer picture of the biblical God's way with the world than one that portrays

God as looking only to merit and demerit. Whether one refers to God's calling male and female His "good" image, God's declaring His steadfast love (*'hesed*) for Israel, or God's incarnating in Jesus Christ, the Deity's covenantal care does not wait on humanity's maturation or achievement. God loves us first (1 John 4:10), while we are yet insensate in the womb (Ps. 139:13–16, Jer. 1:5) and while we are yet sinners in society (Rom. 5:8). A gracious providence does not overturn temporal justice, but it does precede, uphold, and even temper that justice.

The Priority and Durability of Sanctity

When the image of God is identified with dignified selves, this tends to encourage social elitism, if not genocidal cruelty, toward the "undignified" souls. As Kurt Bayertz writes, "[i]n Ancient times, the concept of dignity usually referred to respect for individuals with a high social status: a Greek king or a Roman senator, for example."[48] The ancient world valorized socioeconomic class, whereas the modern world worships self-conscious autonomy. But invidious contrasts between "us" and "them" are implicit in both. The best way to combat such elitism, to reiterate, is by conceiving of the *Imago* primarily as the bearer of sanctity and only secondarily as the fount of dignity. Indeed, the image of God endures even when dignity is lost or never appears, so long as the sacred need to receive or ability to give *agape* abides. "God is love" is the one unequivocal thing we can say of the Deity (1 John 4:8), and His image must reflect this fact. If Adam and Eve are made in God's image prior to their exercising any autonomous agency (Gen. 1:27), achieved dignity cannot be essential to the *Imago*; and if Cain, the first murderer, retains his status as divine image even after his guilty act (Gen. 4:8–16), loss of dignity cannot be destructive of the *Imago*.

The priority of sanctity is indicated by the fact that we are normally touched by innocent children and pity guilty adults regardless of calculations of merit or demerit. Because of their sanctity, we honor other human beings both before and after we respect them. Drawing on various etymological sources, James F. Keenan allows that "[t]he overarching effect of sanctity is veneration and inviolability; the overriding reason for both is its sacral quality, a point found in the Scriptures, e.g., in 2 Maccabees 3.12 and 1 Corinthians 3.17."[49] To appreciate sanctity is to adopt a "do no harm" and "help if you can" attitude that permits dignity itself to emerge or reemerge. We wonder at the freshness of a newborn but also at her frailty, at the complexity of a child but also at her incompleteness; we justly punish a thief or a murderer, but we also sorrow over her criminality (at least once she is caught) and usually seek to reform her.

The Hebrew-Christian Bible is not the only text to gesture toward an egalitarianism that treasures human life; writings of the Stoics also come to mind.[50] The Bible is unique, however, in attempting to base its universalism not on reason and volition but rather on the social and sexual body. A much more stable equal regard can be grounded in instinctual need and inherited potential, the solidarity of the flesh, than in contemplative aptitude and authentic agency, which tend to generate hierarchies of achievement. We are all mortals who must be fed and clothed, and who require affection and encouragement, but we are not all geniuses or paragons. Of course, bodily criteria can also lead to elitism—we are not all beauty queens or Olympic athletes—but I associate the image of God with physical need and potential, not physical charm or prowess. It is the ill and dependent in whom sanctity most shines and to whom charity most reaches out, not the healthy and self-supporting.

The *Imago* as Finite and Fallen

Even as medical doctors can learn about physical health by studying disease, so moral theologians can learn about the image of God by examining how it is "stained" or "warped" by sin. One powerful way to look at original sin is as an attempt to appropriate for personal use, exclusively for one's self, what should be accepted as an impersonal gift for all souls. Christian scholars have sometimes interpreted the biblical story of the Fall of Adam and Eve as a *felix culpa,* a fortunate fault, in which the naïve first parents take their initial steps toward informed, responsible adulthood. Indeed, it is sometimes suggested that God wanted, or should have wanted, Adam and Eve to eat of the fruit of the tree of knowledge to complete their moral education and to realize themselves as images of God. Without the initiation into moral knowledge, the argument goes, creatures would have remained dull and benighted. This reading is a colossal anachronism, however, and a dangerous misunderstanding of both human nature and the nature of sin.

One basic point must always be kept in mind in reading Genesis 2–3. God does not prohibit Adam and Eve from *looking at* and *learning from* the tree of knowledge of good and evil; rather, He forbids them to *eat* of it. All other trees in the garden are "fair game" as food, so to speak, but there is this one exception: the tree of ethical values. The previous verses of Genesis have depicted God as majestic Creator, capable of declaring creation "good" even before human creatures are made. Right at the beginning, then, humanity is implicitly warned against a hubris that would see itself as the measure of all things. After humans appear,

God gives them "dominion" over an exceptionally broad range of creatures; the Creator is not stingy. There are limits, however: the ethical values inherent in Eden are to be apprehended with awe rather than seized as one's own. Unlike seeing and appreciating, eating is a form of appropriation that internalizes and destroys the reality at which it is directed. Eating would turn what is external into a part of one's very self, and it is an "all-consuming" pride that thinks it is the sole inventor of values that is forbidden, then punished, in the Garden. When Adam and Eve ate the forbidden fruit, they denied their finitude and became the first moral subjectivists. They clutched the apple of God's eye and claimed it as their own product/produce.

It was not their curiosity or sexuality that cost Adam and Eve Paradise, but that they made an idol of their creative dignity. It is no wonder that their first-born son, Cain, became a murderer: when parents valorize their own dignity, children violate others' sanctity, if only to assert themselves or get attention.

An Objection and a Reply

It may be objected that my account of the image of God is too expansive or permissive. If the *Imago Dei* is minimally a function of the need to receive or ability to give agapic love, does this not mean that plants and animals also bear the divine image? Don't cherry trees and chipmunks, sea kelp and freshwater salmon, all profit from forms of charity? And, if so, aren't they all made in the image of God and possessed of sanctity rights? In a phrase, not likely. By "the need to receive or ability to give *agape*," I refer to what is almost surely a distinctly human phenomenon.[51] Plants and animals have independent value and can be both benefited and harmed by human behaviors, but flora and fauna do not strictly need loving intercourse with humans to flourish. They can, in principle, get along without us. Domesticated and zoo animals rely on human beings for food and shelter, and many would now die without ongoing support from homo sapiens. This is a contingent dependency, however, and is not inherent to the nature of the beasts as such. God might have declined to create Adam without thereby consigning the rest of biological creation to futility and extinction, but God could not have refrained from creating Eve without thereby condemning Adam to misery and death. Human beings require the company and cultivation of their own kind, love of *neighbor*, and without it we waste away and/or perish. (Many animal species display complex and interdependent social relations, of course, but the birds and the bees do not need us the way we need each other.) The self's catchphrase may be *cogito, ergo sum* ("I think, therefore I am"), but the soul's is *amor, ergo sum* ("I am loved, therefore I am").[52]

Consider a parent speaking animatedly to a babe in arms. The adult is not aiming to communicate information to the child, for the latter is too young to comprehend, nor is the adult looking for an immediate behavioral response. Rather, the parent is calling the baby into personhood by engaging its passive potential for language. The parent is loving the baby unconditionally, meeting its impersonal needs and engaging its nascent capacities, in a touching human communion. Without such agapic love—dignity reaching out to sanctity—the baby will literally die, or be so deeply stunted as never to achieve normal cognitive and emotional function. A few animals may be self-aware enough to qualify as "persons," and these few may well have a right to life, but it seems implausible to say that they either need agapic love or love others agapically.[53] Again, they evidently don't need agapic (or any other kind of) love *from us,* as part of their natures. No matter how devoted a trainer may be to her thoroughbred horses or a botanist to his hybrid orchids, there are inevitable constraints on the love that can or should pass between species.[54]

V. Democracy and Human Rights

Types of Rights

Democracy is often identified with the defense of "human rights," but to understand this identification we must unpack both words in the quoted phrase. I have begun in previous sections to interpret what it means to be "human," maintaining, among other things, that the soul of humanity is intimately tied to the image of Deity. More specifically, I have argued that God's image inheres in embodied need and potential rather than in disembodied intellect and will. (Christ himself needs to love and be loved.) I now turn to the meaning of "rights." The main point here is that the need-based rights of nonpersons must have an equally important place in a good society as the achievement-based rights of persons, perhaps even a more important place.

Rights are standardly divided into two basic types: positive and negative. Positive rights are claims to goods and opportunities that ought to be provided to one by others. One can claim the goods and opportunities (e.g., education or health care) as due one actively from without. Negative rights, on the other hand, refer to goods and opportunities that ought not to be tampered with by others. One can insist on various omissions by others, their passive noninterference with one's internal powers (e.g., with life and liberty). The positive/negative distinction is quite plausible, but it leaves undecided the basis for the relevant rights. Are we due provision of or noninterference with the goods and opportunities as a function of past performance (achieved merit), or are the rights in question grounded in our nature as such (shared need or potential)? Are the rights merely "legal" or "pragmatic" and dependent on cultural variables, or are they "natural" or "human" and applicable to everyone everywhere? (Voting at age eighteen is a legal right in the United States, but immunity from enslavement at any age is a universal human right. Why?) In answering these questions, we need to draw yet another contrast. Whether positive or negative, rights that depend on achieved merit I call "dignity rights," while rights that presuppose only shared need or potential for care I call "sanctity rights."

Respecting dignity rights is a matter of justice, of giving selves their "due" based on their personal actions and intentions. Honoring sanctity rights is a matter of love, of giving souls their "due" based on their impersonal liabilities and prospects. Dignity rights are earned, a function of reward, whereas sanctity rights are gifted, a function of inviolability. One can lose dignity rights by acting unethically or breaking the law or declining radically in autonomy. A drunk driver may lose the right to operate a motor vehicle, for example, and an end-stage Alzheimer's patient may be institutionalized and restrained. In contrast, one can never lose sanctity rights so long as one lives, since these rights do not turn on achieved merit or demerit. Even fetuses and capital felons, for example, have the right to life, in my judgment, because they remain images of God capable of giving or receiving love. In fact, it is a duty of love to affirm these lives.

The right to receive and the duty to give love differ from the rights and duties associated with contractual or reciprocal justice, but they are no less real. Indeed, the right and the duty are so fundamental to human life that they are almost too important to be called by those terms. The language of "rights" and "duties" usually suggests an adversarial relation in which conscious claims and counterclaims must be adjudicated by principles of fairness. I write, nevertheless, of love's "right" and "duty" to avoid the impression that *agape* is merely supererogatory, a matter of private discretion or optional philanthropy. On the contrary, love of neighbor, attentive to the sanctity of life, is the indispensable social good. The point to grasp is that a "duty of justice" is a matter of rewarding achieved merit, punishing demerit, or keeping promises or contracts, while a "duty of charity" is a matter of responding to God's call or the claim that another creature has on one simply by virtue of sharing the image of God. Duties of justice turn on reciprocity or retribution, while duties of love are more un-conditional and possibly unilateral. Duties of justice are founded on personal dignity, in sum, while duties of love are based on impersonal sanctity.[55]

Human Beings and Democratic Values

Many secular critics see Judaism and Christianity as placing individual human beings at the timeless center of the universe—God's special darlings—and thus as being falsified by Copernican and Darwinian revelations of humanity's cos-mic marginality and biological contingency. There is no denying that Western religion has at times encouraged an overweening pride in human nature. As I have indicated, however, one of the chief aims of Genesis 1–3 is to *decenter* "man." The tree of knowledge, rather than Adam and Eve, is "in the middle of the gar-den" (Gen. 3:3), and the point of the creation stories and their sequels is to high-light the fact that humanity is finite and fallen. There are limits to human intel-lect and will, limits on dignity-based rights, to put the point in modern terms. The Lord loves human beings, and He creates Adam and Eve purposefully, but they are an *image* of God, not the Deity Himself. It was the effort to deny their dependency on God and one another, to insist on boundless dignity rights, that caused Adam and Eve to trouble each other and thus to suffer and even to die.[56] They wanted to be left alone with their own autonomous creativity, and that is just what God gave them east of Eden.

Many religious critics see liberal democracy as similarly placing individual human beings on the timeless throne of the universe, and thus as being falsified by Aristotelian and Thomistic revelations of humanity's social nature and its re-liance on historical traditions and divine graces. There is no denying that Western democracy has at times encouraged an atomistic individualism that loses sight of civility and the common good. One of the chief aims of the Declaration of In-dependence and the U.S. Constitution, however, is to *dethrone* "man." Monar-chic sovereignty belongs to the Lord God alone. Humanity's knowledge, sympa-thy, and power are all finite and fallible, and these facts ought to dictate limited government and cooperative practices undertaken by otherwise competing per-sons and groups. Freedom to make major personal choices is important, but freedom does not exhaust democratic values. The American Revolution rallied around rights to "*life,* liberty, and the pursuit of happiness," while the French Revolution called for "liberty, *equality,* and *fraternity.*" Life and equality are not earned by individual performance but given as features of humanity. Equal regard, particularly for the least well off, is part of love's democracy—a "sacred" matter, as even the Deist Jefferson saw.

Sanctity Rights and Democratic Politics

If personal intellect and will generate dignity rights (to exercise free speech, to pursue happiness, to have valid contracts kept, to vote, to practice religious faith, etc.), then impersonal needs and potentials produce sanctity rights (to life, to health care, to education, to equal regard, to fraternal consideration, etc.). Again, one does nothing to merit the gift of life and the nurturance necessary to sustain and develop it, and attention to no positive achievement in time will render all human selves equal. Intellectual and moral accomplishments vary dramatically across individuals. It is not our rational and volitional works but rather our bodily vulnerabilities and potentials that most deeply unite us. We are all subject to injury and death, and we all need unconditional care to mature into autonomous agents capable of dignity.

Some contemporary philosophers conceive of democratic politics as concerned solely with the recognition and protection of dignity rights. Ronald Dworkin and Peter Singer, for instance, agree that only the interest-based rights of self-aware agents have substantive legal weight. Dworkin grants that some things without self-consciousness possess sanctity (e.g., great works of art and fetal human lives), while Singer doubts that sanctity exists. But both thinkers would restrict the liberal state to upholding the goods and opportunities associated with achieved selfhood. Consciousness has value, according to Singer, but only persons who are *self-*conscious actors across time have the right to life; personal freedom and equality must be supported by judicial and legislative means, according to Dworkin, but the steel of the law should not be used to enforce controversial judgments about what is impersonally valuable. For Dworkin, dignity decisively trumps sanctity in political and legal contexts; democratic respect for freedom of conscience precludes enforcing axiological views about the status of fetuses or the comatose, say, since these views are not generally agreed upon by all citizens. For Singer, again, dignity and pain avoidance are the only goods for the utilitarian to attend to; some animals (e.g., mature chimps) have personal dignity and thus should be seen as having the right to life, but some humans (e.g., newborn babies) lack personal dignity and thus should be seen as subject to swift, elective death.[57]

The problems with a political-legal ethic that focuses so exclusively on present dignity are (1) that it inevitably violates sanctity, and (2) that it neglects the necessary conditions for the emergence and preservation of dignity itself. Postpersons, such as those with senile dementia, and nonpersons, such as the retarded and future generations, have little or no legal standing when extant dignity dominates. As far as the state is concerned, there can be no compelling obligation to preserve or protect their lives. This is worrisome enough, but even more troubling is the fact that prepersons, such as fetuses and infants, have little or no standing either. They are not yet rational selves, so, on this view, they have few if any rights. One may be required not to visit pointless pain on such "impersonal" beings, but they have no right to life and most wrongs associated with their treatment relate to the interests of their family or caretakers. For Singer, a deformed (or perhaps merely unwanted) baby under twenty-eight days old may be killed at its parents' behest, so long as no unnecessary suffering is involved.[58] Dworkin holds that a fetus does not have interests and so is not a rights-bearer, at least not until very late in pregnancy—roughly thirty weeks of gestational age. Hence, most abortion is not an injustice to the fetus itself, not a violation of its rights, and the law must not restrict abortion beyond the minimal conditions set by *Roe v. Wade*.[59]

If fetuses and infants, not to mention generations as yet unconceived, have few if any rights, then there is little morally relevant distinction between abortion, infanticide, and so denuding the environment that future human life is impossible. Indeed, there is no legal obligation to care very much for things impersonal, beings not yet possessed of dignity, since dignity rights are the only kind with clout. This is clearly self-defeating, however, for both individuals and groups. Any society that attempts to prescind from normative verdicts about the status of impersonal goods—from life's beginning to its end—will undercut any basis on which to promote the necessary conditions for the personal. Just agents were once loved patients, even as majestic oaks were once tiny acorns, and you cannot secure the former without cultivating the latter.

Democratic society is defined by a commitment to the liberty and equality of its citizens, but if only autonomous agents count as democratic citizens, then liberty has undercut equality. Democratic equality has, at its best, looked not to personal excellence (what makes us heroic) but to impersonal need and potential (what makes us human); democracy has stood for inclusive regard for the rights of all, that is, especially the weak and marginalized. Among the weakest and most marginal are those who do not possess dignity: the very young, the very old, the very challenged, and the very guilty. These human lives still embody sanctity, however, and a democracy worthy of the name must count them as citizens bearing sanctity rights to care and protection. The needs and potentials of infants, for example, should translate into their right to receive love, even as the realized freedom and dignity of adults should translate into their duty to give love. Otherwise, both decency and democracy falter.

VI. Conclusion: Cultural Prescriptions

I began this essay by noting a small but significant change of wording in Thomas Jefferson's draft of the Declaration of Independence. The change was emblematic of the fact that for some proponents of the Enlightenment, including both Benjamin Franklin and Immanuel Kant, the self-evidence of human equality *to* reason was but a corollary of reason's being itself *the foundation* of equality. Shared reason was not merely the recognizer and revealer of universal human rights but also their main, perhaps their only, ontological basis. I have maintained in these pages that a Christian understanding of human nature, the body politic, and the body of Christ must reject this line. Amid our concern with "self-realization," "personal freedom," and "death with dignity," we must not forget about "soul cultivation," "impersonal need," and "life with sanctity." We are more than cognition and volition, so an emphasis on rationality must always be counterbalanced by an equally (if not more) profound attention to embodiment. If we look for inspiration and guidance solely from reason and rational appetite, the sources of dignity, we rely on weak reeds, but, more important theologically, we insult the meaning of the *Imago Dei*.[60] Without a stereoscopic vision of both our autonomous selves and our embodied souls, we cannot escape a cynicism about life that blinds us to its intricacy and depth.

We must see clearly the good and the bad in ourselves. Human intentionality and freedom are remarkable faculties, but biblical Christianity will always remind us that these faculties make possible both dignity and depravity.[61] Indeed, since the Fall out of Eden, our intellects and wills have been marked by prejudice and perversion, not always and everywhere but often and anywhere. The Fall of humanity means that no homeopathic cures for social evils are now possible. Inordinate pride in our own autonomy constituted the original sin, and more such pride only makes things worse. Defenders of liberal democracy who would prescribe for its citizens more private freedom and a more neutral public sphere, for instance, fail to see that it is precisely "freedom" and "neutrality" run amok that most threaten democracy itself. The ills associated with elective abortion, globalized capitalism, and Islamic terrorism cannot be overcome with sleight-of-hand slogans like "Hands off my body," "Let the market's invisible hand reign," and "Don't tie the hands of the military." The treatment for modern and postmodern selves (and societies) must be allopathic: we must be drawn out of our selves. The malaise of individual dignity can best be remedied by an appreciation of something outside of and antecedent to that dignity: human sanctity.

We must look to the original gift of life for existential meaning, rather than merely to our (supposedly) autonomous achievements. We are souls before, while, and possibly after we are selves; we are called eventually to be just, but we are made from the outset to be loved and loving. We are created to depend on and serve one another in time and in the flesh, and, once we grasp this fact, we may even glimpse the Creator who cherishes us all exactly as we are. To be loved by God, the One who made and then redeemed us, is to be empowered to love both selves and souls, our own and others'.

Love of souls is the perilously neglected political virtue of our time. It is a distinctly "democratic" virtue, in that the common needs and potentials with which it is occupied are most evident in the *demos,* the most wretched and most defenseless class. Love in a liberal society today must be attentive to liberty, equality, and *vulnerability.* Love of souls is also a distinctly "Christian" virtue, in that Jesus identified himself with the least well off in society. No society—democratic or undemocratic, Christian or un-Christian—can long survive unless its members are willing and able to identify with and sacrifice for others—to love them for their own sakes. Our interdependency is a sociological fact.

Let our selves rejoice in whatever rationality and dignity they can rightly claim, but let them also pay grateful tribute to the sacred souls from which they must spring. As I have said repeatedly, for personal selves to emerge out of impersonal souls requires unearned care, from "private" parties such as family and friends but also from civic institutions such as hospitals, schools, churches, and governments. (God's grace undergirds all of these caregivers, need I say, even as God's image is the recipient of care.) A liberal polis will not put all power of nurturance and protection into the hands of the nation state—subsidiarity and federalism are wise practical principles—and not all liberal citizens will talk of the "image of God." In my estimation, however, the sanctity of human life is a gift of God, and reverence for that sanctity should preclude a number of practices now countenanced by Western cultures: elective abortion, active euthanasia, capital punishment, and unbridled warfare—to name only a few cultural evils. More positively, reverence for sanctity should enjoin better child care, national health insurance, greater pro bono legal work, a more equitable tax system, and a discriminate military—to name only a few cultural goods. These prescriptions are controversial and obviously require detailed defenses not possible here,[62] but the spirit behind them is at once Christian and democratic.

However pressing casuistical issues are decided, no community can live without some conception of, and moral and legal commitment to, its own dependent and vulnerable humanity. The more a society attends charitably to the least among its members, as well as in the world at large, the wider will be its democratic politics and the deeper may be its Christian faith. The politics and the faith are not identical—we must say "no" to all political idolatry—but they can and should be mutually supporting.

NOTES

1. Walter Isaacson, *Benjamin Franklin: An American Life* (New York: Simon and Schuster, 2003), 312; Isaacson is following Becker, Van Doren, and Maier in this observation.

2. According to St. Thomas, "man is said to be the image of God by reason of his intellectual nature," and, properly speaking, "this image of God is not found even in the rational creature except in the mind." See *Summa Theologica*, I, Q. 93, arts. 4 and 6, trans. Fathers of the Dominican Province (Westminster, Md.: Christian Classics, 1981), 471 and 473. Thomas goes on to suggest, however, that other powers of the soul (such as the will) may be called, secondarily, a "trace" of God or in the "likeness" of God (ibid., arts. 6, 7, and 9).

3. See *A Latin Dictionary*, comp. Charlton T. Lewis and Charles Short (Oxford: Clarendon Press, 1987), 577 and 1626. For similar points, see the entries for "dignity" and "sanctity" in *The Compact Edition of the Oxford English Dictionary* (Oxford: Oxford University Press, 1971), vols. I and II, 726 and 2633, respectively.

4. See, for example, U.S. Catholic Bishops, "Statement on Capital Punishment" (Washington, D.C.: United States Catholic Conference, 1980), 7.

5. *A Latin Dictionary*, pp. 578 and 1626.

6. Kant, *Groundwork of the Metaphysics of Morals*, in *Immanuel Kant: Practical Philosophy*, trans. Mary J. Gregor (Cambridge: Cambridge University Press, 1996), 4:433–4:436, 83–85.

7. A passive potential (e.g., for language) must be engaged or cultivated by others in order to be realized.

8. The word "innocence" is usually contrasted with "guilt," and young children are standardly judged to be without guilt (leaving aside the issue of original sin). But children's innocence/guiltlessness is deeper than that of adults. Calling an adult "innocent" implies that she has not committed some specific wrong, while calling a child "innocent" refers to his being anterior to attributions of praise and blame altogether. Though a human being possessing sanctity, a young child is not yet a morally responsible agent possessing dignity.

9. "... and they brought to [Jesus] all the sick, those who were afflicted with various diseases and pains, demoniacs, epileptics, and paralytics, and he cured them" (Matt. 4:24). This verse could just as easily end with "and he loved them." Love is curative precisely in looking not at worth but at need, not at dignity but at sanctity.

10. *The Oxford English Dictionary*, vol. IX, S–Soldo (Oxford: Oxford University Press, 1933/78), 80.

11. See J. O. Urmson, "Saints and Heroes," in *Moral Concepts*, ed. Joel Feinberg (Oxford: Oxford University Press, 1969), 61–62.

12. *The Oxford English Dictionary*, vol. V, H–K, 345.

13. How active/passive the human being is in acquiring/exercising the theological virtues is much debated in Christian theology, with Catholics sometimes allowing more

synergy between divine grace and human freedom than Protestants. I myself am an Anglican Arminian, holding that faith, hope, and love are supernatural gifts offered by God to all. We can do nothing on our own to achieve them, so we are "passive" in that sense; but we can freely accept or reject them, so the relevant grace is not irresistible. The cardinal virtues, on the other hand, are much more subject to human will. Again, to achieve a cardinal virtue is, thus far, to become dignified; to receive a theological virtue is, thus far, to be sanctified.

14. See Kant, *Groundwork of the Metaphysics of Morals*, 4:421, 73; and Luke 6:20–21.

15. For a discussion of this distinction, though without reference to Kant, see Robert Pinsky, *Democracy, Culture and the Voice of Poetry* (Princeton: Princeton University Press, 2002), 64–73.

16. See the discussion of Adam and Eve below. What about cloning as a means of reproduction and homosexuality as a denial of male/female complementarity? Human cloning is now neither biologically possible nor morally defensible; until much greater technical mastery is had, it is irresponsible to risk the harm likely to be done to the subjects involved. Homosexuals still often speak of "masculine" and "feminine" partners, though these gender roles are no longer so directly tied to sexual difference. The deep need for romantic cooperation by two parties endures.

17. It is notable that the procreation that sustains the generations requires a bodily act in which rational self-control is let go and passion brings two together as "one flesh" (Mark 10:8). *Pace* Augustine, sexual intercourse as such does not violate personal dignity, but two persons (a man and a woman) must set aside their insistence on autonomy if sanctity is to be "reproduced." And without sanctity, no dignity. Beyond biological reproduction, sustaining children also involves loss of autonomy, as all new parents can attest. Sex can also be quite calculated and calculating, to be sure, but it is normally the denying or delaying of sexual intercourse that requires rational self-control, not its present enjoyment. Viagra and vibrators have not made sex entirely vapid and volitional.

18. See Martha C. Nussbaum, *Upheavals of Thought: The Intelligence of Emotions* (Cambridge: Cambridge University Press, 2001).

19. Peter Singer has argued for exactly this premise and conclusion; see his *Practical Ethics* (Cambridge: Cambridge University Press, 1993), *Rethinking Life and Death: The Collapse of Our Traditional Ethics* (Oxford: Oxford University Press, 1994), and *Unsanctifying Human Life,* ed. Helga Kuhse (Malden, Mass.: Blackwell Publishers, 2002).

20. "A human being cannot renounce his personality as long as he is a subject of duty, hence as long as he lives; and it is a contradiction that he should be authorized to withdraw from all obligation, that is, freely to act as if no authorization were needed for this action." See Kant, *The Metaphysics of Morals*, 6:422, 547.

21. Some liberal apologists would celebrate personal dignity, and its attendant rights, as the singular *political* value, allowing room for sanctity as a private or familial concern but without extending it substantive legal protections. John Rawls approximates this view—see his *Political Liberalism* (New York: Columbia University Press, 1993)—as does Ronald Dworkin, discussed below.

22. See, e.g., Martha C. Nussbaum, "Non-Relative Virtues: An Aristotelian Approach," in *The Quality of Life*, ed. Martha C. Nussbaum and Amartya Sen (Oxford: Clarendon Press, 1993); her *Sex and Social Justice* (Oxford: Oxford University Press, 1999); and her *Women and Human Development: The Capabilities Approach* (Cambridge: Cambridge University Press, 2000).

23. *The Oxford English Dictionary,* Vol. IX, S–Soldo, 80.

24. As Søren Kierkegaard's pseudonym Anti-Climacus puts it, rather playfully:

> A human being is spirit. But what is spirit? Spirit is the self. But what is the self? The self is a relation that relates itself to itself or is the relation's relating itself to itself in the relation; the self is not the relation but is the relation's relating itself to itself. A human being is a synthesis of the infinite and the finite, of the temporal and the eternal, of freedom and necessity, in short, a synthesis.

See Kierkegaard (Anti-Climacus), *The Sickness Unto Death,* trans. Howard V. Hong and Edna H. Hong (Princeton: Princeton University Press, 1980), 13. Behind the humor in this quote is the truth that the self is reflexive awareness and choice.

25. Wittgenstein, *Philosophical Investigations,* trans. G. E. M. Anscombe (Oxford: Blackwell, 1958), 178e.

26. I take the phrase "noncognitive well-being" from Stephen G. Post, *The Moral Challenge of Alzheimer Disease* (Baltimore: The Johns Hopkins University Press, 1995), 9.

27. Cf. Peter Strawson's account of "persons" in *Individuals: An Essay in Descriptive Metaphysics* (London: Methuen, 1959).

28. Typical of the Western tendency to identify "soul" with "mind," as well as to associate both with the "self," is Owen Flanagan's recent *The Problem of the Soul: Two Visions of Mind and How to Reconcile Them* (New York: Basic Books, 2002). Flanagan's is a complex and important book, but it employs the sort of intellectualist vocabulary that inevitably leads to "the mind/body problem." Is the mind made in "the humanistic image" of philosophy and theology or in "the scientific image" of biology and chemistry? Is the soul/self nothing but the mutable brain, or does it have a permanent and immaterial essence? For my part, I want to reject Flanagan's initial step of equating human identity with the "mental" powers of reflection and free will. This step makes the brain the privileged organ of inquiry and the soul/self nothing but a synonym for rational agency. Our shared humanity is more than rational agency, I have been arguing, and when the soul is seen as seated in the entire body and as possessed of needs and potentials antecedent to self-consciousness, this fact comes into clearer focus.

29. Kierkegaard (Vigilius Haufniensis), *The Concept of Anxiety,* trans. Reidar Thomte (Princeton: Princeton University Press, 1980), 41.

30. Schneewind, *The Invention of Autonomy* (Cambridge: Cambridge University Press, 1998), 3, n. 2.

31. Ibid., 6.

32. Kant, *Groundwork of the Metaphysics of Morals,* 4:396, 52.

33. Ibid., 4:434, 84.

34. Ibid., 4:436 and 4:434, 85 and 84.

35. Ibid., 4:440, 89.

36. Ibid., 4:398, 53.

37. *The Oxford English Dictionary,* Vol. V, H–K, 346.

38. Kant, *Groundwork of the Metaphysics of Morals,* 4:393, 49.

39. Kant, *Critique of Practical Reason,* in *Immanuel Kant: Practical Philosophy,* trans. Mary J. Gregor (Cambridge: Cambridge University Press, 1996), 5:122, 238.

40. Ibid.

41. "*Morality* is . . . the relation of actions to the autonomy of the will, that is, to a possible giving of universal law through its maxims. . . . A will whose maxims necessarily har-

monize with the laws of autonomy is a *holy,* absolutely good will. The dependence upon the principle of autonomy of a will that is not absolutely good (moral necessitation) is *obligation*. This, accordingly, cannot be attributed to a holy being." See Kant, *Groundwork of the Metaphysics of Morals*, 4:439, 88. Given its "subjective imperfection" (meaning "pathological" loves and wayward "inclinations"), "the human will" must flee bodily idiosyncrasy and rely on autonomously chosen imperatives, an autonomy that is not attributable to "the *divine* will." See Ibid., 4:414, 67, and 4:399, 55.

42. Karl Barth is the premier Christian theologian of the last century to interpret the image of God, as referred to in Genesis, in terms of sexual dimorphism and relatedness. See his *Church Dogmatics*, III/2 and III/4, trans. Harold Knight, G. W. Bromiley, J. K. S. Reid, and R. H. Fuller (Edinburgh: T. and T. Clark, 1960). In *CD*, III/2, 324, Barth concludes that man's humanity is "fellow humanity," that "[b]ecause [God] is not solitary in Himself, and therefore does not will to be so *ad extra*, it is not good for man to be alone, and God created him in His own image, as male and female."

43. Against a purely "soulish" reading, David J. A. Clines has written: "The human person according to the Old Testament is a psychosomatic unity; it is therefore the corporeal animated person that is the image of God. The body cannot be left out of [the] meaning of the image; the person is a totality, and its 'solid flesh' is as much the image of God as its spiritual capacity, creativeness, or personality, since none of these 'higher' aspects of the human being can exist in isolation from the body." See Clines, "Humanity as the Image of God," in *On the Way to the Postmodern: Old Testament Essays 1967–1998*, Vol. 2 (Sheffield, England: Sheffield Academic Press, 1998), p. 31 in the Internet reprint (http://www.shef.ac.uk/~biblst/ Department/Staff/BibsResearch/DJACcurrres/Postmodern2/...).

44. See Phyllis Trible, "Eve and Adam: Genesis 2–3 Reread," in *Womanspirit Rising: A Feminist Reader in Religion* (San Francisco: HarperSanFrancisco, 1979), 75 and 79. While I find Trible's defense of an egalitarian reading of the second creation account generally persuasive, I believe she goes too far in construing the pre-Eve Adam as physiologically androgynous (74, 76, and 78). He is a "man" (*adam*) made of "soil" (*adamah*), and before Eve is formed out of his rib he is not yet aware of himself as a male, but the latter is an epistemic point about what he realizes, not an ontological point about what he is. It is exactly because Adam is a human male without a human female that he is dissatisfied with both solitude and the animals. To think Adam initially either hermaphroditic or sexually undifferentiated renders it impossible to understand why he pines for a partner and why he is so enthusiastic about being given Eve. Eve awakens Adam to conscious masculinity, but only because he is already biologically male and in some sense incomplete without her. (God's incompleteness theorem is offensive to some feminists, but note that it is Adam who is depicted as poignantly needing Eve. Can I help it if the Deity is a romantic?) To emasculate the body of pre-Eve Adam is to suggest that human sexual differentiation was not part of God's original plan for creation, a storyline much more Aristophanic and Greek than Mosaic and Hebrew. See also Trible, *God and the Rhetoric of Sexuality* (Philadelphia: Fortress Press, 1978), 72–143; and Brevard Childs, *Old Testament Theology in a Canonical Context* (Philadelphia: Fortress Press, 1986), pp. 188–95.

45. Some would interpret the image of God as purely relational, as not a matter of any innate feature or faculty of human beings but of God's loving gaze directed toward them. As a recognition of humanity's dependence on God and a strategy to insure its humility, this tack has some appeal. There is a poetic simplicity in thinking of human nature as like a mirror that reflects God's image: the image appears on the mirror, but it is

not an intrinsic property of the mirror. The problem with this reading, however, is that it undermines the Genesis account of God's *creating* Adam and Eve and calling them (and everything else) *good* (Gen. 1:31). If we would do God the honor of believing that He can bring into existence (and love) realities other than Himself, realities with a finite integrity of their own, we must see the *Imago* as an ontological facet of human nature. Otherwise, God seems solipsistic and "creation" but an autoerotic game.

46. If one helps one's wife with the kids, for example, this may be an expression of moral dignity if it is pursuant to a promise or otherwise part of an agreement regarding the division of family labor, or it may be an act of neighbor love if it is more spontaneous and gratuitous. The point is that loving kindness is a moral excellence that typically rises above calculations of desert, contract, and compensation. I thank Terence Cuneo for moving me to clarify this distinction.

47. As David Clines observes, "whereas in the rest of the ancient Near East the image of God was limited to the king, in Genesis it is regarded as characteristic of humankind generally, without distinction between king and commoner, man and woman, or Israelite and non-Israelite." See "Humanity as the Image of God," 25.

48. Kurt Bayertz, "Human Dignity: Philosophical Origin and Scientific Erosion of the Idea," in *Sanctity of Life and Human Dignity*, ed. Kurt Bayertz (Dordrecht, Boston, and London: Kluwer Academic Publishers, 1996), 73.

49. James F. Keenan, S.J., "The Concept of Sanctity of Life," in *Sanctity of Life and Human Dignity*, 3.

50. See Bayertz, "Human Dignity," 73.

51. I speak here of creaturely *agape*. God loves agapically, but I am concerned with the image rather than the original of Love.

52. Perhaps better is *amatus sum, ergo sum* ("I have been loved, therefore I am"), but perhaps best is *amor, ergo amo* ("I am loved, therefore I love").

53. My Emory colleague, Frans de Waal, has described behaviors among apes that look very much like "altruism" and "empathy"; see his *Good Natured: The Origins of Right and Wrong in Humans and Other Animals* (Cambridge, Mass.: Harvard University Press, 1996), 19–20, 56–57, and 228. He cautions, nonetheless, against projecting too robust a moral sensibility onto the higher primates. I can only acknowledge that if chimpanzees, say, genuinely love their neighbors, then they too are made in God's image. Better to expand the moral community to include some animals than to contract it to exclude some humans.

54. Edward Albee's play *The Goat, or Who Is Sylvia?* is a powerful study of just how wrong-headed and destructive bestiality can be. Albee deftly suggests that Martin's claim to be in love with Sylvia, a female goat, stems from his forgetfulness of who he is, especially in relation to his wife, Stevie. Martin first sees Sylvia while stopping in the country to buy some (forbidden?) fruits and vegetables, and he subsequently represents an Adam who, unlike the original, would pronounce the animals enough. He has carnal relations with the beast. Stevie (whose name is an apparent play on "Second Eve") must finally kill the goat to impress on her husband that she, Stevie, is the partner fit for him—not just sexually, but also morally and spiritually. Martin's "loving" Sylvia radically distorts his needs and potentials, making it impossible for him to love or be loved by Stevie. (Need I mention the injustice the adultery does to Stevie herself?) By "scapegoating" Sylvia, Stevie shows her husband the difference between human beings, who have a right to life, and animals, which typically do not. Only then can Martin recall himself and say he is sorry for the pain and

confusion he has caused. For a contrasting perspective on these matters, but without reference to Albee's drama, see Peter Singer's "Heavy Petting," http://www.Nerve.com, March 2001. Singer does not quite endorse bestiality, but he finds little to object to in it, so long as it is painless to both parties.

55. As indicated above, I equate the "personal" with the idiosyncratic, the distinctive features of our individual historical lives; I equate the "impersonal" with the universal, the common elements of our shared human natures. At times, I refer to this distinction as that between "existence" and "essence," without intending thereby to endorse an unnuanced existential*ism* or essential*ism*.

56. Whether human mortality is "natural," a part of God's original plan, or an "unnatural" calamity visited on the species as punishment by God, Genesis at least suggests that the *fear* of death, seeing it as threatening to meaningful life, is the result of human self-centeredness, the folly of grasping at one's life as a possession.

57. See Dworkin, *Life's Dominion: An Argument about Abortion, Euthanasia, and Individual Freedom* (New York: Knopf, 1993), *Freedom's Law: The Moral Reading of the American Constitution* (Cambridge, Mass.: Harvard University Press, 1996), and *Sovereign Virtue: The Theory and Practice of Equality* (Cambridge, Mass.: Harvard University Press, 2000); and Singer, *Practical Ethics, Rethinking Life and Death,* and *Unsanctifying Human Life.*

58. Singer, *Rethinking Life and Death,* 217. Singer has had second thoughts about the twenty-eight-day boundary; see his "Dangerous Words," an interview with the *Princeton Alumni Weekly* (January 26, 2000), 19.

59. Dworkin, *Life's Dominion,* 18–19.

60. My distinction between the soul's sanctity and the self's dignity is akin to the Eastern Orthodox distinction between the "image" and the "likeness" of God. Rather than reading Genesis 1:26's reference to God's "image" (*tselem*) and "likeness" (*demuwth*) as a hendiadys, the Orthodox tradition treats the divine image as an ontological given for all humanity and the divine likeness as a (partial) historical achievement for some persons. I thank Terence Cuneo for calling this parallel to my attention.

61. See Reinhold Niebuhr, *Christian Realism and Political Problems* (New York: Charles Scribner's Sons, 1953), 101–2; and John Witte, Jr., "Between Sanctity and Depravity: Human Dignity in Protestant Perspective," in *In Defense of Human Dignity,* ed. Robert Kraynak and Glenn Tinder (Notre Dame, Ind.: University of Notre Dame Press, 2003).

62. I try to provide such defenses for many of these proposals in Jackson, *The Priority of Love: Christian Charity and Social Justice* (Princeton: Princeton University Press, 2003), and "A House Divided, Again: Sanctity vs. Dignity in the Induced Death Debates," in *In Defense of Human Dignity.*

3 | EVOLUTIONARY NATURALISM AND REDUCING THE DEMAND OF JUSTICE

JOHN HARE

This essay discusses two recent attempts to provide an evolutionary and naturalistic account of why we are under the obligation to be just in our dealings with each other. Larry Arnhart, who is a political theorist and one target of my essay, aims to follow Aristotle in understanding natural justice and natural right as "resting on a biological conception of natural teleology."[1] Michael Ruse, who is the other target, rejects this position, arguing for the claim that an evolutionary account of justice does not need any such foundation.[2] I am going to pose a dilemma about whether to claim a naturalistic foundation for the demand of justice or to deny that it needs one. My conclusion will be that foundationalist views such as Arnhart's and antifoundationalist views such as Ruse's reduce the demand of justice unacceptably. The connection with the theme of this book is that a liberal polity, if it is going to justify a strong notion of rights, must appeal to an objective demand of formal justice. I will not try to defend this conceptual connection between liberalism and formal justice. But I will explain in attacking Arnhart what I mean by "formal justice," and in attacking Ruse what I mean by "objective." Roughly, the demand of formal justice is that each person should count as one, and no person as more than one. And, roughly, a normative claim is objective if it is made true by facts outside us, which we can either recognize or fail to recognize. If my attacks are on target, the views of both Arnhart and Ruse present a threat to the project of a liberal polity.

Arnhart and Ruse both deny, for very different reasons, that there is an objective moral demand of formal justice. But there are at least two types of evolutionary ethics that accept such a demand, and which I will not try to cover in this essay.[3] Each of them can be understood as originating in the views of Darwin, though these views in Darwin are not consistent with each other. One possibility is that biological evolution gives us a picture of human beings that is at odds with an ethics of formal justice and, therefore, if we are to sustain such an ethics, we need to balance it with some other source of normativity. Darwin, for example, sometimes suggests a tension between biology and social norms. Donald Campbell follows these suggestions by founding a naturalistic ethics on social or cultural evolution that is not itself based on biological evolution, but is in tension with it.[4] Darwin also tends toward a kind of romanticism about progress in nature, following Alexander von Humboldt.[5] This is the belief in a kind of immanent life force that produces, first, life itself, and then higher and higher forms of life which emerge finally into freedom, culture, and the recognition of the equal dignity of every human being. These views and the relationship between them I will have to set aside for the present discussion.

I. Larry Arnhart

Arnhart argues this way: the good is the desirable, and the desirable is what is generally desired by human beings. I will call this "the double identity." By "generally desired" he means that these desires are found in most people in every society throughout human history, though not necessarily in every person, since there may be defective individuals who lack them. The connection he makes with evolution is that it is evolution which has given us these desires, operating selectively on our species in the hunter-gatherer stages of our development during the Pleistocene era. Evolution gave us these desires, he says, because they enhanced survival and reproduction.[6] He lists twenty of these desires, and the framework of his argument is that if a desire is general in this sense, belonging to this list of twenty, then its fulfillment is good.

I do not want to deny that there are desires that are general in this sense. That is an empirical question, and we should listen to what the comparative anthropologists tell us about it. Arnhart has done ethical theory a service by bringing together much of the germane scientific literature, not just from anthropology but from ethology and cognitive and social psychology. What I want to deny is the double identity. This opposition will be no surprise to Arnhart because I am arguing as an adherent of the Augustinian and Kantian tradition in ethics, which he attempts to undermine. I want to argue that if we think of the good the way Arnhart does, we will end up reducing the demand of justice unacceptably.

One quick way to reject Arnhart's project is to say that he is trying to deduce an "ought" from an "is." Hume is sometimes interpreted as arguing that such an inference is always invalid because it introduces into the conclusion a normative term which is not present in the premises.[7] I am not going to use this argument, because I think it begs the question against Aristotelian teleology, and there are defensible versions of the teleological view of substance, including human substance.[8] The argument, I think, is *too* quick. Nonetheless I will try to show that Arnhart's particular derivation of normative conclusions from descriptive premises does not succeed.

The dispute between us has many predecessors. When Socrates raises the question "What is justice?" in the first book of the *Republic,* the answer he gets from Polemarchus is that "justice is to benefit one's friends and harm one's enemies."[9] Socrates is not happy with this answer because it is one of the governing convictions of his life that it is always wrong to do harm, even in retaliation.[10] Arnhart is on the side of Polemarchus in this dispute, which shows already that he does not accept the demand of formal justice. He wants to deny that there is an ethical demand to love our enemies and, indeed, he denies that there is any valid principle of ethics that requires disinterested benevolence. The following quotation gives the flavor. It comes in a discussion of Darwin's inconsistency about ethics. Arnhart says:

> Darwin is wrong in thinking that female sympathy—as rooted in maternal care—can expand into a disinterested universal sentiment of humanity. After all, even maternal care manifests itself as a love of one's own offspring and a willingness to defend them against strangers. And although sympathy can be expanded to embrace ever-larger groups based on some sense of shared interests, this will always rest on loving one's own group *as opposed to other groups.* Darwin's appeal to universal humanitarianism can only be explained as a utopian yearning for an ideal moral realm that transcends nature, which contradicts Darwin's general claim that human beings are fully contained within the natural order.[11]

Arnhart thinks Darwin is misled here by a false sense that there is something wrong with motivation directed towards one's own happiness. Arnhart has a brief section condemning the doctrine of total depravity and what he calls, following Frans de Waal, "Calvinist sociobiology." He continues:

> But if I am right about this, if human beings are not bound together by a universal sentiment of disinterested humanitarianism, then deep conflicts of interest between individuals or between groups can create moral trage-dies in which there is no universal moral principle or sentiment to resolve the conflict. When individuals or groups compete with one another we must either find some common ground of shared interests, or we must allow for an appeal to force or fraud to settle the dispute. The only alterna-tive, which I do not regard as a realistic alternative, is to invoke some tran-scendental norm of impartial justice (such as Christian charity) that is be-yond the order of nature.

I want to state briefly what such a norm might be. Stating it does not demon-strate it; I am not going to try to do that. But I will try to show that the revision of morality that Arnhart has to make is more substantial than appears at first sight. The norm I have in mind is the Golden Rule in its reformulation by Kant as the first and third formulas of the Categorical Imperative.[12] Suppose my friends and I are watching a soccer game, and we decide to stand up for the whole game to get a fuller view, thus preventing the family in the row of seats behind us from seeing any of the play.[13] If I want to judge this decision morally, the first formula forbids me from making ineliminable singular reference to any other individual and, in particular, myself. I have to prescribe that the person who wants to stand may do so even in the hypothetical case in which I am in the row behind him and cannot see any of the game. And, according to the third formula, I have to share the morally permitted ends of those affected by my act, for example, the purpose of those behind me who want to see the game as well. That is, I have to make those ends my own ends. If I do this kind of moral thinking I will find that I am not morally permitted to stand up throughout the game, and that I ought to sit down.

What is the role in this scenario of desires and motivation directed towards one's own happiness?[14] One way to look at the issue is by considering what Kant himself would say about it. According to Kant, it is not that desires are made ir-relevant by this kind of moral thinking. The goal is that inclination and duty should be aligned with each other; this is how Kant appropriates the doctrine of sanctification. But desires, even if they are general in Arnhart's sense, are not authoritative because even our typical desires can be directed to immoral ends. Kant, we might say, also appropriates the doctrine of total depravity. This is not the view that we have no good in us. On the contrary, we are born with what Kant and Calvin both call "a seed of goodness," which hears the call of the moral law. Rather, the doctrine is that there is also a fundamental innate propensity to evil on top of this that "prevents the seed of goodness from developing as it otherwise would" into the fruit of a morally good life.[15] The natural desires we are born with are thus a mixture of good and bad, with a basic ranking, in Kant's terms, of our own happiness above our duty to others. It is worth adding that, contrary to what Arnhart says, Kant and Aquinas are here on the same side of the dispute.[16] Both of them see the need for a combination of inclination and reason in the human moral life. Both hold that all humans have the same moral worth, which must be acknowledged. For example, Aquinas talks of an honor or subjection "which regards some dignity of a man absolutely" because "in respect of that dignity, a man is made to the image or likeness of God."[17] And they both hold that we are, unfortunately, born with an innate but imputable tendency to put ourselves first and so fail to acknowledge this equal worth in others.

How is it that Arnhart reaches the conclusion that there is no authoritative norm of formal justice? I think the key is the claim that the good is what is generally desired. When Arnhart looks at the desires he thinks evolution gave us in our hunter-gatherer stage, he does not find a desire to respect human dignity as something valuable in itself. What he does find (among the list of twenty) are desires for social status, for political rule (though this is, he says, a natural male desire, not a natural female desire), for war (again, a male desire), for wealth (that is, enough property to equip one for a good life and to display social status), and for justice as reciprocity. I will come back to several of these desires later, but it is this last desire that I want to focus on because it will be the meaning of "reciprocity" which determines how successful the arguments are about women and slaves that I will end with.

What is justice as reciprocity? It is fairness in exchange—in Polemarchus's terms, a benefit for a benefit and a harm for a harm. Arnhart takes the notion from Hume, and for Hume justice as reciprocity extends only as far as utility. A person will be motivated towards reciprocity by the desire for this kind of justice to the extent that she perceives that she will benefit or that she will avoid harm to herself. If we imagine, therefore, a society in which those whom we exploit will not be able to harm us because of their weakness, we will not be moved by justice as reciprocity to end the exploitation even if we are resented for it. This is Hume's conclusion—that no inconvenience would result from the exercise of such a power and, therefore, the restraints of justice would be totally useless, though we might be motivated by compassion and kindness.[18] For justice as reciprocity to be involved here, the subservient population not only would have to resent the subservience, but to be able to resist and make us feel the effects of their resentment. If we know they will not succeed, there are no rules of reciprocal justice to stop us because there is no penalty enforced for breaking them. If, however, we think that those we are exploiting may well rise up against us and prevail, then we will be motivated by justice as reciprocity to acknowledge their present demands.

It is important to distinguish this sense of reciprocity from a different one. The Golden Rule in its Kantian formulations embodies a kind of reciprocity, but a more morally ambitious kind. It assumes already that we acknowledge the other as a person of equal worth and, therefore, make her ends our own ends. This acknowledgment is not, however, built into justice as reciprocity as Arnhart conceives it.[19]

Aristotle is the hero of Arnhart's book, and I want to focus on Aristotle's treatment of the moral status of women and slaves because these are the two main cases (along with parents and children) that Arnhart discusses. Aristotle notoriously held that women are inferior to men and, therefore, should never rule either in state or (over adult free males) in household. And he justified slavery on the basis that some people are by nature incapable of ruling themselves. Arnhart wants to let Aristotle off the hook on slavery on the grounds that the ancient philosopher is being deliberately confusing, so as to make us work out his hidden views, which are actually more humane.[20] The evidence for this is supposed to be that there are texts that are hard to fit into a coherent view. But this is often true in Aristotle. *Metaphysics* VII and VIII, for example, contain texts about essence that make it hard to discern a consistent view.[21] But to suppose that Aristotle is deliberately including confusion seems to me quite alien to his character, which is one of constantly searching for more clarity. I think we have to take his statements about women and slavery as reflecting his own views. What is relevant in the present context is to connect these views with his account of human nature. Aristotle thinks that some humans simply do not have the kind of rational control that makes ruling or freedom appropriate and that is especially distinctive of human life.[22] More deeply, humans by nature desire wealth, power over others, and high social status. Here Aristotle and Arnhart are in agreement. For both of them, the human good includes wealth, power, and status. There is nothing in the character of the good thus conceived to make patriarchy or slavery naturally abhorrent. I think that Aristotle is for the most part right about the natural desires we are born with. He is not right, however, in the inference to the human good. We *do* naturally desire these things, but it does not follow from the fact that we desire them that they are good.[23]

One way to see this is to see that the natural desires conflict. I will illustrate this from Arnhart's own treatment of the moral status of women and slaves. He says:

> The natural pattern of desires typical for men is not the same as that typical for women. Men typically have a stronger desire for sexual promiscuity, while women typically have a stronger desire for intimate companionship. Men typically have a stronger desire for dominance, while women typically have a stronger desire for nurturance. Men typically desire the solidarity of comradeship, while women typically desire the solidarity of kinship. Because of their typical desires, the distinctive virtue of men is courage, while the distinctive virtue of women is sympathy.[24]

We have here a refinement of the initial double identity. What is good is not merely what is generally desired by humans, but what is generally desired by *natural* subgroups of humans, such as males and females. This refinement was already present in the list of twenty natural desires, which implied a conflict between the natural desire profiles of the male and female members of the species. This view is quite compatible, Arnhart says, with a feminist naturalism, and he quotes remarks by Carol Gilligan and other second-wave feminists about "a different voice."[25] But these feminists were not actually in favor of separating the political and domestic spheres and granting a complementary preeminence in the political sphere to males and in the domestic sphere to females. Even if Arnhart is right about what the natural desires are, I think we should resist the proposed double identity and therefore the inference from general desire over human history to the human good. The frustration of natural desire, he tells us, is bad. Males have a natural desire for promiscuous and casual sexual partnership (while naturally desiring fidelity from their long-term female partners in order to secure the paternity of their children). This sets up a *conflict* between what we might call natural male and female mating strategies. Is Arnhart saying that the satisfaction of *both* conflicting desire-patterns is good?

Arnhart does in fact have a term for conflict in natural desires, and he should, I think, use it here too, though he does not. It is the term "tragedy." We get tragedy whenever we get two natural desires in conflict with no resolution by common self-interest, and Arnhart does not give us any way to proceed in such cases except by coercion. He gives a clear account of the meaning of tragedy in the process of arguing that female genital mutilation is wrong and should be abolished, and is *not* merely tragic. It is wrong, he says, because it frustrates natural human desires. It would be merely tragic if there were a conflict between natural desires for it and against it and no common ground of shared interests to mediate the dispute.[26] The proponents of female genital mutilation claim that it fulfills natural male desires to control female sexuality (so as to secure paternity) and perhaps to promote male sexual pleasure. Arnhart thinks rightly that to be consistent he has to show that the practice does not fulfill these natural male desires. For if it does fulfill them, then we will find ourselves in what he calls a tragic dilemma; this is where a dispute is not amenable to universal moral principle but only to force and fraud.[27] In particular, he does not give us a way to rank the natural desires by appeal to some higher principle.[28] What he cannot say, and what I want to say, is that the practice is wrong (not merely tragic) even if it does fulfill natural desires by the ruling males.

If Arnhart is going to be consistent, he should say that male and female mating strategies in general are tragic in the same way. He does say that lifetime monogamy is unnatural, a frustration of natural desires and, therefore, presumably bad. After the children can manage on their own, he says, there is no natural need for the couple to stay together.[29] The natural and therefore best strategy is what he calls serial monogamy, a succession of committed relationships. But he should, I think, go further and admit that for males even in a committed relationship there is a natural desire, which is therefore good to fulfill, namely, to be unfaithful.[30] Arnhart cannot, as far as I can see, have it both ways. Given that what frustrates a natural desire is bad, he cannot both say that males have a natural desire for promiscuity and that what is best (and not merely tragic) for males is monogamous albeit sequential fidelity. If males, by virtue of their natural political dominance, can enforce a double standard, according to which infidelity in females is punished but infidelity in males is not, there will not be any obstacle in *nature* (as Arnhart views it) to their doing so.

The sense of tragedy is also the only conclusion I think Arnhart is entitled to in the case of slavery, and I will end this section with this point. He thinks that there is a natural human desire for exploitation, "[l]ike other social animals, human beings are naturally inclined to exploitation through coercion and manipulation."[31] But there is also a natural inclination on the part of slaves not to be exploited. The result is, one would think, tragedy—one natural desire pitted against another.[32] But Arnhart does not in fact conclude with tragedy. He concludes that slavery is wrong and should be abolished because it is inconsistent with justice as reciprocity, which is a natural human desire. This is the argument I want to consider. It all hangs on the meaning of reciprocity. As I understand his idea, it is Humean, and, as I said before, in Hume this kind of justice extends only as far as utility. On this account it is because human slaves, unlike ant slaves, *will* effectively resist exploitation that human slave owners are required by this kind of justice to acknowledge their claims. The problem with this account is that, for millennia of human history, the resistance of slaves was futile. Slavery was only abolished when William Wilberforce and his friends were obedient to the claims of the kind of universalist morality which Arnhart thinks is unrealistic. As Hume conceded, the extent of justice in his sense is dependent on the existing and likely power relations that obtain at the time; if a group is so weak that it cannot effectively resist, the restraints of justice are useless and so inapplicable.

Hume only half-humorously considers the case of women:

> In many nations, the female sex are reduced to like slavery, and are rendered incapable of all property, in opposition to their lordly masters. But though the males, when united, have in all countries bodily force sufficient to maintain this severe tyranny, yet such are the insinuation, address, and charms of their fair companions, that women are commonly able to break the confederacy, and share with the other sex in all the rights and privileges of society.[33]

It is the logic of this I want to point to. Women, says Hume, can properly claim reciprocity because they do have the power of effective resistance through their "insinuation, address, and charms." But slaves have not, in human history, had such advantages. It is in any case false to suppose that women have in fact had this power through most of human history. They have not in fact for most of this history succeeded in overcoming male oppression by flirting. Similarly, there have been slave uprisings and rebellions, but they have almost always been bloodily and brutally suppressed. Arnhart claims that there is a contradiction in treating a slave as not a full human being, and so as not entitled to reciprocity. I agree that there is a moral contradiction once the claim has been admitted that all biological human beings have equal dignity deserving respect. But this claim is the universal moral principle that Arnhart is concerned to reject as unrealistic. If this moral principle is not accepted, there is no logical contradiction in holding that an organism is both human in some ways and not human in others. This is just what Aristotle and defenders of slavery in general usually say. Aristotle softens it by proposing that slaves should be offered freedom if they attain the requisite deliberative capacities by contact with their masters' households. But there is no contradiction (except morally, once the universal principle is granted) in holding that before this time, there are natural slaves. There is no logical contradiction, and there is no requirement of justice as reciprocity if the natural slaves are unlikely to be able to exact retribution for their exploitation. There is only tragedy, the tragedy of one natural desire (to exploit) being pitted against another natural desire (not to be exploited).

Arnhart wants to rest his account of justice on biology, and rejects the view that the authority of the demand of justice requires God's command. This does not mean that he rejects religion. In his final chapter he presents a choice between reason and revelation, neither of which can refute the other. But he says that Darwinian natural right will survive either choice, since "the moral teaching of revelation—at least as conveyed in the Hebrew Bible" (even if not the Christian Bible)—"conforms to the natural desires of human beings as rooted in human biology."[34] Humans, he continues, will seek the uncaused ground of all causes because of their natural desire to understand. This "will lead some to a religious understanding of God. It will lead others to an intellectual understanding of nature. Yet, in either case, the good is the desirable. And perhaps the greatest human good, which would satisfy the deepest human desire, would be to understand human nature within the natural order of the whole."[35] In this passage Arnhart indicates that he thinks religion is not needed to justify obligations of justice, though it may be helpful for the religious type of person. But then my criticism returns. After one finishes Arnhart's book, the impression is strengthened that if one is looking for a "ground" for the demand of *formal* justice, nature under Arnhart's description is not going to provide one, and appeal to some higher religious source is required.

So I end this section with the conclusion that Arnhart has told us a great deal that is useful about natural human desires. But he has not produced an argument that successfully founds the sense of justice on an evolutionary view of human nature. If we do try to derive justice from general human desire, we will not be able to say that the exploitation of women and slaves is wrong. We will only be able to say that it is tragic. This is what I meant by saying that the double identity requires a substantial revision of morality. When we reject, as unrealistic, the principle of the equal dignity of human beings, we reduce significantly the ethical demand for how we should live.

II. Michael Ruse

In the second section of this essay, I will examine the view of a theorist who accepts that we cannot found the sense of justice on general human desires in Arnhart's sense, but who nonetheless supports a version of evolutionary ethics.[36] The most important difference between Michael Ruse and Larry Arnhart lies in the fact that Ruse finds a fallacy in the derivation of conclusions about how we ought to live from premises about what we naturally desire, while Arnhart does not.[37] But this is not a failure in evolutionary ethics as such, Ruse thinks. It would be such a failure if formal justice *needed* a foundation, if evolution could not supply it, and, therefore, if the foundation had to be found somewhere else (in Reason, for example, or God's will). But Ruse thinks the first premise here is mistaken. He thinks that formal justice does *not* need a foundation, and so there is no failure when evolution does not provide one. He is following John Mackie on this point, and it is worth spending some time distinguishing the sense in which these two philosophers are and are not skeptics about ethics.

Mackie's views about value are analogous to his views about color.[38] Mackie thinks that when ordinary people make judgments about color—for example, that an apple is red—they are making an error. They are claiming that a property resembling their sensation of redness actually exists in the apple. But, says Mackie, such a property would be very odd. It would both have to cause our sensation physically and have to resemble the sensation that it causes. What is actually happening here, he says, is that people project their sensation onto the world.[39] It is the same with value. Ordinary people have the experience of commending an action or a person as just. Mackie says that they then project that experience onto the world by supposing that there is an entity out there, justice (for example, a Platonic Form), which they are receiving through some kind of intuition. The truth is, he says, that there are no such entities, and no objective good in the sense of a normative entity outside us that we either recognize or fail to recognize.[40] He thinks the sense that there are such entities is a projective illusion.

Mackie's view is a kind of skepticism. But it is not skepticism about first-order ethics, about whether there are right and wrong responses to the proposal to break a promise or to kill innocent people. Mackie is sure that we have moral obligations not to do these things. His skepticism is about the second-order question, sometimes described as a metaethical question, about the ontological status of the right and the good.[41] Mackie and Ruse want to say that the conviction that the right and the good exist as separate entities outside us is an error or an illusion; we have mistaken the direction of dependence, supposing that the evaluation depends on the value rather than the value on the evaluation.

Ruse adds to this that objectivity in Mackie's sense is an illusion that is *adaptive* for us, and is caused by a genetic program aimed at our survival and reproduction. The idea is that the illusion of the objective existence of justice in Mackie's sense makes us more likely to cooperate with each other in promoting the good, and cooperation is the key to our success in survival and reproduction. Evolution, therefore, gave us the genes that produce this illusion. The sense of justice is thus objective in a different sense, but not in Mackie's sense. It is, objectively, adaptive for us, and the genes that produce it are really objectively there, whether we know about them or not.

Both philosophers give us the same argument that the objectivity of value must be a projective illusion. Ruse says that once we have given a causal explanation of our being moved morally, "we see that it is *impossible* (although, thankfully, not necessary) to satisfy the call for a reasoned justification."[42] Mackie makes the point by arguing that Plato's Form of the Good, if it existed, would have to be a very odd kind of entity. It would have to be a cause of our being moved morally and it would also need to have "to-be-pursuedness" or normativity somehow built into it.[43] Perhaps God could be such an entity, Mackie says, but he does not believe in God and he does not think any other kind of entity could play this double role.

Mackie is wrong, I think, about both color and value. John McDowell has argued that ordinary people are not in error in their color judgments in this way, and that the notion of resemblance which Mackie imputes to them is not, as Mackie says, coherent and false, but rather, incoherent.[44] I do not want to get into that dispute here. But it is worth noting that there has been a great deal of discussion of Mackie's views since his book came out in 1977. It is hard to know what Ruse thinks about this discussion because he does not refer to it.[45] On this occasion, I am not going to go through this discussion. My conclusion is that there is no incoherence in the notion of a value outside us, drawing us towards itself or repelling us.[46] In a value judgment, however, we are not merely reporting such an attraction or repulsion, but endorsing the pull towards it or the push away from it. Mackie is right that evaluative judgment standardly expresses the will, but he makes the mistake of thinking that values must be either things completely independent of us or things that we invent and project onto the world. The point of the prescriptivist view I prefer is to deny that these are the only two possibilities.

Mackie's conclusion is that, since there are no such value entities outside us, moral realism is an error, a projective illusion. But if I am right about the coherence of the idea of a magnetic attraction (or repulsion), this argument against moral realism fails. We can develop a view which I call "prescriptive realism," which says both that values are there in the world independently of the evaluator and that evaluative judgment expresses the evaluator's will.[47] For example, a good relationship has within itself the power to draw its members towards reconciliation after one of them has committed an offense against the other. Prescriptive realism sees no objection to saying that the value (the "goodness" in the relationship) is there even if one of the members or even both of them are temporarily blind to it or resisting its force. But when the offended party makes the *judgment* that it is wrong to nurse the grudge because the present barrier between the two of them is incongruous and false to the true nature of the relationship, then he or she is expressing a commitment to dismantle the barrier, by forgiveness and reconciliation. The role of evaluative judgment is to endorse the sense of attraction or repulsion, since the person or act being evaluated *deserves* to cause that response.

Ruse takes over Mackie's argument against realism, which is an argument from the exhaustive dichotomy between what we discover and what we invent. If this argument fails because the dichotomy is not exhaustive, then Ruse needs another argument to show that the objectivist or realist picture is mistaken. As far as I can see, he does not have one.

There is an additional reason for discomfort with Ruse's position. Suppose we agree with him that there is no foundational ground for formal justice, in the sense of a neutral set of premises derivable from formal logic, which is acceptable to the reason of any human being and which does not already presuppose the truth of what we are trying to ground. Suppose we agree also that we are nonetheless justified in believing what is ungrounded in this way, as long as there is no "defeater" for that belief.[48] For example, we may not be able to ground our belief in the external world in a foundationalist way, but our belief that we are having an experience of the external world (for example, that we are seeing a goldfinch) may nonetheless be justified in the absence of some defeater such as a hallucinogen or hypnosis or a malicious neighbor with a holograph. But Ruse cannot take this kind of position about formal justice because he *does* give us a defeater against the authority of moral judgment. If we came to see, as Ruse teaches, that the objectivity of the demand of justice is an illusion produced by our genes, that would tend to defeat the sense that the demand has authority over us and would therefore lower the force of the demand. I mean this point both normatively and factually. We ought to find the demand less authoritative, just as we ought to find that the exposure of an optical illusion reduces our confidence in a perceptual belief we formed because of the illusion. That is the normative point. But also, the exposure would in fact be likely to reduce our tendency to act in accordance with the demand. This objection to Ruse has been made by others. For example, Robert Richards expresses the doubt that people will continue to behave morally if they come to believe that the objectivity of morality is an illusion, and he therefore tries to use evolutionary theory to demonstrate that morality is, after all, objective.[49] Since Ruse's position is that the illusion of moral objectivity is useful to us adaptively, he ought to agree that the exposure of the illusion would be damaging to us.

One way to put the difficulty here is to say that Ruse's account produces a lack of fit or harmony between the actual design function of formal justice for the human species and what the demand of justice feels like from inside moral experience.[50] To illustrate what I mean by this, consider the following thought experiment. Suppose, like the Epicureans, we thought of the gods as looking at us from their own world and being entertained by our misfortunes. They look at us in the same way we look at soap operas on television. Suppose, further, that the gods set us up in this world with exactly this sort of entertainment in mind; suppose this was our design function. There would then be a lack of fit between the way we think of the point of our moral lives and the actual point with which our lives were established. Suppose, finally, that we discover that this is how things are. We discover that we are literally, as Macbeth suggested metaphorically in a moment of despair, "poor players that strut and fret their hour upon the stage," and our lives are "a tale told by an idiot, full of sound and fury, signifying nothing." What impact would this have on our lives? I think that this kind of discovery would have the same kind of impact on our moral lives that Descartes's demon in the *Meditations* is imagined to have on our quest for knowledge. Descartes imagines that a very powerful demon undertakes for his own malicious purposes to make all our knowledge claims false. Descartes thinks he has an argument to show the demon is bound to fail. But if we came to believe such a demon existed and was succeeding in his plans, we would not try so hard to get our knowledge claims right. What would be the point? In the case of the thought experiment about the Epicurean gods, we would stop trying so hard to be just. Why should we care so much about the role which our sense of justice was designed to play, namely, to give our life stories an entertaining plot line for their intended audience?[51]

The situation with our genes in Ruse's picture is like the situation with the Epicurean gods in the thought experiment. We take our judgments to be objective in the sense that we think we are responding to values that are actually there. But the mechanism that is in fact moving us, in Ruse's picture, is adaptation, or enhanced survival and reproduction. Take, for example, the judgment by the Good Samaritan that he should help the traveler by the side of the road who had been wounded and left for dead. He thinks that what is moving him is simply the need of another person unrelated to him by kin or tribe, in fact an enemy of his own people. But according to Ruse, what is actually moving him, by biochemical mechanism, is the survival and reproduction of his own genes.[52]

Ruse has two responses to this objection. The first is that those of us who have a genetic disposition to see the demand of justice as objective could not behave other than morally even if we tried.[53] This is, I suppose, an empirical question. There are many people who do manage not to behave justly, but perhaps they are born without the genetic mechanism in its fullness that the rest of us have.

There is also some preliminary evidence against Ruse in those experiments that tend to show that when people believe that egoism is true, they are inclined to be less helpful to others.[54] Thus several studies compare economists with people in other disciplines in terms of a variety of measures of cooperative behavior. The pattern is that economists tend to be less helpful. This is not because those already disposed like this choose economics. A before-and-after study was done on students enrolled in two introductory economics courses and an introductory astronomy course.[55] The students were asked at the beginning and at the end of each course what they would do if they found an addressed envelope with a hundred dollars in it, and if they were sent ten computers by a store and were only billed for nine. The students scored the same in the economics and astronomy courses at the beginning of the semester, but the economics students were more willing to act dishonestly at the end. It seems plausible that the difference results from exposure to the theory endemic in economics that motivation is fundamentally egoistic. I speculate that the same would be true after a semester of Ruse's philosophy course.

Ruse's other response is that the belief in the objectivity of the demand of justice is as useful to us as eyesight. We would not, therefore, reject it just because of discovering its origin. But here we need to ask, "Useful for what?" Is it useful for the good of all, impartially conceived, or for our own good, conceived more narrowly in terms that preserve essential reference to ourselves? If the first, then the usefulness of the belief in the objectivity of the demand of formal justice will move us only if we are already committed to being impartially just. Belief in objective justice would be, on this reading, useful for promoting objective justice. This is no doubt true, but it is probably not what Ruse has in mind. He means that belief in the objectivity of the demand of formal justice is useful for our own advantage. But then he has a large job of justification to do. Perhaps I can make the point more vivid by analogy. Suppose scientists were to discover that their work was not directed by the quest for objective truth, as they had thought, but that this drive was an illusion produced by their genes. I think many of them would stop trying so hard.

In Plato's *Republic*, Socrates has to face the question of why it would not be more useful for one's own advantage to have other people believe in justice but to practice unbridled egoism oneself. This is the question about the authority of justice raised by Glaucon's story of the ring of Gyges.[56] Some have thought that this question can be answered on prudential grounds. David Gauthier, for example, in *Morals by Agreement*, has a sustained argument to show that it is prudentially rational to be moral, not merely to encourage others to be so.[57] But two points can be made against such a project. The first is that justice, in the tradition from Augustine and Anselm and Duns Scotus to Kant, requires motivation not primarily by the affection for advantage (to the self) but by the affection for justice itself (the pull towards what is good in itself, independently of advantage to the self). Anything justified or motivated for the most part instrumentally could not, according to this view, be justice.[58] This objection will not be telling for Ruse because he is arguing against this very tradition of thought at just this point.

The second point is that there is evidence (to which I have already referred) that making justice instrumental or useful to a more fundamental egoism does in fact diminish the force of the demand of justice. This same point can be put the other way round. Belief in the objective demand of justice is strengthened by an overall view which gives a good fit between what we believe to be the actual function of the sense of justice for our species and what the demand of justice feels like from the inside. Donald Campbell thus supports (for social utility) what he calls the "preachments" of the traditional religions, even though he does not think them true, because they give this kind of fit.[59] The problem for Campbell is that he realizes that he cannot let his own views get out into the general public (and he used to say, in a self-deprecating way, that this was anyway very unlikely). He acknowledges that if people come to see the traditional preachments and worldviews as *merely* socially useful and not true, in the same way Campbell himself sees them, people will be less likely to act in accordance with the moral demand which the worldviews support. We could put the point in terms of a publicity standard. The publicity standard is that a normative theory should be able to make public what it claims as the source or origin of the normative demand without thereby undercutting the demand. It is, moreover, probably constitutive of being a good citizen in a liberal democracy to be willing to articulate publicly such a source or origin. I do not see how Ruse can avoid failing the publicity standard.

Ruse has written a book with the intriguing title *Can a Darwinian Be a Christian?* His answer to this question is, "Absolutely!"[60] His project in this book is to make peace between Darwinism and Christianity, and his antirealist theme that I have been describing is largely missing. He hopes to achieve this peace by first describing a theistic evolutionist position, in which God is said to use evolution to achieve the divine purposes in creation. Then he describes Christian ethics in terms of a natural law position in which the good is the natural and the natural is the good which God intends.[61] The result of all this is a position like Arnhart's, according to which religion is useful for the religious type of person, but is not necessary in the project of justifying morality. Ruse, however, abandons justification for explanation, holding that religion is simply "a full expression of our humanity." According to such a view, what particular morality one ends up with will depend on what modern biology says human nature is like, for "one's morality is being constrained and defined by what one takes to be the process and product of evolution."⁶² Ruse does not discuss how his position here is consistent with his skeptical position on metaethics that I have been describing in the rest of this section. I think the likely reconciliation is as follows. He thinks there *is* no justification for the demand of justice, and there does not need to be one. Christians will appeal to God in this role, and Ruse is trying to show that there is nothing in such an attempt that contradicts evolutionary theory (as long as the Christians do not attempt a literal reading of the Bible). But since the justice that is under discussion is a justice that coheres with human nature as evolved, a Darwinian need have no quarrel with those who want to provide justification by means of an extra religious loop. But then my criticism returns in full force. What if the demands of formal justice do *not* cohere with human nature as evolved, but are in radical tension with it?

To conclude, then, very briefly. I have tried to present a dilemma for evolutionary ethicists. They have to either undertake the foundationalist project or refuse it. If they undertake it in the way Arnhart undertakes it, they will be liable to the sorts of objections I have raised against Arnhart. If they refuse it in the way Ruse refuses it, they will be faced with the sort of defeater objection that I have raised against Ruse. In either case we have a problem; these philosophers have reduced the demand of justice. If the project of a liberal polity depends on an objective demand of formal justice, the reduction of this demand places this project in jeopardy.

NOTES

1. Larry Arnhart, *Darwinian Natural Right* (Albany: State University of New York Press, 1998), 4; henceforth cited as *DNR*. Arnhart has expansive notions of "right" and of "justice," and I am assuming the scope of his notions for this essay, though I am going to disagree with his account of the foundations of justice. Any account of justice will have to make distinctions between formal and substantive justice, for example, and between justice which is the whole of virtue and distributive justice. But it is not the purpose of my essay to elaborate these distinctions, though I shall sometimes make use of them. In reply to this essay, Arnhart has to some extent modified his views; but he has not yet published the modifications, and I cannot tell to what extent he has met these objections.

2. Michael Ruse, "Evolutionary Ethics in the Twentieth Century," in *Biology and the Foundations of Ethics*, ed. Jane Maienschein and Michael Ruse (Cambridge: Cambridge University Press, 1999).

3. I have given a fuller treatment of these types, including the emphasis on group selection rather than individual selection, in the address "Christian Scholarship and Human Responsibility," in *Christian Scholarship . . . For What?*, ed. Susan Felch (Grand Rapids, Mich.: Calvin College, 2003). This address also appears in "Is There an Evolutionary Foun-

dation for Human Morality?" in *Evolution and Ethics: Human Morality in Biological and Religious Perspective,* ed. Philip Clayton and Jeffrey Schloss (Grand Rapids, Mich.: Eerdmans, 2004).

4. Donald T. Campbell, "On the Conflicts between Biological and Social Evolution and between Psychology and Moral Tradition," *American Psychologist* 30 (1975): 1103–26.

5. See Robert J. Richards, "Darwin's Romantic Biology," in *Biology and the Foundation of Ethics,* 113–53. See also Philip Hefner, *The Human Factor* (Minneapolis: Fortress Press, 1993).

6. Arnhart, *DNR,* 17, 30, 66, 81–82, 124.

7. The prohibition of this introduction is sometimes called "Hume's law." It is doubtful whether Hume himself made the argument in the form I have given. See John Finnis, *Natural Law and Natural Rights* (Oxford: Oxford University Press, 1980), 36 f.

8. See Peter van Inwagen, *Material Beings* (Ithaca, N.Y.: Cornell University Press, 1990). I have made use of his account informally in John E. Hare, *Why Bother Being Good?* (Downers Grove, Ill.: InterVarsity Press, 2002), 136 f.

9. *Republic* 334b.

10. See *Crito* 49a–e and *Gorgias* 508b–509c.

11. Arnhart, *DNR,* 146, emphasis added. See also 76, "Throughout most of human history, the social instincts within a tribe never extended beyond the tribe."

12. Kant gives us the two formulas in *Groundwork of the Metaphysic of Morals* 4: 421 and 429. He expresses his hesitations about the biblical formulation in *Groundwork* 4: 430.

13. The case is from an indignant letter written to the *Grand Rapids Press,* 13 May 2002, by the father of a family in the row behind a group of adult males who stood up throughout the game, despite his protests.

14. Arnhart suggests, in *DNR,* 226, that Kant thinks moral rationality requires a suppression of the emotions, and (quoting Damasio) that this "cool strategy advocated by Kant" is typical of a psychopath.

15. The quotation is from Kant, *Religion within the Boundaries of Mere Reason,* 6: 28. By the phrase "on the top of this," I mean to indicate that the original seed of goodness is prevented by something additional to it, though still innate. Kant is here translating the doctrines of Creation and Fall.

16. Arnhart, *DNR,* 258–66.

17. *Summa Theologiae* II-IIae, Q. 103, A. 3, ad 3.

18. See Jonathan Harrison, *Hume's Theory of Justice* (Oxford: Clarendon Press, 1981), 276.

19. This is disguised by the fact that he also talks about "the simple fairness of reciprocity in the Golden Rule" (*DNR,* 196). But his general doctrine is that the Golden Rule does not exist in nature, but is a construction by Christians and Kantians imposed because of a misperception of what nature is actually like.

20. Arnhart is here relying on a typical interpretive strategy of Leo Strauss. Indeed, Arnhart's book begins and ends with quotations from Strauss. It is worth pointing out that Jonathan Lear, whom Arnhart cites as an ally in this interpretive strategy (*DNR,* 173), does not in fact take such a position. See Jonathan Lear, *Aristotle: The Desire to Understand* (Cambridge: Cambridge University Press, 1988), 197 and 208.

21. For a vivid statement of the difficulties, and an attempt to reduce them, see Daniel Graham, *Aristotle's Two Systems* (Oxford: Oxford University Press, 1987).

22. See *Nicomachean Ethics* (*NE*) IX, 8, 1168b28 f.

23. Here is another tension in Aristotle's thought, though not (I think) a deliberate one. Aristotle thinks that there is a divine or godlike bit in a human being, and that it is this that aims at the good, so that the real good or *telos* may not be the same as the apparent good, which is the object of our other desires. This godlike bit aims at contemplation. In the *Eudemian Ethics* he says that we aim at the service and contemplation of God (*EE* VIII, 3, 1249b21). Arnhart says (*DNR*, 254) that "Aristotle thinks human beings as mortal animals can be happy." But Aristotle's own statement (*NE* X, 7, 1177b32f) is, "We ought not to follow the proverb writers, and 'think human, since you are human,' or 'think mortal, since you are mortal.' Rather, as far as we can, we ought to be immortal and go to all lengths to live a life that expresses our supreme element; for however much this element may lack in bulk, by much more it surpasses everything in power and value." Moreover, Arnhart claims (*DNR*, 243) that Aristotle quickly rejects the thought that happiness is the gift of the gods. But in the passage Arnhart quotes (*NE* I, 9, 1099b8–24), Aristotle in fact explicitly postpones the question to another enquiry, and then (when he picks it up again at X, 8, 1179a25) says, "For if the gods pay some attention to human beings, as they seem to, it would be reasonable for them to take pleasure in what is best and most akin to them, namely understanding; and reasonable for them to benefit in return those who most of all like and honor understanding."

24. Arnhart, *DNR*, 123.

25. Ibid., 127.

26. Ibid., 248. The notion of common interest here is tricky. The woman may have an interest in self-preservation and in marriage given the established order that she cannot change, but even if these produce submission to the institution, they will not remove the tragedy. The idea of common interest, on a Kantian view, removes the tragedy only if it is constrained by the fundamental principle of formal justice.

27. Ibid., 160. See also 149.

28. The best we can do, in such cases, is to rely on what Arnhart calls "prudence," which discerns in the case of tragic conflicts what is the least evil way to proceed.

29. Arnhart, *DNR*, 265.

30. Statistics are hard to be confident about here. An interesting study on a college campus reports that if an attractive stranger of the opposite sex were to approach and propose intercourse, 100 percent of the women in the study would refuse, and 75 percent of the males would accept. R. D. Clark and E. Hatfield, "Gender Differences in Receptivity to Sexual Offers," *Journal of Psychology and Human Sexuality* 2 (1989): 39–55.

31. Arnhart, *DNR*, 168. See also 196.

32. Arnhart does sometimes express himself that way. He talks of Judge Ruffin's "*tragic sense of his moral predicament*" (*DNR*, 170, emphasis added), when the judge tried in 1829 to defend the institution of slavery while at the same time being honest about its reliance on brute force.

33. Hume, *Enquiry Concerning the Principles of Morals*, ed. L. A. Selby-Bigge, revised by P. H. Nidditch (Oxford: Oxford University Press, 1975), 190–91.

34. Arnhart, *DNR*, 275.

35. Ibid.

36. The sense of "found" and "foundation" here is that Arnhart accepts and Ruse denies that we can justify the claims of justice on us on the basis of the desires which evolution has given us.

37. Ruse agrees "that there is a key difference between statements of fact and statements of morality and that (Julian) Huxley and his tradition have failed to bridge it." ("Evolutionary Ethics in the Twentieth Century," in *Biology and the Foundations of Ethics,* 221). See also *Can a Darwinian Be a Christian?* (Cambridge: Cambridge University Press, 2001), 157; henceforth cited as *CDC.*

38. I have discussed these views at greater length in the first chapter of *God's Call* (Grand Rapids, Mich.: Eerdmans, 2001), 18–33.

39. J.L. Mackie, *Ethics: Inventing Right and Wrong* (Harmondsworth, England: Penguin, 1977), 20.

40. There are other relevant kinds of objectivity, such as the objectivity of an umpire, but in this essay I am using the term "objective" as Mackie does. The umpire is objective in that he refuses to give any individual or any team special advantage (even if the player is his daughter or the team is his own team). Objectivity here is conferred by an evaluative procedure on which all rational agents would agree.

41. The second-order skepticism will affect first-order ethics to the extent that uncovering the "error" will affect the experience of being under the obligation. But Mackie does not want to deny the binding force of ordinary moral obligations like truth-telling and protecting the innocent.

42. Ruse, "Evolutionary Ethics," 218, emphasis added.

43. Mackie, *Ethics,* 40.

44. John McDowell, "Values as Secondary Qualities," in *Morality and Objectivity,* ed. Ted Honderich (London: Routledge and Kegan Paul, 1985).

45. See Simon Blackburn, *Essays in Quasi-Realism* (Oxford: Oxford University Press, 1993), and the elegant piece "The Flight to Reality," in *Virtues and Reasons,* ed. Rosalind Hursthouse, Gavin Lawrence, and Warren Quinn (Oxford: Clarendon Press, 1995). See also David Brink, *Moral Realism and the Foundations of Ethics* (Cambridge: Cambridge University Press, 1989), and Richard Boyd, "How to Be a Moral Realist," in *Essays on Moral Realism,* ed. Geoffrey Sayre-McCord (Ithaca, N.Y.: Cornell University Press, 1988).

46. Iris Murdoch explores the metaphor of magnetic force, taking it originally from Plato, and suggests that we can think of a magnetic center that holds these forces together. See *The Sovereignty of Good over Other Concepts* (Cambridge: Cambridge University Press, 1967), 26 and 32–33, and *The Fire and the Sun* (Oxford: Oxford University Press, 1977), 65.

47. *God's Call,* 46 f.

48. For the notion of a "defeater," see John Pollock, *Contemporary Theories of Knowledge* (Totowa, N.J.: Rowman and Littlefield, 1986), 37 f.

49. See R. J. Richards, "A Defense of Evolutionary Ethics," *Biology and Philosophy* 1 (1986): 286, and Peter G. Woolcock, "The Case against Evolutionary Ethics Today," in *Biology and the Foundations of Ethics,* 292.

50. By "design function" I do not mean to imply that there is a designer. That would be a different argument. Ruse is perfectly happy to use the metaphor of design in a way that is neutral about the existence of a designer. See *CDC,* 113: "If you like, put it this way: the metaphor of design is just as much a feature of Darwin's *Origin* as it is of Paley's *Natural Theology.*"

51. A slightly less far-fetched thought experiment also comes from the Greeks. Some of the sophists suggested that our moral lives are the product of manipulation by those in

political power, who desire to keep even our thoughts under control. Suppose we discovered this was right. Surely we would stop feeling ourselves bound by these "spells and incantations" (Plato, *Gorgias* 484a1).

52. Contrast Arnhart's view of the hunter-gatherer societies where evolutionary pressures were operating on us and helping enemies in that way did not favor genetic survival and reproduction even indirectly.

53. Michael Ruse, *Taking Darwin Seriously* (Oxford: Blackwell, 1986), 253.

54. C.D. Batson, J. Fulz, P.A. Schoenrade, and A. Paduano, "Critical Self-Reflection and Self-Perceived Altruism: When Self-Reward Fails," *Journal of Personality and Social Psychology* 53 (1987): 594–602. See also Elliott Sober and David Sloan Wilson, *Unto Others: The Evolution and Psychology of Unselfish Behavior* (Cambridge, Mass.: Harvard University Press, 1999), 273.

55. R.H.T. Frank, T. Gilovich, and D. Regan, "Does Studying Economics Inhibit Cooperation?" *Journal of Economic Perspectives* 7 (1993): 159–71.

56. *Republic* 359 f.

57. David Gauthier, *Morals by Agreement* (Oxford: Clarendon Press, 1986). I have commented on his argument in *The Moral Gap* (Oxford: Clarendon Press, 1996), 176–82.

58. Gauthier's view is that morality is justified instrumentally and then comes to have intrinsic justification; but the latter depends on the former. This kind of dependence is just what the Augustinian-Kantian tradition would deny.

59. Donald T. Campbell, "On the Conflict between Biological and Social Evolution and between Psychology and Moral Tradition," and "Altruism: Biology, Culture, and Religion," with Judith C. Specht, *Journal of Social and Clinical Psychology* 3 (1985): 33–42.

60. Ruse, *CDC*, 217.

61. Ibid., 203.

62. Ibid.

┌─────┐
│ 4 │   # WHY SHOULD CHRISTIANS
└─────┘   # ENDORSE HUMAN RIGHTS?

PAUL WEITHMAN

Why should Christians endorse human rights? Why, that is, should they endorse the claim that human beings have rights that those to whom they are vulnerable—especially their governments—are bound to honor? These questions are not mooted by the fact that many Christian churches and bodies representing Christian churches, such as the Roman Catholic Church and the World Council of Churches, do endorse rights claims and work on behalf of human rights around the world. For one thing, there is a significant strain in conservative religious thought—at least among American sectarians of various denominations[1]—according to which talk of rights should be abandoned because of its social consequences. Moreover, despite the fact that many Christian bodies *do* endorse rights claims, the reasons *why* they should do so are still not well or widely understood. Indeed they are not well understood even by some of those who argue most powerfully that their churches should endorse these claims. Helping us understand the grounds of some of our most familiar and deeply felt moral commitments has, since Aristotle, been one of the tasks of moral philosophy. It is a task I shall undertake here.

To see why I think the reasons for Christian endorsement of rights claims are not well understood, and to catch a first glimpse of the reasons I want to high-light, note that where rights are honored by agents with the power to violate them, such as governments, two consequences follow. The individuals who have the rights are simultaneously *protected* and *freed* or *liberated*. They are protected from certain harms, punishments, and threats for engaging in the conduct that rights protect and they are thereby left free to engage in that conduct. These two consequences may not be separable in fact. Their relationship may be such that, like two sides of the same coin, they are always found together. Or it may be, as some critics of liberalism would argue, that while rights can confer some pro-tection, the liberation they are said to confer is illusory or inadequate.[2] But who-ever has the better of this argument, we can clearly distinguish the protectionist and liberating effects of rights in thought. That is all I need for my purposes. For quite often those who argue that Christians should endorse rights claims point to the importance and value of the protective function of rights. Understandably worried about the human tendency to abuse our freedom, they neglect or down-play the value of the liberating function of rights. What I want to maintain here is that the arguments for rights that are premised exclusively on the protective function of rights are incomplete and that the Christian endorsement of rights should be premised on their liberating function as well.

Where the rights in question are those connected with rights to religious prac-tice and where the actions they leave us free to perform are religious in character, my conclusion seems obvious enough. What I have in mind, however, are argu-ments for a broader range of rights than those specifically connected with reli-gious belief and practice. I want to contend that arguments for these rights should be premised on the liberating as well as the protectionist function of rights. More specifically, I want to argue that Christians should endorse this broader range of rights because:

1. It is necessary for governments and other powerful agents to honor these rights if human beings are to be able to assure themselves that their most fundamen-tal commitments are authentically their own.
2. Christians should value peoples' ability to assure themselves that their most fundamental commitments *are* authentically their own.

I want to begin by stating my opening question somewhat more precisely and by explaining why I take it to be an interesting question. I will then spend some time on an answer that I find unpersuasive, not because it is wrong but because it is incomplete. Finally, I shall try briefly to defend the answer to the question that I have sketched in these prefatory remarks.

I

The question I am interested in is why Christians should endorse rights claims *now,* at the beginning of the twenty-first century and why they should have done so in the recent past—say, for the last century or so. I shall not be concerned here to ask whether Christians or various Christian churches should have endorsed rights claims or should have recognized rights at various points in the more distant past. This question is certainly worth asking, in part because answering it would help us determine where the church has failed to live up to its moral responsibilities and duties over the course of its history. Attempting to answer it would also force us to ask what conceptual frameworks and presuppositions must be in place before rights claims can or should be endorsed as such. There may have been periods in which it would have been inappropriate or indeed impossible to endorse rights claims as such because the requisite background conditions were not in place; yet it may also be that during those periods the church should have recognized and institutionalized other legal protections for the vulnerable. While these matters are well worth pursuing, I shall not pursue them here.

The rights with which I am concerned are the rights to speak, write, and publish freely; to assemble peaceably for a variety of legitimate purposes, including religious and political purposes; rights of association; and those rights associated with the freedom of religion. I shall not, however, ask directly about rights which guarantee the integrity of the person, the prima facie inviolability of the home, or the rule of law, except insofar as violations of these rights are responses to political, religious, or philosophical belief or expression. These are the rights for which an exclusively protectionist argument seems strongest. I do not want to deny its strength. I simply maintain that those who give an exclusively protectionist justification of all rights mistakenly extend that justification from cases in which it is strong to cases in which it needs to be supplemented. Nor shall I have anything to say about various property rights such as the rights to hold and bequeath ownership stakes in the means of production and capital formation. Some American scholars are especially concerned to argue that Christians should endorse these rights in strong form.[3] I shall not comment on their efforts here.

Furthermore, when I ask whether Christians should endorse rights I am not asking whether they should endorse what these rights are said to entail in one or another liberal democracy that has specified rights through political and judicial contestation. Different liberal democracies have worked out the implications of rights claims in different ways and so differ on whether, for example, citizens have a free-speech right to deny that the Holocaust occurred, an unfettered privacy right to procure an abortion, or a liberty right to procure the cooperation of a willing physician in ending their lives. I am not trying to adjudicate among these specifications of rights or to argue that Christians should endorse one rather than another. I am simply asking why Christians should accept an abstract set of rights claims of the sort typically found in human-rights instruments like the American Bill of Rights.

Even if answering this question does not give us much guidance on some of the most pressing questions of contemporary politics, it is, I believe, an interesting question. I hope that the answer I propose will have some interesting implications even if the implications are not straightforwardly political.

For one thing, Christianity has, from its beginnings, understood itself as an evangelical movement. It has understood itself as a movement with the responsibility to spread the good news to all nations. Often enough in the course of Christianity's subsequent history, various Christian denominations have enlisted political power in their evangelical efforts. I take it to be interesting to ask: what premises could such an evangelical movement accept that would allow it to accept the right of free faith and other rights associated with liberal democracy? More crudely put, it is interesting to ask the following question: given that a religion claims each person would be better off if she accepted its tenets than if she did not, what reasons might adherents of that religion have for claiming that such acceptance ought to take place in a context in which persons have a right to free faith and other rights associated with liberal democracy? The answer will be interesting for what it tells us about religion, as well as for what it tells us about social possibilities and, in particular, about the possibility of arriving at what John Rawls calls an "overlapping consensus" on liberal principles of political morality.[4]

As I have already indicated, the condition or answer I defend here is that people ought to be able to recognize the fundamental commitments they make as authentically their own. This is a condition that has, I believe, been accepted by some Christian denominations even if this is not always recognized by those who have written about Christian support for human rights. Identifying this condition and seeing that it has been accepted has historiographic implications. It helps us write the history of the encounter and reconciliation between liberal democracy and various Christian denominations by telling us where we might look for significant influence and transformation.

The condition that people ought to be able to see their most fundamental commitments as authentically their own is, I believe, a condition which owes much to various writers from the German and French Enlightenments.[5] It is a condition that has its origins in the insistence by these thinkers that the conditions of human life and practice be transparent to human reason.[6] If this is correct, and if Christian denominations have in fact endorsed this condition, then this shows that they have taken on board something important from the Enlightenment. And if the adoption of this condition is an *authentic* development of the Christian denominations that have adopted it, then this raises the possibility that those denominations owe a debt to the thinkers from whom this condition was taken over—to those thinkers who recognized how Christianity could faithfully adapt to the social, political, and cultural forces the various enlightenments put in play. Since Enlightenment-bashing is currently so fashionable in some circles of American philosophy and religious ethics, I take this to be a significant conclusion.

Finally, there are prominent strains of liberal democratic thought according to which the strongest argument for the rights and liberties with which I am concerned is that they allow and protect specifically *political* belief, speech, and activity. This, it is said, is the belief, speech, and conduct liberal democracies should deem most worthy of protection. Other forms of expression such as artistic and religious expression are thought to have weaker claims. I believe this is a mistake, which can be avoided by an argument for rights of the sort I shall sketch below—an argument according to which rights claims are to be honored because honoring them secures the conditions for seeing that my fundamental commitments are my own.

II

To return to the main line of argument, the question before us is: why should Christians now endorse, in abstract form, the rights to freedom of thought, expression, and assembly associated with liberal democracy? Before defending my own answer I shall look at a sort of answer that is commonly brought forward but that seems to me inadequate.

As I indicated in my introductory remarks, it is common for Christian thinkers to answer that Christians should endorse human rights because rights serve a protective function. This is a line of argument interestingly explored by Nicholas Wolterstorff in a recently published paper.[7] American Jesuit ethicist John Langan is blunter in a wise, articulate, and systematic paper on human rights. Responding to well-known criticisms of rights by Alasdair MacIntyre, Langan writes:

The point to be borne in mind is that in affirming human rights we are not saying that a society that accepts such norms will be the best society or even that it will not suffer from serious distortions in its judgments about the urgency and weight of major human values. Positively, the point is that affirmation, and observance of human rights, serves to provide a minimum below which society should not fall and helps to protect people from various kinds of threats and evils. A society that affirms and protects human rights may suffer in various ways as a result of inappropriate uses and extensions of human rights norms. It may suffer from extensive individualism, materialism, commercialism, egoism, and other corrupting tendencies. But so long as human beings honor rights, certain things they can do to each other are excluded. There can be numerous misuses of human freedom, but there will be no repetitions of Auschwitz or Cambodia, of Stalinist show trials or legalized racial segregation. Furthermore, so long as free speech and free assembly are available, there will be opportunities for persuading people to renounce the sinfulness and selfishness of their ways. Human rights affirmations should not be conceived as ways of guaranteeing the kingdom of God on earth but as ways of preventing some great evils which it is reasonable to fear.[8]

Note that in this passage Langan seems to be arguing that the recognition of rights protects us against two quite different things. It protects us, or "helps to protect" us, "from various kinds of . . . evils." But the fact that Langan uses the phrase "various kinds of *threats* and evils" suggests that he thinks protection against threats is important as well; this draws some confirmation from a phrase that appears later in the passage, where Langan says that "human rights affirmations" are "ways of preventing some great evil *which it is reasonable to fear*" (emphasis added). I do not want to maintain that these arguments are wrong. Rather, I wish to claim that the first of them is incomplete and that the second suggests how it might be completed, but that following the suggestion takes us beyond protectionist considerations.

Let us begin with what we might call the *first protectionist argument* according to which Christians should endorse rights because they protect us or help to protect us from the very great evils Langan catalogues. The fact that they help to protect us against these evils would not itself show that Christians have reason to endorse them, given all the problems that Langan acknowledges a culture of rights brings with it. I think he must have something stronger in mind—namely, that the widespread recognition of rights is *necessary* to protect us from these evils. If recognition of rights were necessary to protect us or some of us from very great evils of the sort Langan catalogues, that would seem to be a very powerful argument for Christians to endorse rights claims and to urge governments to do so as well.

But note that the argument would leave much *unsaid* about why Christians should do this. For one thing, we would still need to be told why these evils—obviously heinous though they were—are evil. The self-evident horror of torture, cruelty, and extermination can make it seem in poor taste to ask this question, but I think that we should. Some of the answers that occur to us most immediately do not take us far.

These evils cannot be horrible simply because they result in physical pain, though they undoubtedly do. The answer to the question of why it is horrible to do such things to human beings requires appeal to something distinctive about the way human beings anticipate, experience, and remember pain and are degraded when it is willfully and arbitrarily inflicted. Nor will it help simply to appeal to human dignity and to argue that these evils are evil because they are incongruous with human dignity or rob people of it. This is true as far as it goes, but it does not go very far. The notion of human dignity is precisely what needs to be understood. The answer to the question of why these evils are evil will have to appeal to some definitive human capacities in virtue of which we have dignity. Once that appeal is made we are, I believe, on the road to a much richer defense of rights than the protectionist one this passage supplies.

Furthermore, we want to understand why Christians should endorse rights to freedom of religion, of speech, of the press, of assembly, and of association. The horribleness of the evils cited does not help us here. It is true that if these rights are respected, then people will not be tortured, imprisoned, or exterminated because of their religious, philosophical, or political beliefs. But if there is any explanation to be had here, it goes the wrong way 'round. The importance of respecting people's rights to freedom of religion, speech, assembly, and association seems to explain why it is especially bad to imprison or torture people for, say, their religious views. The horribleness of imprisoning them for these views doesn't explain why they have the right of free faith in the first place. To assert that it does is a bit like saying that we should recognize people's property rights because if these rights are not widely recognized people will regularly be deprived of their property by armed robbers. But if there were no such rights, then acts of armed robbery would not have the distinctive kind of badness they undeniably possess. It is the prior existence of the right to property—or the prior existence of the right to freedom of conscience—that needs to be explained.

Finally, it is not clear that recognition of rights as we understand them *is* necessary to prevent the evils and enormities catalogued. Rights impose a whole cluster of duties on others and confer a whole cluster of immunities on their bearers. Among these are immunities from torture and arbitrary imprisonment. But human rights also confer immunities from lesser harms—for example, an immunity from low-grade harassment by public officials on account of the rightholder's political, religious, or philosophical views and expressions. So recognition of clusters of immunities that are subsets of the immunities conferred by rights might suffice to protect us against the enormities on the list and might do so without courting the abuses of liberty that are said to concern MacIntyre. Why, then, should Christians endorse as rich a cluster of immunities as are conferred by the rights with which I am concerned?

We can make some progress by turning to the second line of argument Langan seems to suggest in the quoted passage—that recognition of rights protects us from fear or threat. Why is it important to be protected from or to live without the fear that we will be persecuted or harassed for our political, philosophical, or religious views? An important part of the answer, I want to suggest, is that only if we are free from fear of persecution or harassment can we assure ourselves that the commitments we make on fundamental matters are authentically our own. Recognition of rights is necessary if we are to enjoy this freedom. It is this argument for rights that I now want to explore.

III

The first and most formidable difficulty with the argument I am proposing is that it is very difficult to get a grip on the notion of a commitment's being authentically one's own. We have, I believe, strong intuitions that bear on the matter. There are some commitments that we think somehow express or follow from deep facts about us, commitments we could not give up without giving up something very important about ourselves. But to the extent that we can get a grip on the notion itself, we often put our hands on the wrong things and grab in the wrong places.

For example, we are all familiar with the experience of *sensing* that a commitment is one of those with which we most closely identify, one we hold with fervor and with a feeling of conviction that would move us to risk a great deal for it. Yet it is clear enough that a commitment's being authentically one's own cannot be a matter of its being accompanied by such a feeling. The feeling is neither necessary nor sufficient for a commitment's being one's own. While some commitments are accompanied by the feeling, that feeling could be misplaced because the commitment to which it attaches is one I hold because I am in the grip of some delusion. As for the necessity of such a feeling, I am suspicious of using accompanying *feelings* to individuate states such as beliefs or commitments and to mark significant differences among them.

Nor can a commitment's being one's own be simply a matter of its centrality to one's plan of life. It cannot, that is, be simply a matter of having built or planned one's life around the belief, as one might build her life around her political convictions. We can readily imagine tragic examples of people who discover that they do not really accept the conviction that they previously took to be central but that never actually was. They come to see that they have been deluding themselves. Such commitments seem, intuitively, never to have been authentically theirs at all.

Somewhat more controversially, I do not think it is either necessary or sufficient for a commitment's being authentically one's own that it be made under conditions of freedom, even though we may intuitively think these are the sort of conditions under which commitments ought to be made. Badly mistaken, even tragic, commitments of the sort discussed in the previous paragraph can be made under such conditions. Moreover, it seems to me that a commitment can be one's own even if made under conditions in which freedom is clearly lacking. Someone whose political beliefs are formed under conditions of childhood indoctrination can, it seems to me, come to hold political convictions as authentically his own. The same is true of religious commitments. I say this is somewhat more controversial a claim than those I have already made because great authors in the liberal tradition can be read to disagree with me. There are passages in *On Liberty* where Mill could be taken to suggest that a belief is one's own only if acquired under conditions of the right kind, though I may be misreading him here.[9] It *may* be that Rawls thinks commitments central to one's plan of life are one's own only if they are acquired under conditions that one would approve of as free, equal, reasonable, and rational. I am inclined to think this is not what Rawls means and that he is talking instead about the subtlely different matter of holding fundamental beliefs and making central commitments *autonomously*.[10] Be that as it may, I am prepared to be talked out of the claim that being formed under the right conditions is not a necessary condition for its being one's own because, if it were, this would give an easier argument for rights than the argument I want to make.

Still, Rawlsian talk of hypothetical consent provides a promising clue, for I think that the best sense we can make of a commitment's being one's own is that it satisfies the following hypothetical or counterfactual condition: a commitment is authentically one's own if and only if it would survive critical reflection. It is authentically my own if and only if I would continue to endorse it after engaging in reflection of that kind. So, for example, a religious commitment is authentically my own if and only if I would continue to endorse it after reflecting on it critically. The same is true of political and philosophical commitments.

Whether this captures our intuitions about what commitments are and are not our own depends, of course, upon how the counterfactual conditions—the conditions of critical reflection—are spelled out. It depends, for example, upon what information we would take into account as critical reflectors, which of our actual beliefs, dispositions, and emotional responses we would take account of and what rules of inference we would employ. About all this I have regrettably little to say, except for one thing. I suggest that it is a necessary condition of such reflection that (1) we be informed of some reasonable competitors to the commitment we are testing and (2) we know enough about what it would be like to accept the competing commitment instead of our own that we can imagine the most important consequences for us of doing so.

What are "important consequences" and "reasonable competitors"? Unfortunately, I do not know and can only make the condition plausible by example. It seems to me that a commitment to a personal, providential, and loving god is authentically my own only if I would continue to affirm that commitment after learning enough about the lives of those who do not accept it that I can imagine what it would be like for me to live such a life. Even this formulation is quite vague. Rather than belabor its vagueness, I want to emphasize that the condition is a counterfactual one. A commitment can satisfy the condition even if I never engage in the requisite critical reflection. All that the condition requires of the commitment is that it be such that I *would* continue to endorse it if I *did* engage in such reflection.

I do not know what other conditions must be conjoined with this one so that we have sufficient as well as necessary conditions for critical reflection. Perhaps none. Note, though, that while satisfying this counterfactual condition may suffice for a commitment's being my own, it clearly does not suffice for something quite different. It does not suffice for me *to be able to assure myself* that my commitment is my own. Other conditions must also be satisfied for that. What I said I would argue for is not the claim that rights are necessary for me to have commitments which are my own. I said I would argue for the claim that rights are necessary if I am to be able to assure myself that my most important commitments are my own. How does the argument go?

If I am to assure myself that one of my commitments is my own, I must have some good reason to think that the commitment in question could pass the critical reflection test. I must, that is, have good reason to think that the commitment in question is one I would continue to endorse if I were informed about plausible alternatives to it and if I knew enough about the lives of people who endorse those alternatives to imagine what it would be like for me to endorse one of the alternatives instead. So if I am to assure myself that my commitments are authentically my own—including my religious commitments—I must have access to information about alternative beliefs and ways of life. Moreover, my judgment about what I would or would not continue to believe and do cannot be distorted by force, punishment, or fear. That is, my judgment about what I would or would not continue to believe must be made under conditions of freedom. Therefore, being able to assure myself that my commitments are my own requires that I be free—free enough to judge what I would and would not continue to believe in and commit myself to—and it requires that I have information about alternatives and about what it would be like to live them out.

My claim is that to satisfy these requirements, I and others must have the rights I am interested in. I and others must have the right to freedom of conscience—the right to adopt what beliefs we like on the deepest questions of human existence without punishment or harassment or the fear of either. We must have the right to speak about our ways of life to others, to publish thoughts about how to live and about what it is like to live our lives, and to assemble with others who choose to live as we do. Only if those rights are honored will the requisite information be available, and only then will people engage in what Mill calls "experiments in living."[11] So if I am to be able to assure myself that my commitments are my own, then I and others must have these rights.

This does not yet show that Christians should endorse these rights or favor their widespread recognition. Widespread recognition and enjoyment of rights will result in many people living in what Christians will regard as serious error and in their spreading what Christians regard as false doctrine. It will result in many people living lives that, to the Christian, look like lives that are far less fulfilling than they could be. And it will probably have the consequence that far too many Christians will take false doctrines far more seriously than other Christians will think they should, at least if they decide to assure themselves that their Christian commitments are their own. Why should Christians be in favor of that?

IV

The answer is to be found in the relationship Christians—both individually and corporately—are called to have with God. Of course, the relationships we actually have often fall far short of what we are called to have. But despite this failure, we aspire to something more. We aspire, I presume, to a richer and more intimate relationship with God than most of us in fact have. What kind of relationship are we called to?

To answer this, we can look to a variety of sources. We can look to the relationship with God enjoyed by the patriarchs, the prophets, the matriarchs, and the saints. These are the women and men our tradition recognizes as holy. We can look to the relationship the disciples had with Christ, to the relationship Christ had with the person he called his Father, and to the many images of that relationship that are found in the Hebrew and Christian scriptures. The variety of scriptural images suggests that our relationship with God is as complex as any other intimate relationship in which human beings are involved. God is presented variously as father, friend, king, champion, deliverer, chastiser, source of life, and sustenance. These all suggest that our relationship with God is to be sustained by a mixture of filial piety, friendship, gratitude, loyalty, awe, and love for the kingdom of believers.

But some of the imagery I find most suggestive and provocative is marital imagery. According to the scriptures, God loves us as one might love a faithless spouse. We are to ready ourselves for God's arrival like virgins awaiting the bridegroom. The church is the bride of Christ.[12] I find this imagery to be of continuing relevance despite the enormous changes in marriage over the last two millennia. It is, I believe, legitimate to make at least this much of it.

The marital imagery reinforces the lessons we take away from the other imagery the scriptures employ. As a good marriage is built on gratitude, love of the way of life one has entered into, and loyalty, so our relationship to God is also built on and sustained by these dynamics, just as the analogy suggests. But the marital imagery complements the other imagery by suggesting an additional dynamic. The best marriages are sustained by the belief that one's partner is special, that the choice one has made to enter into marriage and to stay with it is a choice that is authentically one's own. That is, it is a commitment sustained by the belief or the assurance that it is a commitment that could sustain critical reflection—reflection in which one knows some of the alternatives and can imagine what it would be like to live them out.

If we take the marital imagery of scripture and tradition seriously as telling us something about the relationship we are called to with God, then it seems to me that we Christians should want a relationship with God that is sustained by the same forces that sustain the best marriages. We should want a commitment that we think would survive critical reflection in which we know about alternatives and can imagine what it would be like to live them out. That, I have argued, requires that we have rights. If Christians value the kind of relationship with God that they can have only if they and others have rights, then they should value rights as well.

NOTES

This essay was originally prepared for a conference hosted by the Societas Ethica in Berlin in August of 2001. I am grateful to the officers of the Societas Ethica for their kind invitation to participate in the conference. An earlier version of this essay was published in the conference proceedings *The Sources of Public Morality,* ed. Ulrik Nissen (LT Verlag, 2003).

1. See, for example, Stanley Hauerwas, *After Christendom? How the Church Is to Behave if Freedom, Justice, and a Christian Nation Are Bad Ideas* (Nashville, Tenn.: Abingdon Press, 1991), 45 ff.

2. Gerald Doppelt, "Rawls's System of Justice: A Critique from the Left," *Noûs* 15 (1981): 259–308, esp. 275, 285 ff.

3. This is a recurring theme of Michael Novak. See, for example, William Simon and Michael Novak, *Liberty and Justice for All: Report on the Final Draft of the U.S. Catholic Bishops' Pastoral Letter "Economic Justice for All"* (Washington, D.C.: The Brownson Institute, 1986), 15–16.

4. John Rawls, "The Idea of an Overlapping Consensus," in his *Political Liberalism* (New York: Columbia University Press, 1996), 133–72.

5. The ethical value of authenticity is most famously associated with Jean-Jacques Rousseau. See Jean Starobinski, *Jean-Jacques Rousseau: Transparency and Obstruction,* trans. Arthur Goldhammer (Chicago: University of Chicago Press, 1971) 198–200; for some qualifications, see Charles Taylor, *The Ethics of Authenticity* (Cambridge, Mass.: Harvard University Press, 1991), 27–28.

6. On the connections between transparency and the liberal tradition, see Jeremy Waldron, "Theoretical Foundations of Liberalism," in his *Liberal Rights* (Cambridge: Cambridge University Press, 1993), 35–62.

7. Nicholas Wolterstorff, "Do Christians Have Good Reasons for Supporting Liberal Democracy?," *The Modern Schoolman* 78 (2001): 229–48.

8. John Langan, S.J., "Christianity and the Requirements of Human Rights," delivered at the meeting of the Pacific Division of the Society of Christian Philosophers, Los Angeles, Calif., March, 1987 (unpublished, on file with author).

9. See John Stuart Mill, *On Liberty* (New York: Penguin, 1988), 101–3.

10. I defend this interpretive claim, with references, in my *Religion and the Obligations of Citizenship* (Cambridge: Cambridge University Press, 2002), chap. 7.

11. Mill, *On Liberty,* 120.

12. See Ephesians 5:25 ff.

5

CAN A NATURAL
LAW THEORIST JUSTIFY
RELIGIOUS CIVIL LIBERTIES?

TERENCE CUNEO

The purpose of this essay is to explore how a natural law theorist of the Aristotelian-Thomist variety might justify the provision and protection of religious civil liberties. My thesis divides into both a negative and a positive component. The negative component is that some of the more prominent attempts to ground religious civil liberties in the principles of natural law theory are unpersuasive. More specifically, I shall argue that Robert George's attempt to ground religious civil liberties in the good of "religion" is suggestive but ultimately in need of repair.[1] The positive side of my thesis is a suggestion for how natural law theorists might justify religious civil liberties. I shall contend that natural law theorists ought to present a multipronged justification for the provision and protection of religious civil liberties that, among other things, appeals to the ways in which participation in certain religious traditions forms and sustains what I will call a person's "effective identity."

I. What Is a Natural Law Theory?

Lying at the core of any natural law theory are three claims: (1) a claim concerning the nature and constituents of genuine human flourishing; (2) a claim concerning the nature and the content of practical reasons; and (3) a claim concerning the proper role and limits of the state. In this section, I want to say just enough about each claim in order to set the stage for the subsequent argument.

On the Nature and Constituents of Human Flourishing

As I understand it, the natural law theorist's thesis concerning the nature of human flourishing says that genuine human flourishing (over some duration of time) consists in the sufficient participation in a sufficiently wide array of "basic goods." I shall understand basic goods to be certain kinds of activities and functional and experiential states. More exactly, I shall understand basic goods to be *kind-predicables,* the sorts of entities that can be multiply and/or repeatedly predicated of human persons (and other living creatures).[2] I shall further assume that for a person to "participate" in a basic good is just for that person to exemplify that good.[3] It is typical for natural law theorists to claim that there is a small number of basic goods that are general in nature. So John Finnis is, I judge, representative of the natural law tradition when he claims that there are eight basic goods that are constitutive of human well-being: bodily life; knowledge of reality (including aesthetic appreciation); practical reasonableness; excellence in work and play; friendship or harmony between individuals and groups of persons; harmony among one's feelings, judgments, and choices; harmony between oneself and the wider reaches of reality including a more-than-human source of meaning and value; and marriage.[4] Of course, other natural law theorists offer somewhat different and more expansive lists of the basic goods.[5] But it is ordinarily goods such as these that represent the constituents of authentic human flourishing according to a natural law view.

To this let me add two points of clarification. First, natural law theorists ordinarily add to their account of the nature of human flourishing a thesis about intrinsic goodness. Their claim is that participation in one or another basic good is itself intrinsically good. That is to say, the goodness that consists in the participation in any basic good does not inherit all its goodness from the way in which it causally or noncausally contributes to some other state of affairs that is good; rather, such participation is good in itself.[6] Second, it is worth noting an important divide between more traditional natural law theorists who, following Aquinas, give a deeper metaphysical account of what makes it the case that certain types of activities and experiential states are basic goods, and those, following Finnis and Germain Grisez, who do not. More traditional Thomists claim that any adequate account of what makes it the case that something is an aspect of human flourishing must appeal to a teleological account of human nature according to which human beings have an *ergon* or function. Finnis and his followers have vehemently denied this.[7] In what follows, I will not attempt to adjudicate this controversy.

On the Nature and Content of Practical Reasons

Definitive of natural law theory is the thesis that a person's participation in a basic good is a reason of a sort. A little more precisely, the idea is that, necessarily, for any agent S and basic good G, there is a prima facie reason for S to positively value the participation in G in and for itself.[8] When I say that there is a reason for a person to "positively value" the participation in a basic good, I mean that there is a reason for that person to prize, cherish, honor, esteem, respect, appreciate, etc., that participation—where prizing, cherishing, etc., is thought of as involving a whole range of appropriate emotional, desiderative, and actional responses to that participation. The reasons to positively value the participation in a basic good, I shall further assume, are both general and "basic" in character. These reasons are general insofar as they direct all persons in the appropriate circumstances to positively value any instance of a basic good. They are basic in at least two ways. They are, first of all, basic insofar as any explanation of an intelligible piece of practical reasoning must terminate by citing one or another such reason.[9] Second, they are basic insofar as they cannot be inferred from other more fundamental reasons.[10] Robert George, for example, writes that "intrinsic values, as ultimate reasons for action, cannot be deduced or inferred. . . . As basic reasons for action, the value intrinsic goods have cannot (and need not) be inferred from more fundamental reasons for action."[11] George does not say what he means by "more fundamental reasons" here, but I shall assume that he means *explanatorily* more fundamental reasons. So the idea is something like this: P is a basic reason to act only if P cannot be deduced from some other reason Q that explains why P is a reason to act. In any event, it is the panoply of general principles that specifies that we ought to positively value the participation in one or another basic good that comprises the "natural law."

On the Proper Role and Limits of the State

The third and final feature of natural law theories I wish to highlight is a thesis concerning the proper role and limits of the state. Put succinctly, the natural law theorist says that the proper and central role of the state is to provide the basic material, institutional, educational, and social circumstances in which a flourishing life can be chosen and lived. Notice that the proper function of the state is best understood as providing the circumstances in which a flourishing life can be chosen and lived; it is to provide its citizens with the *opportunity* to flourish. According to the natural law account, the state itself cannot guarantee that its citizens will choose a flourishing life, let alone flourish. The state can, however, take various steps to promote and protect (either directly or indirectly) the flourishing of its citizens. Thus, most natural law theorists have thought it proper for the state to enact "morals laws" of various kinds that render illegal certain types of activities that are thought to be inimical to the authentic flourishing of persons (e.g., recreational drug use, prostitution, and so on). However, it should be emphasized that, according to most natural law theorists, the state's ability to implement and enforce morals laws is limited in several ways.[12] For one thing, the natural law limits the measures the state can take to provide for or protect the flourishing of its citizens. The state is never to act in such a way that expresses an intention to destroy, frustrate, or inhibit the participation in, or the opportunity to participate in, the basic goods. For another, as Aquinas himself made clear, the state cannot demand too much of its citizens. Passing morals laws of an especially stringent sort may be futile, and may be the occasion for social foment and even greater vice. So most natural law theorists agree that it is permissible and advisable for the state to allow its citizens to engage in certain kinds of activities that, strictly speaking, contravene the natural law.

II. Our Central Question

The central question I raised at the outset of this essay asks: does a natural law theory of the Aristotelian-Thomist variety have the resources to offer an adequate justification for the provision and protection of religious civil liberties?

Interestingly enough, Aquinas thought it did. It was Aquinas's conviction that it is the proper role of the state to provide for and protect the various religious civil liberties of at least some of its citizens.[13] Aquinas reasoned that it is

the proper role of the state to provide for and protect the necessary components of the flourishing of its citizens. But the flourishing of any person consists in that person's enjoying eternal felicity. As such, the state has a duty to do
what it can (within certain limits) to help bring about and not prevent its citizens' enjoying eternal felicity. On the assumption that Christianity is the one
true faith, the state ought to allow its citizens to engage freely in Christian
modes of worship. For in doing so, the state can clearly facilitate and not hinder
its citizens from enjoying beatitude. Moreover, the state has reason to allow its
citizens to engage freely in Jewish and pagan modes of worship as well, not because such engagement directly (or indirectly) contributes to the eternal felicity
of the citizenry, but because, if the state were to disallow it, this would likely cause
unnecessary social unrest and would harden non-Christians to the truth of the
Christian gospel.

Needless to say, Aquinas's rationale for providing religious civil liberties is not
something that is particularly attractive to contemporary natural law theorists—
and for at least three reasons. First of all, some natural law theorists do not hold
that theism, let alone Christianity, is true. So, Aquinas's deepest rationale for allowing religious civil liberties is simply unavailable to some natural law theorists. In addition, even if the truth of theism forms part of the content of the
natural law, it is certainly one of its more controversial aspects. Thus, if a natural
law theorist were to appeal to the truth of theism to ground religious civil liberties, her theory would not command widespread assent. Finally, most contemporary natural law theorists are apt to draw a much sharper distinction between
church and state than did Aquinas. So, even if theism is true and even if it forms
part of the content of the natural law, most natural law theorists do not claim that
it is the *state's* responsibility to help bring about the eternal felicity of its citizens.
If anything, this responsibility belongs to the church.

So the contemporary natural law theorist who wishes to find a basis to justify the provision and protection of religious civil liberties will have to find another rationale than the one Aquinas offered. Perhaps the most sustained attempt to develop such a rationale is found in Robert George's book *Making Men
Moral: Civil Liberties and Public Morality*. I propose that we explore it in some
detail.

George's Account

One of the more interesting features of George's approach is that, unlike many
contemporary liberal views, it does not attempt to ground religious civil liberties in the good of personal autonomy. As George makes clear, according to a

natural law scheme, personal autonomy is not a basic good.[14] The mere fact that a particular action would realize a person's autonomy does not, according to the natural law view, provide a basic reason for taking that action. At most, personal autonomy is a necessary condition for participating in goods such as practical reasonableness, friendship, and the like, but is not itself a basic good. And, thus, in George's view, we cannot hope to find a basis for the provision of religious civil liberties merely by appealing to personal autonomy. Nor, for that matter, does George try to ground religious civil liberties in a fundamental right to religious freedom. Rights, says George, are always derived from more fundamental moral principles and basic human goods.[15] So, according to the natural law view, there is no sense in talking of a fundamental right to religious liberty. Hence, there is no sense in appealing to such a fundamental right to justify the provision of religious civil liberties. Nor, finally, does George endeavor to justify religious civil liberties by maintaining that the state ought to be neutral with respect to all conceptions of the good and, hence, should allow (all other things being equal) persons to pursue whatever form of life they please. At the core of natural law theories is the conviction that the state ought not to remain neutral with respect to all conceptions of the good, but ought to promote and protect the genuine flourishing of its citizens. So, the appeal to neutrality does not figure in the natural law theorist's attempt to provide a rationale for the provision of religious civil liberties. However, if these three paradigmatic liberal justifications for the provision and protection of religious civil liberties are unavailable to the natural law theorist, where else might the natural law theorist turn?

George's suggestion is that we ought to anchor religious civil liberties in what he calls the basic good of "religion":

> I maintain that the right to religious freedom is grounded precisely in the value of religion, considered as an ultimate intelligible reason for action, a basic human good. Like other intrinsic values, religion can constitute a reason for political action; government need not, and should not, be indifferent to the value of religion.[16]

And what is the basic good of religion? Here it is worth quoting George at some length:

> Irrespective of whether unaided reason can conclude on the basis of a valid argument that God exists—indeed, even if it turns out that God does not exist—there is an important sense in which religion is a basic human good, an intrinsic and irreducible aspect of the well-being and flourishing

of human persons. Religion is a basic good if it provides an ultimate intelligible reason for action. But agnostics and even atheists can easily grasp the intelligible point of considering whether there is some ultimate, more-than-human-source of meaning and value, of enquiring as best one can into the truth of the matter, and of ordering one's life on the basis of one's best judgment. Doing that is participating in the good of religion. Just as one has reason, without appeal to ulterior reasons . . . to pursue knowledge, enter into friendships and other forms of community, strive for personal integrity, develop one's skills and realize one's talents, one also has reason, without appeal to ulterior reasons, to ascertain the truth about ultimate or divine reality and, if possible, to establish harmony and enter into communion with the ultimate source(s) of meaning and value.[17]

If I understand George correctly, participating in the basic good of religion has two main components: first, it involves inquiring into whether there is an ultimate source of meaning and value; and, second, it involves ordering one's life on the basis of one's best judgment about whether there is such an ultimate source (which I shall hereafter simply call "God").

How, then, do we get from the claim that religion is a basic good to the conclusion that the state ought to provide and protect religious civil liberties? George never explicitly spells out his argument. But something like the following, I surmise, is what George has in mind:

1. Every person and institution, including the state, has basic moral reasons not to intentionally inhibit the opportunity for persons to choose to participate in the various basic goods, but has reason to intentionally protect such participation.
2. Religion is a basic good.
3. Therefore, every person and institution, including the state, has basic moral reasons not to intentionally inhibit the opportunity for persons to choose to participate in the good of religion, but has reason to intentionally protect such participation.
4. Providing for and protecting various religious civil liberties (e.g., the right to assemble and worship in a way one pleases, and so on) is a centrally important way by which the state can intentionally not inhibit but intentionally protect the opportunity for persons to choose to participate in the basic good of religion.
5. Hence, the state has basic moral reasons to provide for and protect various religious civil liberties.

I wish to press two sorts of objections to this argument. I want to maintain, first of all, that even if the participation in the good of religion is intrinsically good, and even if the state has a basic reason to provide for and protect such participation, George needs to furnish further considerations for thinking that these basic reasons are not overridden by other factors. Second, I wish to contend that participating in the good of religion does not provide basic reasons to positively value it and, hence, that religion is not a basic good.

The First Objection

Let us suppose that George is right to say that religion is a basic good and, thus, that participating in the good of religion is itself intrinsically good. That is to say, let us assume that it is intrinsically good to inquire into the nature and existence of God and to order one's life in accordance with one's best judgment about these issues. However, even if it were true that it is intrinsically good that one order one's life according to one's best judgment concerning whether God exists and what God is like, it may still be the case—and sometimes is the case—that the particular *ordering* of a life made on the basis of that judgment is intrinsically bad. Thus, it may be the case—and sometimes is the case—that the badness of a particular ordering is sufficient to defeat the intrinsic goodness of having ordered one's life according to one's best judgment concerning the nature and existence of God.

Consider, for example, a religious sect that espouses a view about reality that we might call "cosmic illusionism." This sect maintains that the way reality appears to us is deeply and systematically misleading. Though reality may appear to have different sorts of entities and various sorts of distinctive components, this is not the case. There are no distinctions to be found in reality; reality is really pure, undifferentiated "consciousness." Let us also suppose that this sect holds that, on account of their illusory nature, the apparent beauties of this world are to be shunned, political life should be scorned, and communal life is to be avoided. Now consider someone who belongs to this sect. After reflection, this person has come to accept the major tenets of this sect and she attempts to order her life according to these tenets. Pretty clearly, though it may be good that our sect member has ordered her life according to her best judgment concerning the existence and nature of the divine, the particular ordering of her life looks to be very bad indeed. As a consequence of adhering to the principles of this sect, this person holds packs of false beliefs about the nature of reality and fails to participate in the goods of aesthetic appreciation, sociality, and marriage, to name a few. In this case, it seems as if the badness of the ordering of our sect member's life is sufficient to defeat the goodness of her having ordered her life on the basis of her best judgments concerning the existence and nature of the divine. And if the badness of the ordering of her life is sufficient to defeat the goodness of having ordered her life on the basis of her best judgments concerning the nature and existence of the divine, it is not immediately obvious why, according to a natural law view, the state should provide for and protect her religious civil liberties. After all, many natural law theorists, including Aquinas, have thought that in some cases the badness of the way in which a person has ordered her life is sufficient to defeat the goodness of that person's having ordered her life as she best sees fit. It was Aquinas's conviction, for example, that heretics ought not to be granted any religious civil liberties and deserved death.

Let me forthrightly admit that I do not think that this is an insurmountable objection to George's argument. I only claim that more needs to be said about why participation in the putative good of religion is of such importance that the state ought to protect the religious civil liberties of its citizens—even when we have good reason to believe that adherence to a particular religion renders the ordering of the lives of those persons who adhere to that religion intrinsically bad.

The Second Objection

The second objection to George's argument is more ambitious. It contends that, contrary to what George says, the putative basic good of religion is not a basic good at all.

The objection can be articulated best if we bring to mind the connection George thinks exists between basic goods and basic reasons. The participation in any basic good, recall, is a basic reason—where (roughly) a reason is basic in case it cannot be derived from a more fundamental reason. On the assumption that the basic good of religion consists in inquiring into the existence and nature of God, and ordering one's life on one's best judgment concerning these matters, it follows that we have basic reasons to engage in these activities. But now consider the following line of reasoning. Suppose a person were to ask herself: "Why ought I to inquire into whether God exists or what God is like?" A perfectly intelligible answer is, "Having knowledge is intrinsically good. Since inquiring into whether God exists and what God is like will make it more likely for me to increase my knowledge, I ought to inquire into whether God exists and what God is like." In this case, we have offered an argument to inquire into God's existence and nature by appealing to the basic good of knowledge. Thus, it appears as if we can deduce reasons for inquiring into God's existence and nature from the value of participating in the basic good of knowledge. But are the reasons that consist in participating in the good of knowledge explanatorily more fundamental than those reasons that consist in participating in the putative good of religion? It appears that they are. We explain what it is to participate in this first aspect of the good of religion by appeal to the good of knowledge; indeed, the former appears to be simply an aspect of the latter. Thus, we naturally explain the reasons we have for participating in this aspect of the putative good of religion by appeal to the reasons we have for participating in the good of knowledge. We do not, however, appeal to the first aspect of the putative good of religion to explain what the good of knowledge is or the reasons we have to participate in it. That would be to attempt to explain what is explanatorily more basic in terms of what is less so.

Now consider another argument. Suppose this same person were to query: "Why should I order my life according to my best judgment concerning whether God exists and what God is like?" And suppose the answer is: "It is constitutive of a person's participation in the good of practical reasonableness that this person attempt to order her life in accordance with her best judgments concerning centrally important issues. Whether God exists and what God is like are centrally important issues. Hence, I ought to order my life in accordance with my best judgment about whether God exists and what God is like." In this case, we have offered an argument to order one's life according to one's best judgment about whether God exists and what God is like by appealing to the good of practical reasonableness. Accordingly, it appears as if we can deduce reasons for participating in the second aspect of the putative good of religion from the value of participating in the good of practical reasonableness. Are the reasons that consist in participating in the good of practical reasonableness explanatorily more fundamental than those that consist in participation in this second aspect of the putative good of religion? It appears so. We explain what it is to participate in this aspect of the good of religion by reference to the good of practical reasonableness; indeed, the former appears to be simply an aspect of the latter. Consequently, we naturally explain the reasons we have for participating in this second aspect of the putative good of religion by appeal to the reasons we have for participating in the good of practical reasonableness. We do not, however, explain what the good of practical reasonableness is, or the reasons we have to participate in it, by appeal to this second aspect of the putative good of religion. That would be to attempt to explain what is explanatorily more fundamental in terms of what is less so.

If the foregoing is correct, religion is not a basic good. This is because the reasons we have to participate in the good of religion can be derived from the value of participating in the good of knowledge and the good of practical reasonableness.

Moreover, we have grounds for believing that the sorts of reasons that participation in the good of knowledge and the good of practical reasonableness yield
are explanatorily more basic than those yielded by the participation in the putative good of religion. Participation in the good of religion is just a *way* of participating in these explanatorily more fundamental goods. So, on the assumption
that a thing is a basic good if and only if a person has a basic reason to positively
value the participation in that thing, then it follows that the putative good of religion is not a basic good.

Three Replies

How might one respond to this argument? Here are three different replies.

One line of response runs as follows. To establish that religion is not a basic
good, we would have to show that participating in the basic goods of knowledge
and practical reasonableness fully explains why it is worthwhile to participate
in the good of religion. But the argument just offered doesn't do that. At best, it
offers a partial explanation of why we have reasons to participate in the good of
religion. It ignores the fact that we have additional reasons to participate in the
good of religion. These additional reasons are generated (in part) by the fact that
it is the existence and nature of *God* into which we are inquiring. It is the *object*
of the good of religion that makes it distinctively worthwhile to participate in it.

The fundamental problem with this reply is that, if it is correct, it results in an
inordinate proliferation of basic goods. For consider any subject matter into which
it is worthwhile to inquire. Take, for example, an existentially weighty matter such
as the nature and existence of the soul, the nature of human flourishing, or the
basis of morality. Or consider an existentially less central, though nevertheless
worthwhile, subject such as Rembrandt's use of light, Charlie Parker's use of the
diminished scale, or Chaucer's use of irony. According to the present reply, the reasons a person has for inquiring into any of these issues and ordering her life according to her best judgment on these matters is not exhausted by the fact that in
doing so she participates in the goods of knowledge and practical reasonableness.
The object of each of these inquiries gives a person additional reasons to pursue
them. However, if this "extra worthiness" is sufficient to transform an activity into
a basic good, then we shall have to say that there are basic goods corresponding
to each of these activities—and countless others like them. But George, Finnis,
and company do not say this; they do not say that there is a basic good corresponding to inquiring into the nature of the soul or Rembrandt's use of light. And it is
probably good that they do not. Once we have such a fine-grained account of basic
goods in place, then we will be tempted to say that inquiring into *any* worthwhile

subject counts as a basic good. Moreover, fundamental to Finnis's and George's account of the basic goods is the claim that a good is basic only if it cannot be "reduced to merely being an aspect of" any of the other basic goods.[18] But if being an "aspect" of a good is simply being a manner of participating in it, then it is difficult to see how the present reply can be sustained. An activity such as inquiring into the nature of the soul looks merely to be a way by which we participate in goods such as knowledge and practical reasonableness.

The second response to the argument takes a different route. It says that, while the argument we have offered so far may be successful in showing that the good of religion as George understands it is not a basic good, it is not successful in establishing that the good of religion as Finnis understands it is not a basic good. This is because Finnis offers us a distinct account of the nature of the good of religion that is not vulnerable to the kinds of arguments that we have raised against George's account. Here is Finnis's most extensive defense of the claim that religion is a basic good:

> But is it reasonable to deny that it is, at any rate, peculiarly important to have thought reasonably and (where possible) correctly about these questions of the origin of the cosmic order and of human freedom and reason— whatever the answer to these questions turns out to be, and even if the answers have to be agnostic or negative? And does not that importance in large part consist in this: that if there is a transcendent origin of the universal order-of-things and of human freedom and reason, then one's life and actions are in fundamental disorder if they are not brought, as best one can, into some sort of harmony with whatever can be known or surmised about that transcendent other and its lasting order?[19]

One might interpret this passage to claim that the good of religion is not merely an aspect of the good of knowledge or the good of practical reasonableness. To be sure, participating in the good of religion consists in inquiring into whether there is a God and what God's nature is like. But it is more than this. It also involves (if the more-than-human order is personal) something like having one's will in accordance with the will of the divine. Thus, we might say that the good of religion is a distinct good that is more analogous to the good of friendship and community than the good of knowledge or practical reasonableness.

There are several problems with this reply. To begin with, it does not follow that if the putative good of religion is distinct from the good of knowledge and the good of practical reasonableness it is thereby a basic good. It may still be the case that the reasons we have for participating in the good of religion can be deduced from the reasons that consist in the participation in the good of knowledge or the good of practical reasonableness. In addition, the reply misunderstands Finnis's conception of the good of religion. The reply in question suggests that, according to Finnis's view, the good of religion consists (at least in part) in a person's life and actions being in harmony with God's purposes. But Finnis does not say that. Rather, he says that, *if* there is a God, one's life and actions are in fundamental disorder if they are not in harmony with God's purposes. To be sure, Finnis would also affirm that, if there is a God, then a person ought to order her life in such a way that it is in harmony with God's purposes. But nowhere in his account of the good of religion does Finnis claim that there is a God. Nor does he maintain that the natural law implies that there is a God. So, it is incorrect to say that in Finnis's view the good of religion is distinct from the good of knowledge and the good of practical reasonableness insofar as the good of religion consists in being in harmony with God. And, once Finnis's view is understood correctly, there is, as far as I can tell, no substantive difference between his and George's position.

Let me point to a third way by which we might try to avoid the objection I have raised against the George/Finnis view. It might be said that the interpretation of Finnis just offered is incorrect. Finnis's claim is not that if there is a God, then religion is a good. Rather, Finnis's claim is that religion (i.e., attempting to, and aligning one's will with God) is a good insofar as it can be seen as something that would be worth having. Of course, the nonexistence of God would make this good out of reach in a way similar to the manner in which skepticism would make the good of knowledge out of reach. But even the skeptic who rejects the possibility of having knowledge can see that if knowledge could be obtained it would be good.[20]

I doubt that this last reply is adequate. First of all, even if this reply were correct, it would not imply that participating in the basic good of religion is anything more than a way by which we participate in the goods of knowledge and practical reasonableness (and perhaps friendship). So the present reply is not really a reason for believing that religion is a *basic* good. Moreover, it is presumably the case that participating in the good of religion thus understood is a (basic) reason to act. But it is hard to see how the fact that is picked out by the counterfactual claim *if there were a God, then it would be good to align our will with God's* is a reason to act. The fundamental problem here is that whether the counterfactual participation in a good is a reason to act is (at least in part) a function of (1) whether the state of affairs that is specified in the antecedent of a counterfactual claim (in this case, God's existing) is likely to obtain at the actual world, and (2) the importance of the state of affairs that is specified in the consequent (in this case, aligning our will with God's).[21] Finnis and George, however, wish to characterize the good of religion in such a way that its status of being a good does not depend on whether God exists or whether it is likely that God exists. So suppose we grant that aligning one's will with God's own will would be immensely valuable (assuming that God is as the major theistic religions claim). However, for all that's been said, the likelihood of God's existing may be so low (say, zero) that there is, nevertheless, no reason to pursue that putative good. Moreover, it may be that genuinely attempting to align my will with God's will requires of me immense sacrifices—sacrifices that consist in my not participating in a wide array of basic goods that I know are valuable. And, since for all that we've been told, the probability of theism is very low, it may be that, given these sacrifices, I have no reason to attempt to align my will with God's. Finally, there is a problem regarding religious diversity: when we take into consideration everything that Finnis and George claim, it is reasonable to believe that there are many putative Gods with which we might seek to align our will. And, for all that's been said, there seems just as much a reason to align our will with any one of these Gods as with others. But attempting to align my will with one God's purposes will, in a large range of cases, be incompatible with attempting to align my will with another of God's purposes. But then the putative good of religion directs us to act in a variety of mutually incompatible manners. And that is just to say that participation in this putative good itself gives us no reason to act at all.

What the Natural Law Theorist Should Contend

I have argued that there is no basic good of religion. If the argument is sound, then the natural law theorist should not attempt to justify religious civil liberties by appealing to the putative good of religion. What, then, should a natural law theorist who is interested in justifying the provision and protection of religious civil liberties do?

Let me propose a general argumentative strategy to which natural law theorists should appeal. I suggest that in attempting to justify the provision and protection of religious civil liberties the natural law theorist should attempt to execute an argument that has three main stages. First, the natural law theorist ought to identify the various basic goods the participation in which is intrinsically good. Second, the natural law theorist should make evident the various manners in which participation in certain religious traditions is an instance of, or otherwise contributes to, participation in the basic goods and, hence, why the state has various reasons to grant the appropriate types of civil liberties to participate in those religious traditions. Third, the natural law theorist ought to develop a series of arguments to the effect that (1) the state is incompetent in many cases to ascertain whether the goodness of participation in a particular religious tradition is defeated by other bad features of such participation, and (2) the state will sometimes have broadly pragmatic reasons to provide and protect religious civil liberties even when it has good reason to believe that such participation undercuts the participation in various basic goods. If the natural law theorist can successfully execute these three stages of the argument, then she will have given a sufficient justification for the state to grant religious civil liberties to participate in certain religious traditions. Though to this we should add the following qualification: if the state has good reason to believe that participation in a particular religious tradition has the effect of clearly and deeply damaging the common good, the state may revoke or not grant civil liberties to participate in that tradition.

This, I claim, is the sort of general strategy to which a natural law theorist should appeal. I want to close by considering in a little more depth how the natural law theorist might fill in some of the details of the argument. However, I should emphasize that what follows is just the broadest sketch of such an argument. All too often I simply glide over various intricacies and nuances that would characterize a more fully developed argument.

III. The Positive Argument

Suppose for the moment that the natural law theorist has successfully identified a cluster of basic goods the participation in which is intrinsically good. And suppose, moreover, that this list of basic goods roughly corresponds to the list that Finnis, Grisez, and George offer. What the natural law theorist should then attempt to establish, I suggest, is that participation in certain religious traditions is linked in various ways to the participation in these basic goods and, thus, the state has reasons to provide and protect civil liberties to participate in these traditions. More specifically, I suggest that the natural law theorist can identify at least two general ways in which participation in certain religious traditions is connected with the participation in the basic goods.

The first way in which participation in certain religious traditions is tied to participation in the basic goods is that we can participate in the various basic goods by way of participating in certain religious traditions. In other words, participation in certain religious traditions is often an *instance* of participation in the various basic goods. Indeed, it is this type of answer that has been lurking just below the surface of the second objection we raised earlier against George's view. What that objection brought out is that, while it may be the case that there is no good of religion, the participation in various religious traditions is closely linked to the participation in goods such as knowledge and practical reasonableness. Consider again the basic good of knowledge. And let's suppose that we understand this good rather broadly so that it encompasses other epistemic praiseworthy states such as wisdom, understanding, and aesthetic appreciation. Surely Finnis and George are correct to point out that participation in certain religious traditions is a way by which we endeavor to gain knowledge or understanding of some centrally important issues (e.g., whether God exists, the good for humankind, the nature of right and wrong, and so forth). And surely they are correct to claim that such participation is valuable. Granted, such participation doesn't very often take the form of dispassionate or detached inquiry into these matters. Rather, it often takes the form of engaging in a religious way of life; that is, it often takes the form of engaging in certain rites, consulting certain texts and authorities, practicing certain disciplines, developing various kinds of aesthetic sensibilities, and the like. But as Pascal pointed out concerning the Christian faith, such active engagement is one of the most apt ways by which we can explore the contours of a given religious tradition and its claims to truth.

Or take, as another example, what Finnis calls the good of practical reasonableness. As Finnis describes it, the good of practical reasonableness consists in bringing one's intelligence to bear effectively on the problems of choosing one's actions and lifestyle and shaping one's character.[22] Finnis invites us to characterize the practically reasonable agent (at least in part) as the person who has effectively conformed her actions, lifestyle, and character to her best judgments concerning how she ought to act and live. If this is an accurate depiction of practical reasonableness, then we should affirm that we can, and often do, participate in this good by way of participating in certain religious traditions. In seeking out wisdom concerning the human condition or the nature of God, and effectively conforming our actions, lifestyles, and character traits to our best judgments on these matters, we participate in the good of practical reasonableness.

Knowledge and practical reasonableness, however, are not the only two goods in which we can participate by way of participating in certain religious traditions. There is also the basic good of community and friendship. If we say that a community is instantiated when (and only when) agents have a common end and aim together to realize that end, then many religious groups count as communities.[23] Religious groups instantiate the intrinsic good of community by corporately worshiping God, sharing a vision that they will benefit others in important manners (such as bringing salvation, material and spiritual sustenance, etc.), and so on.

This is to indicate just several manners in which participation in certain religious traditions can be an instance of participation in various basic goods. We could identify still other ways; for instance, we might identify the ways in which persons can participate in the goods of inner peace, excellence in agency, harmony between one's choices and judgments and behavior, and so on, by way of participating in certain religious traditions. But the general point I am trying to make should be clear enough. Let me, then, point to a second way in which participation in certain religious traditions and basic goods are connected.

This second way tells us that participation in certain religious traditions plays a contributory role in forming certain kinds of valuable character traits. A little more specifically, the idea is that participation in certain religious traditions very often plays the *contributory* role of helping to form and sustain character traits that better enable persons to participate sufficiently in a wide array of basic goods.

There are any number of ways in which participation in certain religious traditions plays this contributory role.[24] In what follows, I will consider only one such way. I shall claim that participation in certain religious traditions plays an important role in forming and sustaining the types of traits that are necessary for effective agency itself.

Perhaps the best way to make the point is by having before us two concepts: what Charles Taylor calls a "framework of meaning" and what I shall call a "thick identity."[25] As I understand it, a framework of meaning is a more or less unified cluster of concepts, historical or mythical narratives, moral, aesthetic, or spiritual ideals, and so forth, that offer a portrayal of and direction for attaining genuine human flourishing. Religious traditions are typically constituted by frameworks of meaning; they are, in part, the sorts of things that offer us a vision of human well-being and direction concerning how we might attain it. It follows that one way by which we can assimilate the various ideals, insights, and standards of a given framework of meaning is by being inducted into one or another religious tradition. What I am calling a "thick identity," by contrast, is the natural upshot of a person's assimilating the ideals, insights, and standards of a given framework of meaning.[26] So, a thick identity might best be thought of as that configuration of traits that includes a person's characteristic ways of understanding and interpreting the world, her characteristic ways of behaving and relating to others, her firmest normative beliefs, desires, goals, and so on, that are held relatively constant in the course of practical deliberation.

For our purposes it is important to note that thick identities come in a number of varieties. Among these varieties are what I will call "effective identities." An effective identity is any thick identity that is *practically effective*. An effective identity allows a person to discern particularly salient features of situations, formulate sufficiently clear priorities among her ends, implement action plans that have a reasonable chance of realizing her ends in a wide variety of circumstances, and so forth. Possessing an effective identity thus involves a person's having particular kinds of character traits. Among other things, a person with an effective identity must have a sufficient degree of congruence among her desires, goals, normative beliefs, and so on, together with sufficient congruence between her desires, beliefs, goals and behavior. Moreover, an effective agent must regard herself with sufficient esteem, regard her projects as sufficiently worthwhile, and have sufficient confidence to execute her projects given the proper opportunities. The reason why effective identities are especially noteworthy for our purposes is that having an effective identity is arguably a necessary condition of a person's being able to flourish. Without having the kinds of traits that comprise an effective identity (such as sufficient psychic harmony, self-respect, practical discernment, and so on), a person will be unable to participate adequately in a sufficiently wide array of basic goods.

What I should now like to claim is that the reason certain religious traditions play a contributory role in forming the sorts of character traits that better enable persons to flourish authentically is that they provide the frameworks within which persons can become effective agents. By supplying various sorts of ideals, insights, disciplines, and so forth, certain religious traditions provide the resources by which persons can form and sustain the traits of psychic harmony, self-respect, practical discernment, and so forth. My claim is not, of course, that religious traditions are the only things that play this role. They are only one among many. Nevertheless, I do want to suggest that certain religious traditions play a particularly important and, perhaps, indispensable role in forming effective identities. After all, certain religious traditions are attuned in ways in which many other disciplines, practices, and traditions are not to the sorts of phenomena that undercut effective identity. Loss of orientation, deep dissatisfaction or uneasiness, bitter internal conflict or restlessness, inordinate desire, and moral apathy—these are the ailments of the soul that draw a great deal of attention from most of the great religious traditions. Indeed, one of the central tasks of these religious traditions has been to offer us the sort of insight, edification, community, and disciplines by which we can be steeled against or delivered from these conditions. So, without too much exaggeration, we can say that it is one of the central roles of certain religious traditions to produce in their members the qualities necessary for effective agency. To which we might add that there is evidence that they have had success in the endeavor!

My suggestion, then, is that having an effective identity is among the necessary conditions for a person to flourish, and that participating in certain religious traditions is an important and, perhaps, indispensable way by which these identities are formed. An implication of this is that, according to a natural law view, the state has additional reason to allow and protect the liberties to participate in these religious traditions. In allowing for and protecting these freedoms, the state helps to provide the conditions in which a flourishing life can be chosen and lived.

But as I have indicated already, the natural law theorist must say more than this if she is to provide an adequate justification for the provision and protection of religious civil liberties. Even though participating in certain religious traditions may be an instance of participating in one or another basic good, and even though such participation may help to form the qualities in persons that are necessary for them to flourish, these good states of affairs can be defeated by other bad aspects of this participation. At the end of the day, the participation in certain religious traditions can just as well undercut authentic human flourishing as it can contribute to it. Thus, we are forced to move into the third and final stage of the natural law theorist's argument.

It is at this third stage of argument that the natural law theorist must appeal to more pragmatic considerations. In response to the observation that the goodness of participating in certain religious traditions can be defeated by bad aspects of that participation, the natural law theorist can say several things. First, she should admit that though a central role of the state is to provide the necessary conditions in which a flourishing life can be chosen and lived, the state is in many cases incompetent to discern whether the valuable aspects of participation in certain religious traditions are defeated by the bad aspects of such participation. So, for example, it may be the case that there are valuable aspects of a person's being a Therevada Buddhist or a Presbyterian. It may also be the case that these valuable aspects are defeated by the further fact that the central doctrines of Therevada Buddhism or Presbyterianism to which this person assents, and on which she has based her life, are false. But most would agree, I think, that it lies outside the competence of the state to discern whether that is the case. Whether the central claims made by the adherents of certain religious traditions are true is typically an extremely complex and difficult issue to decide. So we ought not to expect the state to issue accurate pronouncements on this matter. And since it lies outside the ability of the state to decide this issue competently, and since there are clearly valuable features of being a Therevada Buddhist or a Presbyterian, the natural law theorist can claim that the state ought not to disallow religious civil liberties to Therevada Buddhists or Presbyterians.

Other cases will be different. It might be plain from the perspective of natural law theory that the valuable aspects of participation in a given religious tradition are defeated by the bad aspects of such participation. So, for example, it may be clear from a natural law perspective that participation in a sect that advocates cosmic illusionism, and the detachment from aesthetic pleasure, genuine community, political activity, and so on, is an overall bad thing. But, as Aquinas made evident, this doesn't itself imply that the state ought to revoke religious civil liberties in such circumstances. It may be that prohibiting participation in such traditions would only increase social unrest, or promote that religion by creating martyrs, or would make overly stringent demands on the citizenry, or would be impossible to enforce in practice. In cases such as these, the natural law theorist may allow religious civil liberties to participate in certain kinds of religious traditions in order to prevent the occurrence of even greater evils. Of course, none of this should suggest that there will never be cases in which the state ought not to revoke or not permit religious civil liberties to participants in a particular religious tradition. It may be that participating in certain religious traditions is so harmful to the common good that the state must severely limit or ban such participation altogether.

IV. A Final Objection

I would like to close by considering an objection to what I have argued. It might be complained that the position I have defended implies that religion is an instrumental or mere contributory good. According to the view I have outlined, it might be said, participation in religious traditions is good and religious civil liberties ought to be protected, insofar as the participation in religious traditions of certain kinds contributes in various positive ways to the participation in other basic goods. But this approach—so the objection runs—seems wrongheaded. The strategy doesn't accurately reflect that manner in which many religious persons defend their claim to religious civil liberties. The way in which many religious persons defend their claim to religious civil liberties is not by pointing to the fact that participation in religious traditions of various kinds is crucial for, say, forming and sustaining effective identities. Rather, what many religious persons emphasize is how important—how centrally and *intrinsically* important— practicing religion is to them in their ordinary lives.

This objection correctly emphasizes that the success of the present strategy relies on the ways in which participation in religious traditions of certain kinds contributes in positive ways to participation in the basic goods. But it doesn't follow from this that participation in such religious traditions is a mere instrumental or contributory good.[27] Nor have I claimed that the present strategy is the *only* way by which a natural law theorist can justify the provision and protection of religious liberties; there may be other sorts of strategies available. Moreover, when pressed on the issue of why the state ought to provide for and protect religious civil liberties, many ordinary religious persons, I suspect, would not hesitate to appeal to the fact that religious traditions provide frameworks of meaning that render their lives significant. I suspect, then, that the type of justification I have offered doesn't lie as far from those offered by ordinary religious persons as the objection would have us believe.

But suppose for the sake of argument that I am wrong about this last claim and that the strategy I have employed does not resemble closely the manner in which many religious persons defend their claims to religious civil liberties. What follows? Not, I think, that the present strategy is misguided or ought to be disregarded. To the contrary, I would think that it should be welcomed by those who wish to provide a justification for their claims to religious civil liberties. After all, there are plenty of activities that people claim to be especially important to them that do not deserve special attention from the state. What the present strategy offers is a rationale for why there is something special about religion and why the state should take seriously claims that religious institutions and practices of certain kinds should be protected. If what I have argued is sound, it is not only the fact that people are convinced that these institutions and practices are important that justifies the provision and protection of religious civil liberties. It is also the fact that these institutions and practices deserve protection because they contribute in important ways to authentic human flourishing. My aim in the latter part of this essay has been to articulate some of these ways.

NOTES

My thanks to members of the 1998 PEW seminar "Political Philosophy after Liberalism" for their generous input on this topic and an audience at Calvin College in May 1999. I would like to thank Nicholas Wolterstorff, Chris Eberle, Steve Layman, Phil Goggans, Luke Reinsma, and, especially, Mark Murphy for offering helpful comments on an earlier draft of this essay.

1. See Robert George, *Making Men Moral: Civil Liberties and Public Morality* (Oxford: Oxford University Press, 1993).

2. According to George, the basic goods can be "participated in by limitless numbers of persons on limitless numbers of occasions" ("Recent Criticisms of Natural Law Theory," *University of Chicago Law Review* 55 [1988]: 1389). However, in *Making Men Moral,* George also says that basic goods are "not Platonic forms that somehow transcend, or are in any sense extrinsic to, the human persons in whom they are instantiated" (13). I have my doubts whether these two positions are compatible, but will not pursue the issue here.

3. See Germain Grisez, Joseph Boyle, and John Finnis, "Practical Principles, Moral Truth, and Ultimate Ends," *American Journal of Jurisprudence* 32 (1987): 103.

4. See Finnis, "Is Natural Law Theory Compatible with Limited Government?" in *Natural Law, Liberalism, and Morality,* ed. Robert George (Oxford: Oxford University Press, 1996). Finnis's list of basic goods has, however, evolved over the years. Cf. Finnis, *Natural Law and Natural Rights* (Oxford: Oxford University Press, 1980), and "Natural Law and Legal Reasoning," in *Natural Law Theory,* ed. Robert George (Oxford: Oxford University Press, 1992).

5. See, for example, Mark C. Murphy, *Natural Law and Practical Reasoning* (Cambridge: Cambridge University Press, 2001), chap. 3.

6. Here is how Finnis puts the point when speaking of the good of knowledge: "At the same time, finally, it is to be recalled that the knowledge we here have in mind as a value is the knowledge that one can call an intrinsic good, i.e., that is considered to be desirable for its own sake and not merely as something sought after under some such description as 'what will enable me to impress my audience' or 'what will confirm my instinctive beliefs' or 'what will contribute to my survival'" (*Natural Law and Natural Rights,* 62).

7. The literature on this topic is extensive. See, for example, Anthony Lisska, *Aquinas's Theory of Natural Law* (Oxford: Oxford University Press, 1998); Murphy, *Natural Law and Practical Reasoning;* and Alasdair MacIntyre, "Theories of Natural Law in the Culture of Advanced Modernity," in *Common Truths: New Perspectives on Natural Law,* ed. Edward McLean (Wilmington, Del.: ISI Books, 2000). I should add that Finnis, Grisez, and George do not deny that the basic goods are grounded in human nature; to the contrary, they claim that they are so grounded (see George, "Recent Criticisms of Natural Law Theory," 1416). But nowhere, to my knowledge, have Finnis and company offered any account of the sort of dependence relation in question here.

8. Two points here. It is common for natural law theorists to say that the basic goods themselves are reasons, and not that participation in these goods is a reason to behave in a certain way (see, for example, Murphy, *Natural Law and Practical Reasoning,* chap. 3; George, *Making Men Moral;* and Finnis, Grisez, and Boyle, "Practical Principles"). However, since I don't see how a kind-predicable such as "knowledge" could be a reason, I shall speak of the participation in one or another basic good as being a reason. Moreover, when I say that "participation" in a basic good is a reason to behave in a certain way, I assume that we should understand this to mean that either (1) it is a person's actually exemplifying a basic good that is a reason for someone to behave in a given fashion; or (2) that a certain range of possible exemplifications of a good is a reason for someone to behave in a certain way. I will have more to say about clause (2) later in this essay.

9. George, "Recent Criticisms," 1390–94.

10. Strictly speaking, if the basic reasons are facts (as I think they are), then the claim is that the propositions that correspond to these facts cannot be deduced from propositions that correspond to explanatorily more basic facts.

11. George, "Recent Criticisms," 1392; and George, *Making Men Moral,* 12.

12. Finnis and George, for instance, diverge on the extent to which the state can implement morals laws in a given society. Cf. George, *Making Men Moral,* and Finnis, "Is Natural Law Theory . . . ?"

13. See *De Regno,* iv (i. 15) in *St. Thomas Aquinas on Kingship,* trans. Gerald Phelan (Toronto: The Pontifical Institute of Medieval Studies, 1949).

14. Or, more precisely, George holds that, according to one central understanding of the concept of personal autonomy, it is not a basic good. This conception of autonomy

says that "a person's life is autonomous if it is to a considerable extent his own creation." See George, *Making Men Moral*, chap. 6.

15. George, "A Response," in *A Preserving Grace*, ed. Michael Cromartie (Grand Rapids, Mich.: Eerdmans, 1997), 158.

16. George, *Making Men Moral*, 220.

17. Ibid., 221.

18. Finnis, *Natural Law and Natural Rights*, 92.

19. Ibid., 89–90.

20. This is the sort of view defended in Murphy, *Natural Law and Practical Reasoning*, 131–33.

21. For example, the fact *that were I to give a small amount of money to my friend, then I would relieve his financial distress* looks to be a reason to act. It is not unlikely that I can bring about the state of affairs picked out by the antecedent of this counterfactual (giving a small amount of money to my friend) at the actual world. Moreover, the state of affairs picked out by the consequent (relieving my friend's financial distress) is very important. Contrast this with the fact *that were Bilbo Baggins to be alive, it would be good to befriend him*. In this case, the state of affairs picked out by the antecedent (Baggins's being alive) is very unlikely to obtain at the actual world; Baggins is a fictional character. And, thus, though the state of affairs specified in the consequent (its being good to befriend Baggins) is valuable, I nonetheless have little reason to attempt to befriend Baggins because it is so improbable that Baggins is at any time alive at the actual world.

22. Finnis, *Natural Law and Natural Rights*, 88.

23. There are complexities concerning the nature of a community that I am ignoring here. For more on the subject, see Murphy, *Natural Law and Practical Reasoning*, 126–30.

24. See the essays by Coleman and Hollenbach in *Religion and Contemporary Liberalism*, ed. Paul Weithman (Notre Dame, Ind.: University of Notre Dame Press, 1997), that claim that participation in certain sorts of religious traditions helps people to develop certain kinds of character traits whose instantiation is especially important for the health of a liberal democracy.

25. See *Sources of the Self* (Cambridge, Mass.: Harvard University Press, 1989), chaps. 1 and 2.

26. Here I have learned and borrowed from David Wong, "On Flourishing and Finding One's Identity in Community," in *Ethical Theory: Character and Virtue*, ed. Peter French, Theodore Uehling, and Howard Wettstein, Midwest Studies in Philosophy 13 (Notre Dame, Ind: University of Notre Dame Press, 1988).

27. It may be that religion is not intrinsically good according to the way Finnis and George characterize intrinsic goodness. But that may simply be a problem with their account of intrinsic goodness.

6

THE RENUNCIATION
OF CONSCIENCE

MARK C. MURPHY

Nicholas Wolterstorff's 1998 Stone Lectures[1] begin with a reminder of the witness of Polycarp, bishop of Smyrna, a second-century Christian who was martyred for refusing the proconsul's order to disparage Christ and declare full allegiance to Caesar. A soldier's sword eventually had its way with Polycarp, but Polycarp remained loyal to Christ, his king.

Wolterstorff obviously approves—"approves" is far too weak a word—of Polycarp's response in the face of the proconsul's demand. The response—"For eighty and six years have I been his servant, and he has done me no wrong; how can I blaspheme my King, who has saved me?"—hits the mark. And Wolterstorff obviously thinks that the audience of the Stone Lectures will approve as well. There is no effort, because there is no need, to *defend* Polycarp's judgments and actions. It is obvious to all sensible Christians that Polycarp's choice was the right one. Wolterstorff takes his task to be entirely that of understanding more clearly the basis for the rightness of Polycarp's choice rather than that of seeing whether Polycarp chose properly in disobeying the proconsul's order.

Thomas Hobbes, like Wolterstorff, has much to teach us about the nature of political authority, and about how it can be in tension with the demands of divine authority. And Hobbes, like Wolterstorff, is a Christian.[2] But Hobbes's views on the nature of political authority and its potential tension with the demands of divine authority militate in favor of an assessment of the martyr from Smyrna that differs from that presupposed by Wolterstorff. Hobbes's views on divine and human law support the conclusion that, for all of Polycarp's piety, he erred in defying the proconsul. Can we show that Hobbes was wrong and that the rest of us are right about the merit of Polycarp's defiance?

I

Here is how Wolterstorff views Polycarp's situation. Polycarp has two sovereigns: Christ and Caesar (*DCDN* I.1.11). Smyrna, where Polycarp resided, was within Christ's jurisdiction, because the whole world is under Christ's jurisdiction (*DCDN* I.1.3); Smyrna was also in Caesar's jurisdiction, because Smyrna was under the political control of Rome (*DCDN* I.1.12).

To be another's subject, though, is to be bound to obey that other's dictates. Polycarp was subject to Christ and Caesar; but Christ's law directed Polycarp not to revile Him by swearing total allegiance to Caesar, while Caesar's law—or at least that of Caesar's representative, the proconsul Statius Quadratus—directed Polycarp to revile Christ by swearing total allegiance to Caesar. It might look as if Polycarp is bound both to revile Christ and not to revile Christ. But, Wolterstorff assumes, it is obvious that Polycarp would have been wrong to revile Christ. So Wolterstorff argues, in keeping with Christian tradition, that Caesar and his ilk can be our sovereigns only in a *qualified* way. Their authority is only through divine authority: God has delegated authority to them, and their commands bind only insofar as they fall within the scope of the authority that God has conferred upon them (*DCDN* III.5.21).[3] So Polycarp was bound only to Christ's command not to forswear Him; he was not bound to Caesar's command to revile Christ.

Now, Hobbes disagrees with Wolterstorff's assessment of Polycarp's action: he thinks that Polycarp acted wrongly by refusing to perform the action that the proconsul required of him, and he thinks that, even if it were granted that Polycarp acted rightly, it would still be the case that there was something deficient about Polycarp's action, something so deficient that it would be misleading to say of Polycarp simply that he did the right thing.[4] One might think that to hold this view is on its own enough to show that Hobbes was no Christian; as Wolterstorff remarks, "To be a Christian is to acknowledge Christ's sovereignty" (*DCDN* I.2. 6), and one might think that one could hold that Polycarp should have followed the proconsul's directive only if one failed to acknowledge Christ's sovereignty. The question of Christ's sovereignty is a bit of a tricky matter in Hobbes's theological and political views, because Hobbes has unorthodox views on the Trinity: Hobbes thinks that God is a trinity only inasmuch as God was "personated" by Moses (God the Father), Jesus (God the Son), and the Apostles (God the Holy Spirit) (*L* xlii.3). But we can say, at the very least, that Hobbes acknowledges God's sovereignty, and that Christ, personating God, is to be obeyed. God is, on Hobbes's view, the "sovereign of sovereigns" (*L* xxx.10), and it is to Hobbes obvious that God's sovereignty is superior to any earthly sovereign's, so that if there is a conflict between God's law and that of the sovereign's, one should obey God rather than men (*L* xliii.2).

It looks, then, as if Wolterstorff has been given by Hobbes everything that Wolterstorff needs to show that Polycarp was beyond criticism for disobeying the proconsul. If Hobbes allows that God's sovereignty trumps any human sovereignty, so that if there is a conflict between God's law and human law, then God's law is to be obeyed and the human law disobeyed, does it not follow that Polycarp acted rightly, and that there therefore is no basis on which to criticize him?

It does not. There are in *Leviathan* three distinct lines of argument concerning the relationship between divine and human law, the success of any of which would alone be enough to show that Polycarp erred badly in choosing to disobey the proconsul. We will examine each of these three strategies. While, as I will argue, the first two of them are unconvincing, even in Hobbes's own terms, the third is more interesting, harder to defeat, and requires us to think much harder than we might otherwise be inclined to think about why Polycarp must have been in the right in refusing to do what the pronconsul demanded of him.

II

Hobbes's first strategy is the least subtle and least plausible: he denies that, apart from the laws of nature, there are any divine laws that, as divine laws, obligate us.[5] So there is no divine law forbidding Polycarp from denying Christ. So long as there is no divine law forbidding Polycarp from denying Christ, Caesar's order stands unopposed by any law of superior authority, and thus Polycarp should obey it.

The claim that there are no divine laws that we are obligated to obey other than the laws of nature is a hard saying. Here is Hobbes's argument for it. We cannot be obligated by a law unless we know that it proceeds from the lawgiver whose will we are obligated to obey (*L* xxvi.16; xxxiii.23). We can know the content of the laws of nature through natural reason (*L* xiv–xv), and we can know via natural reason that there is a God (*L* xi.25), and that the laws of nature are God's dictates to us (*L* xxxiii.22). So we are obligated to obey the divine law that is knowable through reason. With some limited exceptions, though, the divine law that is knowable through reason cannot license disobedience to the sovereign: for the upshot of those laws of nature is that peace is to be sought, and on Hobbes's view peace can be achieved only by agreeing to near-absolute obedience to the sovereign's dictates (*L* xvii.13). What the laws of nature tell us to do is: whatever the sovereign tells us to do (for the limited exceptions, see *L* xxi.11–17).

What, though, about those divine laws that are revealed to us by inspiration, or through prophets, or from Scripture? Hobbes's arguments with respect to inspiration are skeptical: we have little reason to believe that, when others claim that they are inspired to disobey the law, they are genuinely being told to disobey; and we should turn on ourselves the same suspicion that we turn on others (*L* xxxii.6). Prophets can be false, and even if they perform miracles to testify to their being sent from God, one standard for so testing them (Hobbes argues from Scripture) is that of obedience to the duly constituted authorities. Thus, any putative prophet that commands us to disobey the sovereign ipso facto shows him- or herself to be a fraud (*L* xxxii.5–8).

The biggest challenge for Hobbes in putting forward this line of argument is that of dealing with Scripture, which contains a number of injunctions that seem to be the sort of directive that might come into conflict with the earthly sovereign's dictates. Some of these directives Hobbes pushes to the side as counsels rather than commands, as solid advice rather than obligatory dictates, suggesting that divine advice is not the sort of thing that could justify disobedience to a human sovereign's command (*L* xlii.43–45). But Hobbes is left with some remainders, and we want to know why these remainders cannot justify in some instances disobedience to a human sovereign. One of the more straightforward instances is Christ's injunction not to deny Him, with the attendant warning that one who denies Christ will be denied by Christ before His Father in Heaven (Matt. 10:33). One might think that Polycarp's rejection of Christ and acceptance of Caesar would be just the sort of denial of Christ that Christ forbids. And so Hobbes needs to explain to us why Polycarp should not take himself to be bound by a divine law here. Hobbes's answer is that we do not know that the Bible is the word of God; we only believe it to be so (*L* xxxiii.24; *L* xliii.8). As we must know, and not merely believe, that a dictate came from a legitimate authority for that dictate to count as law, the dictates in the Bible do not measure up.

But this is terribly unconvincing. Hobbes apparently thinks that there is some higher epistemic threshold that must be met in order for us to understand a putatively binding dictate to be law, and that the divine commands revealed in

Scripture do not meet this standard. But it is hard to see why any Christian would accept this line of reasoning. Evidently I think that Scripture meets some positive epistemic standard—after all, I believe it. And, what's more, it isn't just me, as if I have some eccentric view; lots of my fellow Christians also believe it to be true. Hobbes may not wish to label this sort of belief "knowledge." But while we might allow that a law whose promulgation is extraordinarily uncertain and dubious may fail to bind, it is hard to believe that the Christians to whom Hobbes's argument was addressed would find this to be an accurate description of the deliverances of Scripture.[6]

Another worry here is that human law will often fall to the same argument, and in embarrassing ways. It is often the case that whether a law was passed by a duly constituted authority is something about which we can have only testimony as our basis. We cannot have the sort of epistemically highly circumscribed belief that Hobbes labels "knowledge." But these laws can bind us nonetheless. We can, if we like, speak with Hobbes and allow that it is true that we merely believe that these are laws. That does not seem sufficient to call their character as binding dictates into question.

III

Hobbes has another line of argument, more subtle, but which ultimately fails as well. Suppose that we grant that there can be a divine law requiring one not to Φ and a human law requiring one to Φ, and in particular a divine law requiring Polycarp not to blaspheme and a human law requiring Polycarp to blaspheme. One might think that by granting this we must thereby approve of Polycarp's action. But Hobbes claims that this is not so.

What Hobbes appeals to is a doctrine of responsibility. Suppose, for example, that I am bound by a human law to Φ, and Jane is bound by a divine law to ψ. Suppose further that Jane is not going to ψ unless I refrain from Φ. It is extremely plausible to suppose here that these suppositions are not sufficient to warrant the claim that I ought to disobey my human sovereign's dictate to Φ.[7] The violation of divine law that will occur if I obey my human sovereign is, while real and deplorable, *not my responsibility*—it is *Jane's* responsibility. Jane is the one who is acting wrongly, not I. It is only violations of divine law that are *my* responsibility that could justify *my* disobedience to human law.

Now, this point might seem of little help to Hobbes. For in the sort of case exemplified by Polycarp's martyrdom, one and the same person seems to be bound to inconsistent courses of action by divine and human law. It is not like the case of Jane and me, where I am responsible for my actions and Jane is responsible for hers. But Hobbes rightly says that even if a person A performs some action, the normative effects of that action may be attributable to some different person B. For example, if I sign a contract, the normative effects of that action—binding someone to performance—may not accrue to me but to my wife. This would occur if I were my wife's agent, if I had, for example, power of attorney to make contracts on her behalf in a certain sphere. So there is *some* room to move here. It does not follow immediately from Polycarp's uttering the words "I renounce Christ" that the normative effects of that utterance—*having violated an obligation to God, having become blameworthy,* etc.—accrue to Polycarp rather than someone else.[8]

Hobbes claims that if one violates a divine law out of obedience to a human sovereign, then one is not responsible for that violation; the responsibility belongs to one's human sovereign, not to oneself. It is as if the sovereign performed the action through the subject; the subject is a mere instrument of the sovereign's action. So, on Hobbes's view, had Polycarp uttered the words that the proconsul had ordered him to utter, the guilt would not have been on Polycarp, it would have been on the proconsul. Polycarp is bound not to commit violations of human law for which he is ultimately responsible; he is not bound not to commit violations of divine law for which he is not responsible. And so, as the only relevant obligation is that imposed by the human law, Polycarp was wrong to disobey the proconsul.

Hobbes offers as scriptural evidence for this position the story of Naaman (2 Kings 5: 1–19). Naaman was a soldier, and a courageous one; he was also a leper. Sent to Israel to see whether he might be cured of his leprosy, Naaman met with Elisha, who told Naaman that he would be free of his leprosy if he washed in the Jordan River. Naaman, after some hesitation, was persuaded to do as Elisha instructed, and was cured. Naaman (quite understandably) embraced the Lord of Israel as the true God. But he still had duties to the king of Aram and was sufficiently troubled enough by them to voice his worry to Elisha:

> Naaman said . . . "I trust the LORD will forgive your servant this: when my master [the king of Aram] enters the temple of Rimmon [a pagan god] to worship there, then I, too, as his adjutant, must bow down in the temple of Rimmon. May the LORD forgive your servant this." "Go in peace," Elisha said to him.

Hobbes's understanding of this story is, I take it, as follows. We can allow that it would ordinarily be wrong for Naaman to enter the temple of Rimmon and bow down. If Naaman did so of his own accord, then he would be responsible for that action, and blameworthy. Naaman did not do so of his own accord, though, but out of obedience to his earthly sovereign's commands. So Naaman is not responsible for the action. But *someone* must be; there was an act of bowing down before a pagan god, and it was intentional. It must, Hobbes thinks, be the responsibility of the party by whose intention the act was initiated. And so Hobbes concludes generally that "whatsoever a subject . . . is compelled to [do] in obedience to his sovereign, and doth it not in order to his own mind, but in order to the laws of his country, that action is not his, but his sovereign's" (*L* xlii.11).

The philosophical explanation for this doctrine is to be found in Hobbes's discussion of authorship and personation in chapter 16 of *Leviathan*. Hobbes distinguishes between natural and artificial persons: a person is *natural* when his or her words and actions are attributed to him or her; a person is *artificial* when his or her words or actions are considered as standing in the place of those of another person. In some such cases, the artificial person's actions are "owned by those whom [he or she] represent[s]," where to own an action is to be responsible for its normative effects. So Hobbes writes that

> When the actor [the person whose action is owned] doth any thing against the law of nature by the command of the author, if he be obliged by former covenant to obey him, not he, but the author breaketh the law of nature; for though the action be against the law of nature, yet it is not his; but contrarily, to refuse to do it is against the law of nature that forbiddeth breach of covenant. (*L* xvi.7)

The responsibility for commanded actions that subjects believe to be contrary to divine law must, similarly, rest on sovereigns rather than on subjects, for subjects are obligated by covenant to obey their sovereigns. (And we should note that there is really nothing essential to Hobbes's argument carried by the contractarian position he espouses. So long as subjects are bound to obey their earthly sovereigns—and, after all, worries of the sort that we are dealing with here do not arise unless there is such a requirement of obedience—Hobbes can make his point.) As sovereigns are the authors of such actions, the actions are their responsibility, not the subjects', and the subjects can obey their earthly sovereigns while remaining free of sin.

But it seems to me that Hobbes's argument here has little merit as scriptural interpretation or as philosophical argument. On the scriptural side: to take the Naaman account as an argument for this particular account of how the responsibility for blaspheming or idolatry might be shifted, one would need to give reasons to dismiss the variety of accounts in which believers are cast in a highly favorable light for refusing to adjure faith in Yahweh or Christ, even contrary to the demands of those in authority. We need only think here of Shadrach, Meshach, and Abednego (Dan. 3:1–30). But even focusing on the Naaman story itself, it is far from clear that what Naaman is being given leave to do is to perform an idolatrous act. Naaman is being given leave to help his master bow down. Naaman might equally well perform that action in helping his master dress or stretch before exercise. It is not at all obvious that it is the sort of formal cooperation in a sinful act that is to be condemned as itself sinful.

Aside from scriptural worries, the philosophical account is also unpersuasive.[9] Hobbes's argument is that if one does not perform the act contrary to divine law at the behest of another, whom one is obligated to obey, then one will violate the obligation to that other. But he does not explain why it isn't the case that one cannot be obligated to perform an act contrary to divine law, so that the obligation to obey the sovereign does not extend to this case. The point is easiest to see in the context of a contractarian theory of political authority, like Hobbes's, but the point can be made in the context of any familiar account of political authority. It is plausible enough, and most Christians believe, that God is naturally authoritative over us: on the familiar view of God's kingship, we come into the world under divine authority, live our lives under divine authority, and die under divine authority. But if that is the case, then we cannot obligate ourselves by contract to full obedience to our earthly sovereigns. For if God is authoritative over us, then we are bound to do what God commands of us: any obligation that we place ourselves under to obey an earthly sovereign will have to be conditional, that is, conditional on God's not commanding us otherwise. And so Hobbes cannot say that it is because Naaman is obligated by covenant to do as his master commands that Naaman must bow down before a pagan god; for if God is Naaman's sovereign, Naaman could not obligate himself by covenant to bow down before a pagan god if God commanded him not to do so.[10]

IV

Hobbes's argument that there really are no divine laws that could conflict with the earthly sovereign's commands is unpersuasive. So are his arguments that if there were such conflict, one would not be responsible for violating divine law were one to do so out of obedience to his or her earthly sovereign. We have thus seen no reason to call into question Wolterstorff's initial assessment of Polycarp's action as highly praiseworthy. But Hobbes employs a third strategy. Like the second strategy, the third strategy appeals to the notion of responsibility. But it does not attempt to shift the responsibility for one's violations of divine law out of obedience to the earthly sovereign from oneself to one's earthly sovereign. Rather, the idea is that that for which one is ultimately responsible is not the actions that one performs but rather the decision procedure by which one decides to perform, or not to perform, those actions. One's responsibility for the performance of a certain action is derivative from how one made the choice.

Consider the distinction made by Alan Donagan between first-order and second-order moral properties.[11] First-order moral properties attach to acts, states of affairs, even character traits: acts are right (or wrong), states of affairs good (or bad), character traits virtuous (or vicious). Second-order moral properties attach to agents in light of their performance or pursuit of these acts, states of affairs, or character traits: agents are blameworthy or praiseworthy, culpable or inculpable, and so forth. Second-order moral properties attach to agents in virtue of their responsibility vis-à-vis objects of first-order moral assessment.

Now, it is a commonplace that an act performed by an agent can receive a negative first-order moral assessment while the agent performing the act receives a positive second-order moral assessment. An act can be wrong while the agent of the action is not blameworthy. An act can be wrong while the agent of the action is even praiseworthy. It is wrong to kill innocent people, but one might, perhaps through an irresistible compulsion brought about by mental illness, be blameless. It is wrong to kill innocent people, but one might, as a result of a mistake of fact that no reasonable agent could have failed to be prey to, kill an innocent person as part of a heroic and self-sacrificial plan of action; one might then even be praiseworthy for his or her performance of the morally wrong act. In such cases it is a shame that the wrongful action was performed, but we may well admire the agent for his or her performance of it.

It is, or should be, also a commonplace that an act can be right but the agent blameworthy. One might perform the proper action, but one might have reached the conclusion that this action is to be performed in a slipshod, negligent, but ultimately lucky way. It might be right to support candidates that oppose the death penalty. But if one reaches this decision in a hasty way, if one's deliberation on this weighty matter is instead quick and dirty, one might well be blameworthy in doing the right thing by casting ballots for abolitionists.

From the point of view of deliberation, one's attention should be on first-order moral features. In deciding what to do, we should aim at what is right, or good, or virtuous, not what we must do to be praiseworthy rather than blameworthy. There are various explanations for this, but I will rest content with the point rather than with an account of it. But nevertheless I think that we can see that there is a certain primacy to the second-order. Whether our actions turn out to be right, or the states of affairs that we promote turn out to be good, or the character traits that we foster turn out to be virtuous is to a large degree outside our control. But how I go about responding to these items and their first-order moral features is something that is up to me—or is up to me to a much larger degree, at any rate. And it seems to me that this primacy looms even greater in a Christian context. From a Christian perspective, we are even more aware of the extent to which our doings are subject to the unfathomable workings of divine providence, that every pursuit is a matter of cooperation with God, and that our role is relatively small indeed; and, on the other side, that it is far more important that we do our part in a responsible way rather than that we generate just the right results. In deliberation, we care about getting things right; but in the perspective of what is ultimately of importance, what matters is the state of our souls in choosing rather than what we actually effect by our choices.

This primacy of the second-order leaves a path for an argument by Hobbes against Wolterstorff's assessment of Polycarp's situation. Suppose that Hobbes's argument for the consistency of divine law and human law fails, as I have argued in section II. It may well be that Polycarp's action was right. But that does not mean that Hobbes's view of Polycarp as being deeply in error is not closer to the mark than Wolterstorff's assessment of Polycarp's choices as entirely worthy of praise. For all that we have seen, it may be the case that while Polycarp's action was right, his way of choosing was improper, so that he was *blameworthy* in making the right choice. And given the primacy of the second-order from a Christian perspective, that would mean that Hobbes's assessment of Polycarp is more to the point than Wolterstorff's.

Hobbes's third, and most interesting, argument against Wolterstorff's view relies on his doctrine of the renunciation of conscience. Hobbes holds that in the absence of political authority, each of us may and should act on his or her own private conscience, but when there is a political authority in place, that political authority is the public conscience by which each subject ought to be guided (*L* xxix.6–7). It is hard to know exactly what Hobbes means when he says we are to give up acting on our own private consciences and act on the public conscience instead. But here is what I suggest. We might think of the process of deliberation leading to decision and action as consisting in several stages. There is the *collection of information,* where we gather and think over the various facts, and relationships among those facts, that are relevant to the eligibility of the various courses of action that are thought by the agent to be open to him or her. There is the *settlement on a verdict,* a combination of judgment and decision in which the various facts considered in deliberation are brought together to bear on the choice, so that one of the various options is selected as the action to be performed. And there is the *execution*, whereby the agent carries into effect the decision reached in the verdict stage. What I suggest is that Hobbes's view is that in the state of nature each of us carries out the collection of information and the settlement on a verdict stages privately: it is up to each of us on his or her own to come to a judgment and decision about how the various facts relevant to the decision bear on the choice to be made. But when we enter political society, things are, or should be, different. We should at that point let the political authority carry out, to whatever extent it wishes, the verdict stage for us. In any matter on which the public authority has seen fit to render a dictate about how a subject should act, the subject should allow that dictate to serve as the verdict concerning how the various relevant facts come together in a judgment about what is to be done. This is a sort of practical disposition: one allows the sovereign's judgment to take the place of one's own in one's deliberation.

This has a seedy sound to it. Perhaps we can make it less seedy by imagining cases in which it might seem like renouncing one's conscience in this sense is not such a bad idea. Suppose that God were to tell you that your deliberative capacities were about to be undercut, so that your verdictive capacity will become massively unreliable. Further, God informs you that there is a moral sage to whom God has given the gift of inerrancy in moral matters: whenever this person says that one ought to Φ, then it is true that, all things considered, one ought to Φ. And God tells you one more thing: that if, by any chance, you would like to have produced in yourself a deliberative disposition to accept the sage's judgments as your own verdicts in deliberation, God would be happy to make it so.

Well, what should you do? There is a very strong case in favor of the view that you ought to renounce your conscience to that of the moral sage. You have it on divine authority that the sage will never steer you wrong. And you have it on divine authority that, should you wish it, you can have a firm disposition to accept the sage's dictates in the place of your own private verdicts. So there is a strong argument that the thing to do here is to ask God to give you the practical disposition such that when the sage says that you ought to Φ, then the verdict that you will reach regarding Φ is that it is the right thing for you to do.

One might think that the view that we ought to renounce our consciences in this way is subject to devastating criticisms, one Kantian in flavor and the other Thomistic. The Kantian objection is in the vicinity of autonomy: there is something valuable about the making of verdicts on one's own that makes it wrong to form, or to attempt to form, such a disposition.[12] We should concede that it is, generally speaking, a great good for one to exercise one's verdictive capacity in deliberation on one's own. But we should be wary of the tendency to inflate this good in a way that devalues other goods. For deliberation is about the pursuit and promotion of goods, and if one's verdictive capacity is massively unreliable, one is sure to respond improperly to these goods on innumerable occasions. And, further, when we get clear on what the goods of deliberation are, it is not so clear that the exercise of one's verdictive capacity, in circumstances when that capacity is massively unreliable, is such a good thing after all. This is not a judgment of the comparative value of the good of exercising one's verdictive capacity independently and the goods to be lost by exercising one's verdictive capacity in a massively unreliable way. Rather, this is the judgment that the exercising of one's verdictive capacity is not such a great good as such; it is only under certain favorable conditions that it is a great good. The verdictive capacity is a capacity for judging and deciding: for making well-grounded judgments about the relative merits of various courses of action, and for making free and independent choices among the various eligible options that are not ruled out as unreasonable. But in the case as described, whenever the sage makes a pronouncement, there is a fact of the matter about which option to adopt; so it is not as if one is sacrificing the good of free and independent choice among eligible options by going along with the sage's verdicts. And if there is an intrinsic good to the making of judgments about the relative merits of various courses of action, it would seem that this good can be enjoyed only when one's faculties of judgment are truth-tracking. Here is an analogy. I think that there is a good in coming to judgments in nonpractical matters, say, about scientific matters. But there would be little or nothing intrinsically good in my relying on my independent judgment in coming to an opinion on a matter in quantum physics. I am clueless in such things; my judgments could be no more than guesses, and there would be nothing praiseworthy about my getting them right should I happen to hit on a true view. So, in this case, the preconditions of the good of reaching verdicts independently are not realized or are realized so tenuously that this good can be enjoyed meagerly or not at all.

The Thomistic objection appeals to the claim that it is never right to act against one's conscience because in acting against one's conscience one is attempting to do what one judges to be wrong.[13] It is never right to act against one's conscience, even when one's conscience errs; so the fact that one might more reliably choose rightly by adhering to the sage's dictates rather than one's own is not enough to make it a permissible option. But it seems to me that the course of action suggested here is not subject to this Thomistic criticism. For what is being suggested here is that one allow the sage to determine what one takes to be the right thing to do, not that one judge for oneself what the right thing to do is and then act contrary to it if the sage's advice differs from one's own judgment. So it is perfectly compatible with gaining the practical disposition of letting the sage's judgments take the place that one's own privately formed verdicts would have had that one never act in a way that is contrary to one's ultimate judgments about what is to be done. So the Thomistic criticism fails to call into question the wisdom of acquiring this practical disposition.

Suppose that we allow, then, that the thing to do here is to ask for this disposition. But suppose further that you do not ask for this disposition, instead choosing to rely simply on your soon-to-be massively unreliable verdictive capacities. How should we describe the situation in which you, through dumb luck, happen to make the correct choice about what is to be done? We should say that while your act is the right one, you are nevertheless blameworthy for acting on your massively unreliable verdictive capacity. You could have gotten it wrong just as easily as you got it right. What's more, things did not need to be that way: you could have become the sort of person whose verdicts were not massively unreliable. One who spurns the chance to trade in one's massively unreliable verdictive capacities for those of the moral sage, even when acting in a way that is objectively morally right, is nevertheless blameworthy.

We may transform this case in the direction of Polycarp's in three steps. In the first step, the situation is the same, except that the sage is now one's political authority: whenever the political authority tells you to Φ it is the case that what you ought to do, all things considered, is to Φ. The sovereign may not be intending to report the truth about what you ought to do, as the sage does; what the sovereign is doing is laying down dictates. Nevertheless, the sovereign's dictates infallibly track what one ought to do. This change does not appear important. What is crucial about the moral sage in the example is not the sort of speech-act that she performs (assertions rather than commands), but that there is a perfect and easily recognizable correspondence between the content of these speech-acts and what you ought to do, all things considered. Since this correspondence is present in the situation in which a political authority is an infallible guide to what one ought to do, our judgment about the case of this political authority should not differ from our judgment about the case of the infallible moral sage.

Next, suppose that this practical disposition is not to be implanted in you by an immediate act of divine power; rather, it will have to be built up in you through education and self-discipline. But the value of having that disposition is not lessened by the greater difficulty in achieving it. And while we will have to contend with some of the costs involved, it is not as if we have a *choice* about whether to devote resources to this sort of moral education and habituation — the question is not *whether* we will employ these resources but in the service of *which* dispositions. So if it is possible to develop this disposition, which it seems to be, and if we are going to have to develop some practical dispositions in order to act well, then our assessment of the worthiness of choosing this practical disposition rather than some other should not be affected by our having to develop it ourselves rather than merely to receive it through divine fiat.

The third and final step moves us all the way to (what Hobbes takes to be) our actual situation. Instead of the sovereign's dictates being an *infallible* indicator of the right thing to do, we will say simply that the sovereign's dictates are just a *much more reliable* indicator of the right thing to do than our own judgments are. This makes matters messier, for now the gap between the goods of rendering verdicts on our own and the goods of adherence to the sovereign's dictates becomes smaller. But if the fact that the sovereign tells you to do something is a very strong indicator that it is the right thing to do—much more reliable than one's independent verdict about what the right thing to do would be—we should still be impressed by the strength of the case for adopting the practical disposition of renouncing one's private conscience to the sovereign's dictates.

We are, Hobbes claims, very unreliable judges of what is to be done: we overestimate what is due to us, we underestimate what is due from us; we overestimate our strengths, we underestimate our weaknesses (*L* xiii.2). The sovereign, whose dictates are concerned with public matters, can render judgments about what subjects are to do that are far more impartial and more likely to be accurate representations of what is required of one with respect to public matters than one's private verdicts would be. Now, one might concede this and say: well, nevertheless, the sovereign might very well give commands about what are *private* matters, matters that do not materially affect the public good and how it should be promoted. But we can just take the argument further: subjects are more likely than sovereigns to deceive themselves about the boundary between public and private. When a subject has a strong desire to do something, even something that individually, or if carried out by a sufficient number of individuals, would affect the commonwealth's interests substantially, that subject is likely to deceive him- or herself into thinking that it is a private rather than a public matter. So sovereigns are more likely to judge what is owed from subjects in public matters more reliably than subjects are, and sovereigns are more likely to judge what is public and what is private more reliably than subjects are.

If that were all there were to Hobbes's argument, there would be something to it, but it would be subject to a very powerful, indeed devastating, objection. Even if it is generally true that the sovereign's judgments are a more reliable basis for choice in public matters than one's own, there may be particular cases in which there are clear mistakes by the sovereign. And so one might think that the disposition to be adopted is not one of submission of one's conscience to that of the sovereign, but rather that of submission of one's conscience to the sovereign when the sovereign is not making a clear mistake. But Hobbes has another argument, an argument from fairness. The idea is that we can see that it would generally have bad effects for folks to have simply a disposition to obey the sovereign only when the sovereign is not making a clear mistake. Even if you, pillar of intellectual virtue that you are, are not likely to confuse the sovereign's making a clear mistake with the sovereign's making just an ordinary not-so-clear mistake, you should recognize that lots of people will not make this distinction properly, and the result will be dissension and instability. And, furthermore, it is not so clear who is capable of making this distinction properly and who is not. The only *fair* thing to do is for all to adopt generally a disposition of obedience, regardless of whether the sovereign seems to be making a clear mistake. Or, better, a disposition that includes not looking too hard into whether the sovereign is making a clear mistake.

Hobbes's claim is that our private judgment is, when operating properly, self-effacing: we should privately judge that we ought to no longer exercise our private judgment in public matters, and we should develop a disposition not to exercise such private judgment in any case in which the sovereign has rendered a verdict.[14] Private judgment drops away in such cases and ceases to be operative. To put it strongly: one does not continue to act on private judgment where the content of the private judgment is "do what the sovereign says, because of reliability and fairness concerns." To continue to do so is to put away private judgment insufficiently: if one must go back to the well in order to replenish one's commitment to acting on the sovereign's dictates, then one will too often have to answer questions such as why is my sovereign authoritative? Is the sovereign's command binding when it seems to go contrary to the law of nature or divine law? If the sovereign has made a clear error, isn't it rule-worship to adhere to its dictates? and so forth. The only recourse is to stop asking and answering on one's own questions about what is to be done in cases in which the sovereign sees fit to render verdicts. That is Hobbes's doctrine of the renunciation of conscience.[15]

If this argument for the renunciation of conscience were successful, then we would know what to say about Polycarp, and it would *not* be what Wolterstorff says about him. We might well allow that Polycarp did the right thing when he refused the proconsul's order. But he is nevertheless blameworthy for what he did, for he was relying on his own lights to decide what to do, when he should have been relying on the proconsul's lights. And since from a Christian perspective how we are as agents is more important than are the particular acts that we perform, Hobbes's assessment of Polycarp is more to the point than Wolterstorff's.

One final point. Hobbes's arguments for the renunciation of conscience appear in the early parts of *Leviathan;* they are matters of natural law. The natural law, in conjunction with facts about human psychology and the condition of human life outside of political authority, dictates that we subordinate our private judgment to that of the sovereign. But Hobbes understands the natural law as divine law (*L* xxxi.7). So it is God himself that dictates that we subordinate our consciences in this way. In subordinating our judgment to that of our earthly sovereigns, we are doing God's will.

V

Where does Hobbes go wrong?

There are a few answers that are plausible enough as far as they go but are, I think, nevertheless unsatisfying. The arguments that appeal to the undesirable feedback effects of the renunciation of conscience or that appeal to the view that sovereigns are generally less reliable than subjects are in guiding those subjects' behavior rightly may, upon inspection, turn out to be sufficiently good reasons for failing to renounce one's conscience in the way that Hobbes has in mind. But, as I will argue, these answers will always have a bit of the tenuous about them, as they rely on empirical premises that may well turn out to be in error. What we want, I say, is an argument that is immune to these tenuous speculations.

Feedback.　One way to argue against Hobbesian renunciation of conscience is to argue that Hobbes has failed to consider feedback effects. Suppose it is true that sovereigns typically generate dictates that are more in line with what subjects ought to do than the subjects' own privately reached verdicts would be. We cannot move from this premise to the conclusion that subjects ought to renounce their consciences to the sovereign's decision making, because there may be feedback effects: the fact that a subject has renounced his or her conscience may become known to the sovereign, and this fact may result in the sovereign's becoming less reliable than the subject. The sovereign may be more tempted to give dictates that are unreasonable if the subject has renounced his or her conscience than if he or she has not; independent judgment serves as an obstacle to this sort of manipulation.

Hobbes is aware of the issue. He considers it particularly in the context of Christian obedience to non-Christian sovereigns: if we are to give our (nearly) entire obedience to sovereigns, whether they be Christian or not, what is to stop these sovereigns from giving commands that are inimical to Christian faith? Hobbes's ingenious point is that the reason why non-Christian sovereigns feel the need to give commands that undercut Christian faith is that Christian faith is often thought to be revolutionary or in some other way subversive of the requirement of obedience to one's earthly rulers. This is not simply an empirical claim about the motivations of the rulers with whom Hobbes was familiar. Rather, it is a claim about what a sovereign cares about qua sovereign: if the sovereign is charged with the preservation of the public good, and citizens' Christian faith undermines that good, then sovereigns will have, as sovereigns, reasons to be concerned about their subjects believing and living the Christian faith. If, on the other hand, one takes one's Christianity to require the renunciation of conscience that Hobbes takes to be a matter of divine law, then the sovereign should, and will likely, lose the motivation that he or she or it would have had to try to undercut one's Christian faith (*L* xliii.23).

The point is, to an extent, generalizable. If a primary interest of sovereigns is that of keeping subjects sufficiently obedient to do their bidding, then sovereigns will have good reason to make sure that the source of obedience is not cut off. If the Christian's source of obedience to earthly rulers is his or her judgment that divine rule requires the renunciation of conscience, then the sovereign will have good reason to see to it that his or her commands do not have a detrimental impact on subjects' Christian faith. This does not—as the case of Polycarp dramatically illustrates—show that every sovereign will in fact minimize this impact. But Hobbes thinks that it goes a long way toward showing that the renunciation of conscience is a safer bet than one might believe.

Unfavorable social conditions.   The feedback argument is just one instance of a more general argument, that is, that Hobbes's view assesses incorrectly the relative merits of one's own private verdict-reaching capacities and one's sovereign's verdict-reaching capacities. One might think that Hobbes is just too optimistic here. There may be some forms of sovereignty in which the sovereign's judgments are likely more reliable than the subject's, and there are some forms in which the subject's judgments are more likely reliable than the sovereign's. There may be no hard and fast evidence on these matters, but we might make rough and ready judgments. And these judgments may very well suggest that under current social conditions no subject, or at least no Christian subject, should be comfortable with the notion that the sovereign is a more reliable judge of what is required of him or her than he or she would be.

Again, Hobbes is not altogether silent here. He would have us recall that only part of his argument is a reliability argument, one grounded in the superior epistemic status of the sovereign's dictates; the other part is a moral argument. Look, he would say, surely you agree that not everyone should be allowed to exercise his or her verdictive capacity free from the constraints of politically authoritative judgment. Imagine what the social world would be like if private judgment failed to yield to a common standard. Now, for some people, this may very well involve yielding one's more reliable judgment to another's less reliable judgment. But this might be the only fair result. (Imagine a household in which the husband is less practically wise than the wife, across the board. It may nevertheless be important that authority over spheres of their lives be distributed, for fairness reasons: it is unfair to burden the wife with too much responsibility, and it is unfair to deprive the husband of having a say in household matters.)

It may be that at a certain point reliability looms so large that matters of fairness have to yield. One's sovereign may be so unreliable that one would have to say that the values to be protected by refusing to renounce one's conscience to the sovereign's public conscience are greater than the values of equality and fairness fostered by everyone equally yielding to authority. But it is not so clear that things are as bad as all that, at least where I am writing today. Imagine two conditions, one in which one acts on (for example) the demands of the United States government and of the demands of the state and local authorities, and can otherwise act as one sees fit, and the other in which one simply decides for oneself on each occasion what the wisest course is. It is far from clear that one would act worse by yielding one's private conscience to the public conscience of the state. One might say, rightly, that there are all sorts of options between wholly private judgment and Hobbesian renunciation of conscience. But if this is the response, one is now in Hobbesian territory. One has conceded that conscience is to be renounced, and the disagreement is over just how far. Think about how far we expect our neighbor to accede to the demands of the public authority: quite far indeed, Hobbes suggests, and he notes that we should hold ourselves to that same standard.

Before we turn to what I take to be a more successful challenge to Hobbes's view, I want to respond to the most straightforward argument against the Hobbesian view: the *foreseeable horror*. One can foresee that one's sovereign might tell him or her to do something horrible, and if one has renounced one's conscience, one will be epistemically defenseless. I think that this is perhaps the most common worry about the renunciation view, and it is also among the least persuasive. To the point: I can foresee that my private judgment might tell me to do something horrible. I might blaspheme, or commit murder, or do some other foul thing, and my conscience might approve of it. I hate to think that I could ever become that sort of person, but I have to allow that it could happen. The point is that, insofar as private judgment and the sovereign's dictates are just rival decision procedures, foreseeable horrors might result from either of them. If all we are looking to is the outcome of these procedures, we should be interested just in measuring the likelihood of their reliability along with the results of correct and incorrect judgments. But this is the sort of tenuous speculation that it seems to me we would do better to avoid. Our assessment of Polycarp as praiseworthy does not depend, I think, on our assessment that Polycarp got the numbers right, that he estimated properly the likely overall effects of the reliance on private judgment as compared to the likely overall effects of renouncing his conscience to the sovereign. Polycarp took a proper stance toward God, a stance that he would not have taken if he had become the sort of person that Hobbes recommends that he become. That is why Hobbes is wrong and Wolterstorff is right.

The important point for Christians is not the Kantian or quasi-Kantian worry that subjects who accept Hobbes's view will miss out on exercising their verdictive capacities. Nor is it even Aquinas's worry, that those who act against conscience will act against their final assessment of what is right to do, and will therefore choose what they take to be wrong. The important point is that Hobbes's view, taken as applying to subject-sovereign relationships of all sorts, cuts one off from friendship with God. Or, to be more precise, if one is able to enter into the relationship with one's sovereign that will produce the benefits that Hobbes envisions, then one will thereby preclude oneself from having a proper relationship of friendship with God.

I understand friendship here along roughly Aristotelian lines. To be friends with another is to live with him or her—to coordinate one's conduct with him or her on a day-to-day basis—in a way that takes the friend's good as a fundamental reason for action.[16] In taking the friend's good as basic, one takes up the other's practical reasoning and decision making into one's own in a way that is not merely strategic. That one's friend wills or wishes for something is a basic reason for one to try to fulfill that wish.

Now, relationships of friendship are essentially non–self-effacing. I think that this is obvious from the nature of friendship as defined in terms of the way that one takes others' choices and decisions into account in one's day-to-day living. But if it is not obvious, then we can just try to imagine what it would be like for friends to decide that their friendship ought to be self-effacing and see whether the resultant state of affairs is a friendship at all. Suppose, for example, that two people love each other very much but each makes the other's life a living hell. Their best efforts to be goods for each other are disastrous, either through over-intrusiveness or sheer hamhandedness. They may come to the realization that the best way to do good for each other is to stop trying to do good for each other. If, they might reason in common, they were no longer to try to live together, but were instead each to simply look out for his or her own interests, each of them may do better, and indeed the circumstances may be such that each simply looking out for his or her own interests might causally contribute to the other's good. So they decide that, in order to be better for each other, they will no longer live together, and will no longer take the other's decisions and judgments into their practical reasoning in the familiar way. I take it that the resulting state of affairs is best described not as a self-effacing friendship but as no friendship at all: they no longer take each other's well-being as basic reasons for action—they no longer coordinate their conduct for the common good of their common life. Whatever *they* call it, *we* can see that they have decided no longer to be friends. I am not claiming here that friends might never have sufficient reason to do this. I am claiming only that if they do this, they have chosen not to have an interestingly different kind of friendship, but instead to have no friendship at all.

The notion that adherence to God's commands is self-effacing brings with it a rejection of the possibility of friendship with God. For one will no longer be able to act on one's judgments of what one believes that God wills of one. To believe that Hobbes's theory of the renunciation of conscience is correct is to believe that God might tell us to reject friendship with God. No Christian can accept this result. That is why Hobbes must be wrong and Wolterstorff must be right about the merit of Polycarp's refusal to blaspheme Christ.

Wolterstorff remarks in his Stone Lectures that, while he is keen to insist on the importance of the fact that Christ is sovereign over all of us, "That [Christ] is our king is far from the only thing to be said about Christ" (*DCDN* I.2.7) and "it is not the deepest thing to be said" (*DCDN* I.2.8). Surely among these other, deeper things to be said is that God loves us and invites us into a loving friendship with Him. And if that is so, then Hobbes's account of the renunciation of conscience cannot be accepted by Christians. For that account requires us to reject friendship with God for the sake of other goods. And that is surely both repugnant in itself and not the sort of requirement that God, who died on the cross to bring us into relationship with him, would impose on us.

NOTES

I thank Nick Wolterstorff, as well as Bob Roberts, Terence Cuneo, Rob Miner, and audience members at the 2002 Wheaton Conference, for helpful criticism of earlier drafts of this essay.

1. These lectures, entitled *Dual Citizenship, Dual Nationality,* are presently unpublished, although some of their content is found in Wolterstorff's "Christian Political Reflection: Diognetian or Augustinian?" *Princeton Seminary Bulletin* 20 (July 1997): 150–68. I cite them in my text as *DCDN* and give the lecture and section number, along with the page number of the photocopied version I have on file.

2. Hobbes is popularly treated as an atheist. Occasionally his atheism is argued for rather than merely asserted. See, for the best such argument I know of, Edwin Curley's "'I Durst Not Write So Boldly' or, How to Read Hobbes' Theological-Political Treatise," in *Hobbes e Spinoza, Scienza e Politica,* ed. Daniela Bostrenghi (Naples: Bibliopolis, 1992), 497–593. For a convincing argument for Hobbes's sincerity—at least, as convincing as can reasonably be hoped for, given our inability to read the hearts of believers (or nonbelievers)—see A. P. Martinich, *The Two Gods of Leviathan* (Cambridge: Cambridge University Press, 1992), pp. 19–39, 339–53.

3. There are a couple of different lines of thought within the Christian tradition of political thought about how God delegates His authority to earthly rulers. On one view, the community designates who is to receive that authority, and then the authority is conferred directly on the ruler by God. On another view, God places political authority naturally within the political community as a whole, which then translates that authority to some particular ruler (perhaps even to itself, politically constituted, as in a direct democracy) through customary law. Wolterstorff's remarks seem all to aim in favor of the former of these views, and at no point does he suggest that political authority resides in the community as a whole prior to the institution of some particular authority.

4. I am going to take Hobbes's positions in *Leviathan* as definitive of his view. Hobbes's positions on the question of Christian disobedience, especially when the sovereign is non-Christian, do show development from *Elements of Law* to *De Cive* to *Leviathan.* But his position is usefully stark in *Leviathan.* I cite *Leviathan* as *L* in my text, using chapter and paragraph numbers; the text is from Edwin Curley's edition (Indianapolis: Hackett, 1994).

5. Of course, this is consistent with our being obligated to perform an action that is the *content* of a putative positive divine law. But our obligation to perform those actions could result, on Hobbes's view, only from their being commanded by the human sovereign, not from their being commanded by God.

6. One might note that there may be many who do not have adequate reason to believe Scripture to be the word of God, and so they would not be under divine law. Even if this were granted, it is beside the point. When Hobbes defines law, he does so in a way that makes it a relational notion between a sovereign and a particular subject: "CIVIL LAW is, *to every subject,* those rules which the commonwealth hath commanded him . . ." (*L* xxvi.3). So the fact that my neighbor might not be bound by a putative divine law would not call into question my being bound by that putative divine law.

7. If there is a divine law requiring one to do everything in one's power to prevent others from violating divine laws, then there would be a conflict. But it is highly implausible that there would be such a divine law. It would almost certainly come into conflict with other divine laws, for one thing.

8. One might object to the move from civil contexts of contract making, etc., to moral contexts of wrongness and blameworthiness. No Christian can enter a general objection of this form, given any orthodox understanding of the Atonement. We are reconciled with God through Christ's sacrifice. Its normative effects embrace us, insofar as we have entered into some sort of special relationship with him. Now, one might say: it isn't right to appeal to what is admittedly mysterious in order to halt an objection. But Hobbes's point would be that understanding authorization and its normative-property transferring power makes the Atonement less a mystery.

9. I consider these points in greater detail in "Hobbes on Conscientious Disobedience," *Archiv für Geschichte der Philosophie* 77 (1995): 277–82.

10. Not only is the account unpersuasive, it is inconsistent with *Leviathan*'s doctrine of authorization. Hobbes holds that "A multitude of men are made one person, when they are by one man, or one person, represented so that it be done with the consent of every one of that multitude in particular" (*L* xvi.13). Hobbes thinks that when there is an earthly sovereign, that sovereign's subjects authorize all of the sovereign's actions (*L* xvii.13). Hobbes relies on this account of authorization in arguing that subjects cannot accuse their sovereigns of injustice:

> Because every subject is by this institution author of all the actions and judgments of the sovereign instituted, it follows that, whatsoever he doth, it can be no injury to any of his subjects, nor ought he to be by any of them accused of injustice. For he that doth any thing by authority from another doth therein no injury to him by whose authority he acteth; but by this institution of a commonwealth every particular man is author of all the sovereign doth; and consequently he that complaineth of injury from his sovereign complaineth of that whereof he himself is author, and therefore ought not to accuse any man but himself. (*L* xviii.6)

No subject, then, can justly punish the sovereign for his or her misdeeds, for "seeing every subject is author of the actions of his sovereign, he punisheth another for the actions committed by himself" (*L* xviii.7). Subjects own all of their sovereigns' actions, and are responsible for all that their sovereigns do, "For that which the representative doth as actor every one of the subjects doth as author" (*L* xix.17). But this account of the authorization of the sovereign is inconsistent with Hobbes's way of shifting the responsibility for bowing down before Rimmon from Naaman to Naaman's master. For there Hobbes argues that subjects may obey the sovereign when the sovereign commands what the subject believes to be contrary to the law of God, because in such cases the action is the responsibility of the sovereign, not the subject. On Hobbes's account of authorization, though, subjects are responsible for *all* of the sovereign's actions. Hobbes will have to give up either this way of dealing with putative conflict between divine and human law or his account of why sovereigns are not subject to punishment by their subjects.

11. Alan Donagan, *The Theory of Morality* (Chicago: University of Chicago Press, 1977), 52–55.

12. See, for example, Kant's "An Answer to the Question: What Is Enlightenment?" in *Kant's Practical Philosophy*, trans. and ed. Mary Gregor (Cambridge: Cambridge University Press, 1996). For an extremely stark contemporary version of this position, see Robert Paul Wolff, *In Defense of Anarchism* (New York: Harper and Row, 1970), 12–18.

13. See Thomas Aquinas, *Truth* (*Quaestiones Disputatae de Veritate*) (Chicago: Henry Regnery, 1952), q. 17, a.a. 3–4.

14. Cf. S. A. Lloyd, "Hobbes's Self-Effacing Natural Law Theory," *Pacific Philosophical Quarterly* 82 (2001): 285–305, though her understanding of the self-effacing character of Hobbes's natural law view is weaker than my own. The idea of a theory, principle, or faculty being self-effacing is present in Sidgwick (*Methods of Ethics,* 7th ed. [Indianapolis: Hackett, 1981], 490), though it is explicitly named such only by Derek Parfit (*Reasons and Persons* [Oxford: Oxford University Press, 1984], 40).

15. There are other options, of course: one might agree that conscience is to be re-nounced, but disagree that it is to be renounced in the direction of the sovereign; instead, one might say, it is to be renounced to the Church. Hobbes would reject this option, for, on his view, the only way for the Church to speak unequivocally is for it to speak through some authorized party (*L* xxxix.4); and, casting aside the papal pretensions to speak for the Church (*L* xlii.81–135), Hobbes reckons that the only realistic candidate to have this role is the sovereign.

16. *Nicomachean Ethics,* trans. Terence Irwin (Indianapolis: Hackett, 2000), 1157b19.

PART II

RELIGIOUS REASONS AND VIRTUOUS CONDUCT

7

RELIGIOUS REASONS IN
POLITICAL ARGUMENT

JEFFREY STOUT

Freedom of religion consists first of all in the right to make up one's own mind when answering religious questions. These include, but are not limited to, such questions as whether God exists, how God should be conceived, and what responsibilities, if any, human beings have in response to God's actions toward them. Freedom of religion also consists in the right to act in ways that seem appropriate, given one's answers to religious questions—provided that one does not cause unjustified harm to other people or interfere with their rights. Among the expressive acts obviously protected by this right are rituals and other devotional practices performed in solitude, in the context of one's family, or in private association with others similarly disposed. I want to focus, however, on a class of acts that express religious commitments in another way, namely, by employing them as reasons when taking a public stand on political issues. What role, if any, should religious premises play in the reasoning citizens engage in when they make and defend political decisions?

I have learned much from Nicholas Wolterstorff's important essay on this question, "The Role of Religion in Decision and Discussion of Political Issues."[1] In this essay I will defend something like Wolterstorff's permissive answer against more restrictive ones offered by contractarians like John Rawls. In doing so, I not only wish to give public expression to my admiration for Wolterstorff's philosophical work in this area, but also to commend his contributions to public life more generally. He has put his principle into practice in a way that has been enormously beneficial to the broader political community. Ours is a time when some prominent Christian thinkers—Stanley Hauerwas, for one—have been distancing themselves from the norms of human rights and justice in order to preserve the integrity of the church's story and witness. Wolterstorff has taught by example, as well as by carefully crafted argument, that such strategies impose a false choice.

The free expression of religious premises is morally underwritten not only by the value we assign to the freedom of religion but also by the value we assign to free expression generally. All citizens of a constitutional democracy have not only the right to make up their minds as they see fit, but also the right to express their reasoning freely, whatever that reasoning may be. It is plausible to suppose that the right to free expression of religious commitments is especially weighty in contexts where political issues are being discussed, for this is where rulers and elites might be most inclined to enforce restraint. Any citizen who chooses to express religious reasons for a political conclusion would seem, then, to enjoy the protection of two rights in doing so—freedom of religion and freedom of expression. And these rights not only have the legal status of basic constitutional provisions, but also possess sufficient moral authority in the ethical life of the people that the framers of the U.S. Constitution affirmed them explicitly in the Bill of Rights.

I have no doubt that the expression of religious reasons should be protected in these ways. Indeed, I would encourage religiously committed citizens to make use of their basic freedoms by expressing their premises in as much depth and detail as they see fit when trading reasons with the rest of us on issues of concern to the body politic. Otherwise we shall remain ignorant of the real reasons that many of our fellow citizens have for reaching some of the ethical and political conclusions they do. We shall also deprive them of the central democratic good of expressing themselves to the rest of us on matters about which they care deeply. If they do not have this opportunity, we will lose the chance to learn from and to criticize what they say. And they will have good reason to doubt that they are being shown the respect that all of us owe to our interlocutors as individuals.

Of course, having a right does not necessarily mean that one would be justified in exercising it. There are clearly circumstances in which it would be imprudent or disrespectful for someone to reason solely from religious premises when defending a political proposal. But some theorists hold, more controversially, that such circumstances are more the exception than the rule. Some of them claim that reasoning from religious premises to political conclusions is always either imprudent, improper, or both. They therefore urge a strict policy of restraint. Others make a concession to free expression by qualifying the strict policy in some way, but still portray the introduction of religious reasons into public discussion of matters of basic justice as improper unless redeemed in the long run by reasons of a different kind.

In a religiously plural society, it will often be rhetorically ineffective to argue from religious premises to political conclusions. When citizens are deeply divided over the relevant religious questions, arguing in this way is rarely likely to increase support for one's conclusions. Sometimes arguing from religious premises not only fails to win support but also causes offence, for there are contexts in which doing so implies disrespect for those who do not accept those premises. Some speakers convey the undemocratic message that one must accept a particular set of religious premises to participate in political debate at all. In the United States, Christians and Jews often convey such a message, wittingly or unwittingly, to atheists and Muslims, and Jews and Catholics can still occasionally sense it in the rhetoric of some Protestants. Therefore, there are moral as well as strategic reasons for restraint. Fairness and respectful treatment of others are central moral concerns.

An influential family of theories begins with such concerns. Political policies, when enacted in law, are backed by the coercive power of the state. To be recognized as a free and equal citizen of such a state is to be treated as someone to whom reasons must be offered, on request, when political policies are under consideration. The reasons that are demanded are not just any reasons. Each citizen may rightfully demand reasons why *he or she* should view the proposed policy as legitimate. It does not suffice in this context to be told why *other people,* on the basis of their idiosyncratic premises and collateral commitments, have reached this conclusion. It is not enough for a speaker to show that he or she is entitled to consider a proposal legitimate. The question on each concerned citizen's mind will rightly be, "Why should *I* accept this?" Fairness and respect require an honest effort, on the part of any citizen advocating a policy, *to justify it to* other reasonable citizens who may be approaching the issue from different points of view.

So far, so good. Proper treatment of one's fellow citizens does seem to require an honest justificatory effort of this sort. When proposing a political policy one should do one's best to supply reasons for it that people occupying other points of view could reasonably accept. I wholeheartedly embrace this ideal. But the theorists I have in mind go further. For example, Rawls argues that the basic norms for our reasoning on political issues would be a set of principles that no reasonable person could reasonably reject.[2] Stephen Macedo, putting the point more positively, claims that "the application of power should be accompanied with reasons that *all reasonable people should be able to accept*" (emphasis added).[3]

It is crucial to take note of what the phrase "reasonable person" is said to mean in this context. Rawls clarifies what he means by it: "Knowing that people are reasonable where others are concerned, we know that *they are willing to govern their conduct by a principle from which they and others can reason in common*" (emphasis added).[4] This definition carries a heavy burden of the argument in Rawls's discussion of "the idea of public reason" in *Political Liberalism* (212–54). What "public reason" requires of citizens is that they be reasonable in the Rawlsian sense. And this means being willing to accept a common basis for reasoning that others, similarly motivated, could not reasonably reject. In short, to be reasonable is to accept the need for a social contract and to be willing to reason on the basis of it. This definition implicitly imputes *unreasonableness* to everyone who opts out of the contractarian project, regardless of the *reasons* they might have for doing so.[5] Someone can be counted as unreasonable according to this definition even if he or she is epistemically entitled, on the basis of sound or compelling reasons, to consider the quest for a *common* justificatory basis morally unnecessary and epistemologically dubious. A loaded definition, if ever there was one.

Contractarians are quick to move from imagining the basis on which citizens "can reason in common" to concluding that *only* by conducting our most important political reasoning on this basis can we redeem the promise of treating our fellow citizens fairly in matters pertaining to the use of coercive power. And this conclusion contains the seed of what I will call the contractarian program of restraint. It is clear that in our society religious premises cannot be part of the basis on which citizens can reason in common, because not all citizens share the same religious commitments, and nobody knows how to bring about agreement on such matters by rational means. Religion is a topic on which citizens are epistemically (as well as morally and legally) entitled to disagree. If so, it follows from the considerations just mentioned that introducing religious premises into our reasoning on basic political issues is at the very least problematic. If the point of the social contract is to establish a basis on which citizens can reason in common, and religious premises are not part of that basis, then introducing such premises in public debate automatically fails to secure the legitimacy of whatever proposal it was meant to support. Contractarians differ over how strict the restrictions on such premises should be, but their entire program strikes me as extremely counterintuitive. As Wolterstorff says, "given that it is of the very essence of liberal democracy that citizens enjoy equal freedom in law to live out their lives as they see fit, how can it be compatible with liberal democracy for its citizens to be *morally re-*

strained from deciding and discussing political issues as they see fit?"[6] The contractarian approach lends support to the view that while the right to express our religious commitments freely is guaranteed twice over in the Bill of Rights, this is not a right we ought to make essential use of in the center of the political arena, where the most important questions are decided.

Some contractarians have argued that we should never reason solely on the basis of religious premises, at least when considering matters of basic justice and what the constitutional framework of politics should look like. Rawls defended one version of this conclusion in the clothbound edition of *Political Liberalism*, but amended it in the introduction to the paperback edition in 1996. His amended view is that reasonable comprehensive doctrines, including religious doctrines, "may be introduced in public reason at any time, provided that in due course public reasons, given by a reasonable political conception, are presented sufficient to support whatever the comprehensive doctrines are introduced to support" (li–lii). According to this "proviso," a citizen may offer religious reasons for a political conclusion, but only if he or she eventually supplements those reasons by producing arguments based in the social contract. The amended Rawlsian view is that religious reasons are to IOUs as contractarian reasons are to legal tender. You have not fulfilled your justificatory obligations until you have handed over real cash. I find this version of the position slightly more plausible than the original, simply because it is less restrictive. It leaves a bit more room for such noted instances of exemplary democratic reasoning as the religiously based oratory of the abolitionists and of Martin Luther King, Jr. But Rawls confesses that he does not know whether these orators "ever fulfilled the proviso" by eventually offering reasons of his officially approved sort (lii, n. 27). So, strictly speaking, the jury is still out on these cases, from a Rawlsian point of view.

I see it as a strong count against Rawls's current position that these particular speakers will barely squeak by on his criteria, if they manage to do so at all. The alleged need to satisfy the proviso in such cases suggests to me that something remains seriously wrong with the entire approach Rawls is taking. Two main types of reason giving are to be found in the relevant speeches. In the first type, the speakers express their own religious reasons for adopting some political proposal. In the second type, the speakers engage in immanent criticism of their opponents' views. As immanent critics, they either try to show that their opponents' religious views are incoherent, or they try to argue positively from their opponents' religious premises to the conclusion that the proposal is acceptable. What they do not do is argue from a purportedly common basis of reasons in Rawls's sense. Rawls does not examine these forms of reason giving in any detail. He does not mention either mode of immanent criticism. Nor does he show why a speaker who combines them when addressing a public audience on constitutional essentials, such as the right to own slaves and the right to vote, needs eventually to offer an argument of some other kind.

Rawls is similarly ambivalent and therefore unpersuasive on Lincoln's Second Inaugural, perhaps the highest ethical achievement of any political speaker in U.S. history (*Political Liberalism*, 254). What gets Lincoln barely off the hook is that "what he says has no implications bearing on constitutional essentials or matters of basic justice." I am not certain that this is true. The speech is about the question of how a nation at war with itself over slavery can remain a union. Lincoln's answer, in effect, is that it can do so only if, at the moment when one side wins the war, the people and the state representing them behave "with malice toward none; with charity for all." This includes behavior intended to "achieve and cherish a just and lasting peace," which in Lincoln's view obviously includes taking the right stand on constitutional essentials and matters of basic justice. In any event, suppose he had addressed such matters directly and at greater length, continuing the theme introduced earlier in the speech, of two parties that both read the same Bible and pray to the same God, whom they believe to be a just judge of wrongdoers. Suppose he had spelled out his immanent criticisms of the self-righteous religious views, the moralistic dualisms, that both sides were then preparing to enact politically. Would the religious content in Lincoln's speech then have been improper? Something is deeply wrong here. The speeches of King and Lincoln represent high accomplishments in our political culture. They are paradigms of discursive excellence. The speeches of the abolitionists taught their compatriots how to use the terms "slavery" and "justice" as we now use them. It is hard to credit any theory that treats their arguments as placeholders for reasons to be named later.

I do not intend to go very far into the details of the debate between Rawls and his critics.[7] My purpose in this section and the next is rather to determine what it is in the contractarian starting point that leads Rawls and others to say such counterintuitive things. If my diagnosis is correct, then the amended version of his position, while it is less paradoxical than the original, does not overcome the basic difficulties in his approach to the topic. My conclusion will be that we ought to reframe the question of religion's role in political discussion in quite different terms.

Let me begin by developing my hunch, which Wolterstorff seems to share, that the trouble is at least partly a matter of epistemology. The contractarians do not seem to have thought through very rigorously the epistemological assumptions they are making. I suspect that they have overestimated what can be resolved in terms of the imagined common basis of justifiable principles, and have done so because at this one point in constructing their theory they have drastically underestimated the range of things that individuals can reasonably reject. They have underestimated what a person can reasonably reject, I suspect, because they have also underestimated the role of a person's collateral commitments in determining what he or she can reasonably reject when deciding basic political questions. What I can reasonably reject depends in part on what collateral commitments I have and which of these I am entitled to have. But these commitments vary a good deal from person to person, not least of all insofar as they involve answers to religious questions and judgments about the relative importance of highly important values. It is naïve to expect that the full range of political issues that require public deliberation—issues on which we need *some* policy—will turn out to be untouched by such variation. Rawls would grant this. Indeed, it is part of his reason for viewing "the diversity of reasonable comprehensive religious, philosophical, and moral doctrines found in modern democratic societies" as a central problem for political liberalism to address (*Political Liberalism*, 36). The question is why constitutional essentials and matters of basic justice are not also affected, for it is reasonable to suppose, when discussing such elemental issues, that the relative importance of highly important values is a relevant consideration. Rawls might wish to deny this on the basis of his doctrine of the priority of the right over the good, but this doctrine also strikes me as the sort of thing that epistemically responsible people have good reason to disagree over.

I am tempted to say that this doctrine is the sort of thing *reasonable* people would be *entitled* to disagree over. For the moment, let me use the term "reasonable" in a way that departs from Rawls's definition. In this sense, a person is reasonable in accepting or rejecting a commitment if he or she is "epistemically entitled" to do so, and reasonable people are those who reliably comport themselves in accord with their epistemic responsibilities.[8] I do not see how the same epistemology can consistently (a) declare the people holding various comprehensive views to be reasonable in this sense and (b) declare the people who dissent from the social contract not to be reasonable in the same sense. To make (a) turn out to be correct, one would need to assume a relatively permissive standard of reasonableness. But if one then applies the same permissive standard of reasonableness to those who dissent from the social contract, (b) is going to be very hard to defend. According to my epistemology, the more permissive standard seems to be the right one to apply in both instances. But if we link the term "reasonable" to epistemic entitlement and apply the term in a relatively permissive way, it will be very hard to make those who reject the contractarian project *on epistemological grounds* qualify as unreasonable.

This appears to be why Rawls has a stake in introducing his definition of reasonableness. The point of doing so is to guarantee that a reasonable person will be committed to the contractarian project of trying to find and abide by a common basis of principles. But this move only begs the question of why the contractarian project of establishing a common basis is itself something no one can reasonably reject in the sense of epistemic entitlement. We still need an answer to this question. There appear to be sound *epistemological* reasons for rejecting the quest for a common basis, reasons rooted in the permissive notion of epistemic entitlement that lends plausibility to the doctrine of reasonable pluralism in the first place. That, then, is the hunch behind my diagnosis. It remains a hunch because recent contractarian theory, not least of all in the case of Rawls himself, tends to be very sketchy when it comes to stating, defending, and applying its epistemological assumptions.[9]

Rawls's current position entails that it would be inherently unfair to rely solely on religious premises in a political argument about matters of basic justice. This would hold, presumably, even in a case where my epistemological suspicions were realized and it proved impracticable to reason on the basis of a principle that all reasonable citizens could reasonably accept. But suppose this did turn out to be impracticable—for the simple reason that some reasonable (i.e., epistemically responsible) people who desire social cooperation have reason for rejecting each candidate principle. Must we then not consider the matter at all? Must we remain silent when it comes up for discussion? Would a requirement of silence in such a case be deemed *reasonable*—in the sense that we would be entitled to impose it, all things considered? For that matter, how could it be deemed *fair* in a society committed to freedom of religion and freedom of expression? I do not see how it could be. As Wolterstorff argues:

> It belongs to the *religious convictions* of a good many religious people in our society that *they ought to base* their decisions concerning fundamental issues of justice *on* their religious convictions. They do not view it as an option whether or not to do so. It is their conviction that they ought to strive for wholeness, integrity, integration, in their lives: that they ought to allow the Word of God, the teachings of the Torah, the command and example of Jesus, or whatever, to shape their existence as a whole, including, then, their social and political existence. Their religion is not, for them, about *something other* than their social and political existence; it is *also* about their social and political existence. Accordingly, to require of them that they not base their decisions and discussions concerning political issues on their religion is to infringe, inequitably, on the free exercise of their religion.[10]

A Rawlsian might object that offering religious reasons, without supplementing them by appeal to reasons that no one could reasonably reject, is inherently disrespectful. But why need this be a sign of disrespect at all? Suppose I tell you honestly why I favor a given policy, citing religious reasons. I then draw you into a Socratic conversation on the matter, take seriously any objections you raise against my premises, and make a concerted attempt to show you how *your* idiosyncratic premises give *you* reason to accept my conclusions. I do not see why this would qualify as a form of disrespect unless it expresses a desire to manipulate. Yet it does not involve basing my reasoning on principles that no reasonable citizen could reasonably reject.

The conception of respect assumed in the Rawlsian objection just introduced seems flawed. It neglects the ways in which one can show respect for another person in his or her particularity.[11] The reason contractarianism neglects these ways is that it focuses exclusively on the sort of respect one shows to another individual by appealing to reasons that *anyone* who is both properly motivated and epistemically responsible would find acceptable. Suppose I am offering reasons R to X for accepting a political proposition P, and do so in the belief that X ought to be moved by R given X's other commitments. Why would it matter that there might be other people, Y and Z, who could reasonably reject those reasons given their collateral commitments? Suppose that Y and Z are also part of my audience. If I am speaking in public, they might well be. Does my attempt to persuade X by appeal to R show disrespect to Y and Z? No, because I can go on to show respect for them in the same way, by offering *different* reasons to them, reasons relevant *from their point of view*.

Consider the sort of immanent criticism that Socrates practices in the Platonic dialogues. He shows respect to his interlocutors in part by trying to discover what they believe and then testing their beliefs for consistency and adequacy. This is a way of taking them seriously as individuals responsible for their commitments. He is trying to find the dialectical paths that will lead each of them in the direction of wisdom and justice, but he realizes that these paths will differ, depending on what their current commitments happen to be. He does not appeal simply to reasons that no reasonable person could reasonably reject. He concerns himself first with what one person who has certain antecedent commitments would have reason to conclude, then with another person who has somewhat different antecedent commitments. In doing so, he purports to show all of these individuals respect, one by one, as the particular persons they are. Citizens, I would argue, can practice immanent criticism on their fellow citizens in a similar spirit.

Perhaps mention of Socrates in this context is more worrisome than the preceding paragraph implies, however. Is not Socrates a master ironist who deceives his interlocutors about his contempt for their vices and commitments? Would not similar deception, if practiced in political contexts, count as disrespectful? Whatever one makes of Socrates's behavior in Plato's dialogues, I grant that some forms of ironic discourse in public settings would involve disrespectful deception of one's interlocutors. But there is no reason to think that immanent criticism must be deceptive in this way.

Imagine that you are an atheist abolitionist in mid-nineteenth-century America. You are engaged in public debate with a Christian defender of slavery. Without dissembling or otherwise showing disrespect, it is surely possible for you to subject the theological and scriptural basis of your interlocutor's political position to immanent criticism. Without pretending to accept the Bible as an authoritative text, you can try to show that your opponent's interpretations of crucial biblical passages are faulty when judged in light of his own collateral commitments. You might present Galatians 3, interpreted in a certain way, as a reason for changing his mind about slavery, while acknowledging openly that this interpretation of Galatians 3 plays no role at all in leading you to accept abolitionist conclusions. To avoid dissembling, you might begin by saying, "I'm no Christian, but I have read the same Bible from which you are quoting, and you seem to have forgotten that it includes Galatians 3." I see nothing inherently deceitful in such an appeal. Immanent criticism of this sort is a principal tool of justificatory discourse, and is often a way of expressing respect for one's interlocutor. But it does not proceed from an already agreed-upon common basis. Instead, it acknowledges that all citizens enter the discursive fray with their own commitments and exercise their powers of reasoning against the background of those commitments.

The case just considered has the following form: you were offering reasons R for X to accept a proposition P given X's collateral commitments C, but without yourself endorsing either R or C. Even if you were not being deceptive, weren't you still manipulating X into accepting P? And doesn't manipulation—or "leveraging," as Robert Audi calls it[12]—smack of disrespect? I suppose it would be manipulative to offer reasons in this way if one disregarded the status of one's interlocutors as responsible agents and treated them as mere means to one's political objectives. Immanent criticism does not, however, seem inherently implicated in treating one's interlocutor as a mere means. Socrates repeatedly engages in it, turning argumentative tactics devised by the sophists to his own philosophical purposes. Plato effectively distinguishes his reason giving from the manipulation of the sophists by portraying Socrates as an immanent critic who treats each interlocutor as a *potential* lover of justice and sound reasoning. As an exemplary immanent critic, Socrates commits himself to learning what can be learned from his interlocutors, the reasons they offer, and the collateral commitments they have made. His regard for them as agents responsible for their judgments and acts is evident throughout. It has nothing in common with the merely instrumental attitude that sophists display toward their interlocutors when using the same *elenchos*-like argumentative techniques. Immanent criticism need not, then, be manipulative. Democratic citizens who employ immanent criticism in public settings need not be behaving sophistically, if they view it as an ad hoc, piecemeal strategy for building a community genuinely responsive to reasons and dedicated to justice. Coalitions of decency are often built one citizen or one small group of citizens at a time.

It appears that contractarians are too caught up in theorizing about an idealized form of reasoning to notice the work that candid expression and respectful immanent criticism perform in real democratic exchange. As I see it, immanent criticism is both one of the most widely used forms of reasoning in political discourse and one of the most effective ways of showing respect for fellow citizens who hold differing points of view. Each citizen keeps track of a range of interlocutors—and does so, necessarily, from his or her own point of view. Any citizen is free to request reasons from any other. If I have access to the right forum, I can tell the entire community what reasons move me to accept a given conclusion, thus showing respect to my fellow citizens. But to explain to them why *they* might have reason to agree with me, given their different collateral premises, I might well have to proceed piecemeal, addressing one individual (or one type of perspective) at a time. Real respect for others takes seriously the distinctive point of view *each* other occupies. It is respect for individuality, for difference. Contractarians, in contrast, seem to be operating on the assumption that discursive sociality must be modeled on a least-common-denominator basis.

Rawls builds this assumption into his conception of a "reasonable person." Such a person is by definition someone who is prepared to play by the discursive rules of the imagined common basis on all essential matters. But why not view the person who takes each competing perspective on its own terms, expressing his own views openly and practicing immanent criticism on the views of others, as a reasonable (socially cooperative, respectful, reason-giving) person? Why limit oneself in the Rawlsian way to the quest for a *common* basis, given the possibility that a common basis will not cover all essential matters? I do not see any convincing answers to these questions in the contractarian theories produced so far. These questions reveal, I think, that the social contract is essentially a substitute for communitarian agreement on a single comprehensive normative vision—a poor man's communitarianism. Contractarianism feels compelled to reify a sort of all-purpose, abstract fairness or respect for others because it cannot imagine ethical or political discourse *dialogically*.[13] Its view of the epistemological and sociological dimensions of discursive practices is essentially blinkered.

Wolterstorff puts the point in a slightly different way:

> So-called 'communitarians' regularly accuse proponents of the liberal position of being against community. One can see what they are getting at. Nonetheless, this way of putting it seems to me imperceptive of what, at bottom, is going on. The liberal is not willing to live with a politics of multiple communities. He still wants communitarian politics. He is trying to discover, and to form, the relevant community. He thinks we need a shared political basis; he is trying to discover and nourish that basis. . . . I think that the attempt is hopeless and misguided. We must learn to live with a politics of multiple communities.[14]

My qualm about this way of putting the point I want to make is that it concedes too much to group thinking. We do have multiple communities in the sense that the points of view many citizens occupy fall into recognizable types. But individuals are the ones who have points of view, and respect for individuals involves sensitivity to the ways in which an individual can resist conformity to type. The basic model of discursive sociality for a democratic society needs to be a dialogical model, it seems to me.[15]

Wolterstorff envisions a multitude of discursive communities conversing both within and across their own boundaries. On my model, each individual starts off with a cultural inheritance that might well come from many sources. In my case, these sources included the training I received in Bible school, the traditional stories my grandmother told on Sunday afternoons, and the example of a pastor committed passionately to civil rights. But they also included an early exposure to Emerson, Whitman, and Thoreau; the art, novels, and music brought into my home by my bohemian older brother; and countless other bits of free-floating cultural material that are not the property of any group. And they included interactions with hundreds of other people whose racial and religious backgrounds differed from mine. It would simply be inaccurate to describe my point of view as that of my family, my co-religionists, or my race. To show respect to me as an individual is precisely not to assimilate my point of view to some form of group thinking. It is unclear to me whether Wolterstorff, in placing as much emphasis as he does on a multitude of discursive *communities,* is prepared to do justice to the kind of individuality that modern democracies can promote. Still, his position represents a major step beyond the contractarian model.

Contractarians derive their idea of public reason from conceptions of fairness and respect that are in fact to be found in the political culture of modern democracy. But they develop this idea in a way that brings it into tension with conceptions of free expression and basic rights that also belong to the same culture. It is not clear why this tension should be resolved by adopting a Rawlsian policy of restraint for all citizens.[16] It seems more reasonable to suppose that one should try to argue from universally justifiable premises, whenever this seems wise, and feel free nonetheless to pursue other argumentative strategies when they seem wise. This would be to treat the idea of public reason as a vague ideal, instead of reifying it moralistically into a set of fixed rules for public discussion. The truth in the contractarian argument for restraint is that it would indeed be *ideal* if we could resolve any given political controversy on the basis of reasons that none of us could reasonably reject. But it is not clear that all important controversies can be resolved on this sort of basis, so it seems unwise to treat the idea of public reason as if it entailed an all-purpose principle of restraint. The irony here is that the contractarian interpretation of the idea of public reason is itself something that many epistemically and morally responsible citizens would be entitled, on the basis of their own collateral premises, to reject.

The contractarian position has a descriptive component and a normative component. The descriptive component is an account of what the norms of democratic political culture involve. It distills a rigorist interpretation of the idea of public reason out of various commitments that are found in that culture. The normative component endorses a principle of restraint as a consequence of that interpretation. I worry that religious individuals who accept the descriptive component of contractarianism as a faithful reconstruction of what the norms of democratic political culture involve will, understandably, view this as a reason for withdrawing from that culture. Why should one identify with the democratic process of reason-exchange if the norms implicit in that process are what the contractarians say they are? I believe this thought is in fact one of the main reasons that such antiliberal traditionalists as Stanley Hauerwas, Alasdair MacIntyre, and John Milbank have largely displaced Reinhold Niebuhr, Paul Tillich, and the liberation theologians as intellectual authorities in the seminaries, divinity schools, and church-affiliated colleges of the wealthier democracies.

We are about to reap the social consequences of a traditionalist backlash against contractarian liberalism. The more thoroughly Rawlsian our law schools and ethics centers become, the more radically Hauerwasian the theological schools become. Because most of the Rawlsians do not read theology or pay scholarly attention to the religious life of the people, they have no idea what contractarian liberalism has come to mean outside the fields of legal and political theory. (There are a few Rawlsians in religious studies, but they are now on the defensive.) The message nowadays in many of the institutions where future preachers are being trained is that liberal democracy is essentially hypocritical when it purports to value free religious expression. The ideology of freedom, according to Hauerwas, masks a discriminatory program for policing what religious people can say in public. The appropriate response, he sometimes implies, is to condemn freedom and the democratic struggle for justice as "bad ideas" for the church.[17] If this message catches on at the grassroots level, it will be very bad news for democracy. Broadly based, religiously motivated political coalitions of the sort that made the Civil Rights movement possible will then become a thing of the past.

One way to counteract this message, while also showing its advocates sincere respect in their particularity, is to offer fair-minded, nonmanipulative, sincere immanent criticism of the new traditionalism. But notice that one can take this Socratic tack with someone like Hauerwas only because he has expressed the religious reasons for his political conclusions in public. One of the benefits democracy derives from the public expression of religious premises is that these premises can then be subjected to public criticism. The people as a whole would not be better served if these reasons were circulated only behind the closed doors of churches and religiously affiliated schools, where they are least likely to face skeptical objections.

One factor to keep in mind when considering the new traditionalism is that Hauerwas and his allies accept the descriptive component of contractarian liberalism. That is, they take this form of liberalism at face value as an accurate account of what the ethical life of modern democracy involves. It is because they view it as a faithful reflection of our political culture that they are so quick to recommend wholesale rejection of that culture. I hold that the contractarians have distorted what this culture involves by wrongly taking a sensible, widely shared, vague ideal to be a clear, fixed, deontological requirement built into the common basis of our reasoning. If I am right about this, the new traditionalists are wrong to reject that culture as implicitly committed to the contractarian program of restraint— what Hauerwas calls "the democratic policing of Christianity."[18] Rejecting what contractarianism and the new traditionalism have in common will permit us, I hope, to reopen the entire question of the role of religious reasoning in public life.

NOTES

1. Nicholas Wolterstorff, "The Role of Religion in Decision and Discussion of Political Issues," in *Religion in the Public Square: The Place of Religious Convictions in Political Debate,* by Robert Audi and Nicholas Wolterstorff (Lanham, Md.: Rowman and Littlefield, 1997), 67–120.

2. See John Rawls, *Political Liberalism* (New York: Columbia University Press, 1993; paperback ed., 1996). For a detailed account of the social contract as a set of principles "that could not reasonably be rejected, by people who were moved to find principles for the general regulation of behavior that others, similarly motivated, could not reasonably reject," see Thomas M. Scanlon, *What We Owe to Each Other* (Cambridge, Mass.: Harvard University Press, 1998), 4 and passim.

3. Stephen Macedo, *Liberal Virtues: Citizenship, Virtue, and Community in Liberal Constitutionalism* (Oxford: Oxford University Press, 1991), 41.

4. Rawls, *Political Liberalism,* 49, n.1, 212–54.

5. "Persons are reasonable in one basic aspect when, among equals say, they are ready to propose principles and standards as fair terms of cooperation and to abide by them willingly, given the assurance that others will likewise do so. Those norms they view as *reasonable for everyone to accept and therefore as justifiable to them . . .*" (*Political Liberalism,* 49; italics added). "By contrast, people are unreasonable in the same basic aspect when they plan to engage in cooperative schemes but are unwilling to honor, or even to propose . . . any general principles or standards for specifying fair terms of cooperation" (ibid., 50). It is clear from the context that the general principles or standards at issue in the latter passage are those that meet the requirement I have italicized in the former passage.

6. Wolterstorff, "The Role of Religion," 94.

7. For useful criticism, see Wolterstorff, "The Role of Religion"; Kent Greenawalt, *Religious Convictions and Political Choice* (Oxford: Oxford University Press, 1988), and *Private Consciences and Public Reasons* (Oxford: Oxford University Press, 1995); and Christopher J. Eberle, *Religious Convictions in Liberal Politics* (Cambridge: Cambridge University Press, 2002).

8. Wolterstorff briefly discusses the relationship between entitlement and reasonableness in Rawls's sense in "The Role of Religion," 91.

9. Ibid., 98.

10. Ibid., 105; italics in original.

11. Wolterstorff makes a related point about respect and particularity in "The Role of Religion," 110 f.

12. Robert Audi, "Wolterstorff on Religion, Politics, and the Liberal State," in *Religion in the Public Square,* 121–44, 135.

13. For illuminating remarks on the importance of attending to the "concrete" other, see Seyla Benhabib, *Situating the Self: Gender, Community, and Postmodernism in Contemporary Ethics* (New York: Routledge, 1992), esp. chap. 5.

14. Wolterstorff, "The Role of Religion," 109.

15. Wolterstorff defends a "consocial" model in "The Role of Religion," 114–16, but what he says there leaves me uncertain whether he is taking sufficient account of

individuality. For a detailed description of a dialogical model, see Robert M. Brandom, *Making It Explicit: Reasoning, Representing, and Discursive Commitment* (Cambridge, Mass.: Harvard University Press, 1994).

16. I am not addressing the distinctive issues surrounding the roles of judge, juror, attorney, or public official.

17. Stanley Hauerwas, *After Christendom? How the Church Is to Behave if Freedom, Justice, and a Christian Nation Are Bad Ideas* (Nashville, Tenn.: Abingdon Press, 1991).

18. The phrase appears as the title of chapter 4 in Stanley Hauerwas, *Dispatches from the Front: Theological Engagements with the Secular* (Durham, N.C.: Duke University Press, 1994), where Walter Rauschenbusch and Reinhold Niebuhr are portrayed as having been complicit in "the exclusion from the politics of democracy of any religious convictions that are not 'humble'" (104).

8

WHAT DOES
RESPECT REQUIRE?

CHRISTOPHER J. EBERLE

I. On liberals and Liberals

There are (at least!) two kinds of liberals. *Mere* liberals—small "l" liberals—assent to a set of claims regarding what makes for a morally appropriate political order: (a) that the state ought to protect a certain set of rights that includes freedom of conscience, freedom of association, freedom of speech, and so forth; (b) that those rights are so important that they ought not be traded off for goods such as economic efficiency; and (c) that each citizen ought to be provided with means to exercise those rights to an adequate degree.[1] *Justificatory* liberals—capital "L" Liberals—are committed to the further claim that: (d) in order for a polity characterized by (a)–(c) to be legitimate, (a)–(c) must be justifiable to the citizens of that polity. That is, in addition to the substantive claims constitutive of a commitment to mere liberalism, justificatory liberals assent to claim that the main aspects of a social order should be amenable to *public justification.*

It is possible to be a liberal without being a Liberal. That is, it is possible to assent to (a)–(c) while denying that each of those claims can and must be amenable to public justification. It is possible, but is it reasonable? Liberals characteristically deny that it is. They claim that the values and commitments that provide a basis for (a)–(c) also provide a basis for (d). What are those commitments? Over and over again, Liberals appeal to the notion of *respect*.[2] Because we must respect our fellow citizens, we should accord them fundamental rights, should not be willing to trade those rights for economic gain, and so on. In addition, because we respect our compatriots, we ought to provide them with reasons that they can accept for the laws to which they are subject. In short, our commitment to *respecting* our compatriots obliges us to provide a *public justification* for restrictive laws.[3]

It seems that the Liberal's justificatory project presupposes important epistemic claims. By all accounts, "justifying" requires the provision of reasons: broadly, Alter justifies a claim to Ego when Alter provides Ego with good reason to accept that claim. Consequently, it seems that, in order for their project to get off the ground, Liberals must provide some account of what makes for "good reasons." Since it is hard to imagine a plausible account of what makes for good reasons that doesn't incorporate epistemic criteria, it seems that Liberalism depends on substantive epistemic commitments.

Given the nature of their project, then, we should hardly be surprised to find that Liberals dip with regularity into the epistemic well. One can hardly read an essay on justificatory liberalism without a healthy dose of references to "rationality," "ideal rationality," "self-critical rationality," "communicative rationality," "reason," "reasonableness," "common human reason," "accessibility," "public accessibility," "in principle public accessibility," "justification," "rational justification," "mutual acceptability," "criticizability," "intelligibility," "provability," "fallibility," "checkability," "replicability," and so on. Unfortunately, the popularity of the appeal to such epistemic concepts is seldom married to an attempt to articulate explicitly just what such concepts involve. This neglect of explication engenders considerable confusion. Although it is clear (or seems to be clear) that the Liberal's project presupposes substantive epistemic commitments, the summary fashion in which those commitments are typically expressed renders it very difficult to arrive at a clear understanding of just what the Liberal is getting at. And, of course, since it is hard to see just what the Liberal is getting at, criticism of Liberalism can be a frustrating affair indeed.

In this essay I will evaluate one excellent exception to this unfortunate trend. Gerald Gaus has developed a sophisticated conception of epistemic justification and employed that conception to articulate a theory of public justification.[4] He has, in short, provided a clear and original answer to the following question: what is a public justification and what sort of epistemic commitments are embedded in a defensible conception of public justification?

II. Gaus's Conception of Epistemic Justification

Gaus's theory of public justification depends essentially on a distinctive conception of epistemic justification, namely, *open* justification. Perhaps the most illuminating way to articulate Gaus's conception of open justification is to follow Gaus in contrasting it with two alternative conceptions, namely, closed justification and what I will call "God's-eye justification." An agent enjoys *closed justification* for some belief only if her other occurrent beliefs[5] provide adequate grounds for that belief (*JL*, 32). For our purposes, the central feature of the closed conception of epistemic justification is as follows: whether an agent is closedly justified in assenting to some proposition P is determined almost entirely by the contents of his evidential set, that is, the other beliefs and experiences he employs to evaluate P. Thus, if Jack believes that he has good inductive evidence that this pizza is untainted—for example, he believes that the delivery boy who just brought it has always delivered untainted pizzas in the past, and if none of Jack's occurrent beliefs override this inductive evidence—then we may assume that the evidence of which Jack is aware provides him with adequate grounds for the claim that the pizza is untainted. Jack is therefore "justified" in believing that this pizza isn't poisoned, whether or not the pizza is in fact poisoned, and whether or not, unbeknownst to him, there exists some evidence that conclusively establishes that the pizza is poisoned. On the closed conception, then, whether an agent is epistemically justified in assenting to P is a function, most centrally, of her other actual convictions and experiences and not of evidential relations of which she is not aware.

By way of contrast, an agent enjoys God's-eye justification for some belief of hers only if that belief is true. According to this conception of epistemic justification, a fact constitutes good reason to believe a corresponding proposition P and, therefore, so long as that fact exists, an agent—who may or may not be aware of this fact—is justified in believing P. If the pizza the delivery boy just gave Jack is poisoned, the fact that it is poisoned provides Jack with adequate reason to believe that it is poisoned. Jack is therefore justified in believing—there is "good reason" to believe—that the pizza is poisoned even if he is entirely unaware that the pizza is poisoned. Thus Gaus:

> Whether [Jack] is justified in believing *B*, we might say, ultimately depends on whether there simply are good reasons for believing *B*. And whether there simply are good reasons for believing *B* does not depend on the nature

of [Jack]'s perspective, but is an objective, entirely external matter. For example: [Jack] has good reasons to believe that the earth is round just because it is true that the earth is round. (*JL*, 32)

Gaus denies that either closed or God's-eye justification provide us with a defensible conception of what it takes for us to justify the moral demands we make of others.[6] The central problem with closed justification is that it ties justification too intimately to an agent's actual convictions: since those convictions might be corrupted by ignorance or prejudice, we should not allow his actual convictions to determine what he is justified in believing. First, Jack might be ignorant of evidence against some proposition P that he would regard as compelling if he was informed about that evidence. That evidence exists that Jack would regard as relevant to the truth of P and that would undermine his belief that P is true renders him unjustified in adhering to P even if his actual beliefs and convictions provide adequate support for P. Second, Jack's actual convictions might be distorted by prejudices that occlude his clear-sighted appreciation of evidence that he regards as relevant to the truth of P, such that, were those prejudices removed, he would reject P. Thus, Jack might be so prejudiced against African Americans that he dismisses forthwith any evidence that might undermine his conviction that African Americans are inherently inferior to whites. Given that his evaluation of the claim that African Americans and whites are equally valuable is distorted by his prejudices, those who understand the way in which his prejudices blind him to the evidence are justified in believing that he has good reason to believe that African Americans are of equal value—in spite of the fact that what he actually has to go on provides adequate support for his racist convictions (*JL*, 32). In short, according to Gaus, it is central to our concept of what it takes to justify interpersonal moral demands that (a) an agent can be *justified* in assenting to some claim even though his actual beliefs and experiences fail to provide adequate support for that claim, and (b) that an agent can be *unjustified* in assenting to some claim even though his actual beliefs and experiences constitute adequate support for that claim. This is because what best completes an agent's complex, incomplete, or fractured belief system might run contrary to what that agent actually believes on the basis of the evidence of which he is aware.

If the closed conception is objectionable because it fails sufficiently to idealize away from an agent's actual convictions, the God's-eye conception is objectionable because it idealizes *entirely* away from an agent's actual convictions—according to the God's-eye conception, whether an agent justifiably assents to a given proposition is not determined *at all* by her actual cognitive commitments. The God's-eye conception drives a gaping chasm between what an agent is justified in believing and the evidence of which she is or can be aware. It implies not only that an agent can have reasons of which she cannot conceive, but that "there could be a fact F that was a reason to accept B, even if humans were incapable of recognizing F, conceiving of it, and so on . . ." (*JL*, 35). Gaus objects:

> It is mysterious what could be meant by saying that [states of affairs that human beings can never cognize] provide *reasons* to believe B. "Reasons for Whom?" is the proper query. Facts become reasons when they enter into cognitive systems with inferential norms and are able to *justify* acceptance of a belief. (*JL*, 35)

Since both closed and God's-eye justification fail to capture an adequate sense of what is required for interpersonal justification, Gaus develops his alternative conception of epistemic justification. According to Gaus, an agent enjoys *open justification* for P only if her system of beliefs, as corrected by information her "system acknowledges as relevant" (*JL*, 129), provides adequate reason for P.[7] This rendering of the concept of epistemic justification, Gaus writes,

> allows for Alf to have reasons for beliefs that are not presently part of his system, but his commitment to the new reasons must be based on his current system as revised by new information. Unlike [the God's-eye conception], open justification genuinely addresses Alf, and genuinely shows that *Alf has reason* to embrace B. On the other hand, open justification does not hold Betty hostage to Alf's current errors, *so long as they are errors from the perspective of Alf's system of beliefs.* (*JL*, 140)

Gaus's conception of open justification depends on a distinction between what an agent's belief system commits her to and the particular convictions to which she adheres. What an agent's belief system commits her to—the *best completion* of her belief system—is determined by particularly deep or fundamental features of her belief system. I interpret Gaus as identifying those deep features with an agent's convictions regarding what counts as genuine evidence.[8] This identification is not implausible since an agent's conviction that, for example, sense perception is a reliable means of acquiring information about the physical world is more fundamental to her noetic structure than are the various beliefs she forms on the basis of sense perception. This feature of Gaus's conception of open justification is closely allied to a further important feature: whether an agent is openly justified in adhering to some claim is a function of what she would believe in certain counterfactual circumstances.[9] When we attempt to determine whether Jill is justified in accepting a given policy, we should not make that determination by identifying whether Jill's actual convictions provide good reason to accept that policy. Rather, we should construct a counterfactual test: we should identify what Jill's simulacrum, Twin-Jill, would have good reason to believe if we impute to her (1) Jill's actual convictions about the kinds of evidence that have evidential force, as well as (2) awareness of evidence of the sort Jill regards as having evidential force but of which Jill is not in fact aware. Gaus's strategy for avoiding the closed conception of justification involves *idealization,* given that we impute to Twin-Jill awareness of evidence Jill does not have, but the idealization is *moderate* since the kind of evidence it is appropriate for us to impute to Twin-Jill is constrained by Jill's actual convictions about what kinds of evidence have evidential force. That the idealization involved is *only* moderate is essential to Gaus's strategy for avoiding the God's-eye conception of justification.

III. Gaus's Conception of Public Justification

The moral impulse driving the justificatory project is a conviction about what respect requires: respect requires that, when citizens impose moral norms on one another, they provide their compatriots with good reasons for those impositions. This intuitive formulation begs for an explication of "good reason," and Gaus's conception of open justification constitutes that explication: a good reason is a claim an agent is justified in accepting given her system of beliefs as corrected by evidence *she* regards as having evidential force. It follows, then, that Jack satisfies his obligation to respect Jill only if he supports policies that Jill has adequate grounds to accept given that Jill's system of beliefs has been corrected by evidence she regards as having evidential force. In general, Jack satisfies his obligation to respect his fellow citizens only if he supports policies *each of them* is justified in accepting given their systems of beliefs as corrected by evidence each of them regards as having evidential force. As an initial formulation of the sort of justification Gaus claims that citizens ought to provide, we can say that *respect requires that citizens support policies on the basis of a rationale which all citizens are openly justified in accepting.*[10] Given this initial formulation, I will now explicate in a little more detail the conditions in which a candidate for public justification is victorious and those in which it is defeated.

First, when is a candidate for public justification defeated? That is, under what conditions does a policy lack public justification? A sufficient condition of a policy's defeat is that there is one citizen whose belief system, even though corrected by information and arguments of a kind she regards as having evidential force, provides her with adequate reason to reject that proposal outright. Each citizen has veto power over any proposal; so long as an agent's suitably corrected viewpoint provides her with reason to reject a given policy, that policy is defeated (*JL*, 133, 146, 159, 171). It is important to clarify immediately this account of what makes for a defeated proposal. A sufficient condition of a proposed policy's defeat is *not* that there is at least one citizen who *believes* that, relative to her viewpoint, she has good reason to reject a given policy. A citizen can be wrong about what her system of beliefs commits her to and, therefore, about whether she is openly justified in dissenting from that policy.[11]

Under what conditions is a candidate for public justification victorious? It is again crucial to note the distinction between what an agent is openly justified in believing and what she believes she is openly justified in believing. Citizens can be wrong not only about the policies they are openly justified in rejecting but also about the policies they are openly justified in accepting. Hence, *it is neither a necessary nor a sufficient condition of a policy's enjoying public justification that that policy garner the actual imprimatur of each member of the public.* What matters is not the actual assent of the citizenry to a proposed policy, but whether or not a policy would be accepted or rejected by a suitably informed and critical citizenry. (As with open justification, whether or not a given policy is publicly justified is a function of what citizens would have good reason to believe in the appropriately specified counterfactual circumstances.)

The epistemic assumptions Gaus employs to construct his theory of public justification are critically important to the success of Gaus's version of the Liberal project. Most importantly, Gaus's integration of his epistemic commitments into his theory of public justification allows him to avoid what he calls *justificatory populism* (*JL*, 130–31). If respect requires, as Gaus allows, that each citizen has adequate reason to accept the policies to which each is subject, and if, as seems plausible, citizens accept (or can easily be brought to accept) beliefs for which they have what they regard as adequate reason to accept, it seems eminently plausible to suppose that a necessary condition for an agent to respect her fellow citizens is that she supports only those policies which all of her compatriots actually accept. According to the justificatory populist, *respect requires public justification* and *public justification requires unanimity.*

However, Gaus will have none of this, for according to Gaus, *respect requires public justification* but *public justification does not require actual unanimity.* Gaus's epistemic commitments enable him to reject justificatory populism: public justification does not require unanimity because agents can be openly justified in accepting some proposal, and thus have good reason to accept that proposal, even though they in fact reject that proposal. Were it not for Gaus's rejection of closed justification, his justificatory project would collapse into justificatory populism, and thus would be vulnerable to Gaus's powerful objections to that version of Liberalism.

IV. Criticism of Justificatory Liberalism

Liberals believe that citizens should refrain from supporting coercive laws for which they lack a public justification. In order for this recommendation to have any bite, Liberals must explain exactly what makes for a public justification, of which Gaus's contribution is exemplary in virtue of his detailed attention to this concept. But I believe, and will now argue, that Gaus's conception of public justification is inadequate.

Against Moderate Idealization

I begin by explaining why we should reject Gaus's moderately idealizing conception of public justification. My argument is as follows:

1. Any of an agent's beliefs about a given policy might be compromised by ignorance or prejudice.
2. Since *any* of an agent's beliefs about a given policy might be compromised by ignorance and prejudice, Gaus must accept an understanding of epistemic justification according to which it is appropriate to idealize away from any of an agent's beliefs about a given policy.
3. Since Gaus must accept an understanding of epistemic justification according to which it is appropriate to idealize away from any of an agent's beliefs about a given policy, he must also accept an understanding of epistemic justification according to which it is appropriate to idealize away from *all* of her beliefs about a given policy.

Ad (1): Recall the following two claims Gaus employs in his criticism of closed justification. First, an agent might adhere to premises that support some conviction C as a consequence of a prejudice to which she is so strongly attached that she will adhere to those premises—and thus to C—no matter how much evidence she has against those premises, as when an agent's racial prejudices so blind her that she dismisses as propaganda any and all evidence against her conviction that blacks are inherently inferior to whites. Second, she might adhere to C only because she is unaware of evidence of a type that she regards as relevant to the truth of C and, moreover, she would reject C if she were aware of that evidence. That an agent's system of beliefs might be compromised in these respects motivates Gaus's claim that, in determining whether an agent is justified in adhering to C, we must idealize away from the prejudices and ignorance that distort her understanding. Of course, Gaus is willing to idealize an agent's actual cognitive situation only in limited respects: we may impute to an agent awareness of only those sorts of evidence she regards as having some probative force. Gaus idealizes, but only moderately.

But the claim that we should idealize only moderately is problematic. If we accept Gaus's reasons for idealizing away from an agent's actual convictions about particular bits of evidence, we have sufficient reason, as well, to idealize away from her convictions regarding what counts as relevant evidence. Why? Because an agent's convictions regarding what counts as relevant evidence can also be compromised by prejudice or limited information. Since beliefs about what counts as relevant evidence as well as beliefs about particular bits of evidence can be compromised by prejudice or ignorance, those sorts of belief can be flawed in both of the respects in virtue of which, according to Gaus, we have good reason to idealize. Hence, either we are prepared to idealize away both from an agent's beliefs about particular bits of evidence and from her beliefs about what counts as relevant evidence or we refuse to idealize at all. But it seems essential to Gaus's version of the Liberal project that we be prepared to idealize, so it is the first option with which we must reckon.

Consider a concrete case. Jerry accepts the claim that the Bible is an infallible source of knowledge. According to Jerry, if the Bible expresses proposition P, then P must be true. Two initial points about Jerry's commitment to biblical authority: first, Jerry's conviction that the Bible is a reliable source of information surely counts as a conviction regarding what counts as relevant evidence. Second, given Gaus's willingness to grant that different agents can reasonably adhere to vastly different worldviews, including religious ones, we have no reason to believe that he would argue that Jerry's privileging of the Bible is irrational or unreasonable.[12]

Surely it is possible that Jerry's commitment to biblical authority is compromised by prejudice. Suppose that, in Jerry's case, Freud was correct in claiming that religious beliefs are generated and sustained by wish fulfillment. What follows from that supposition? Allowing one's wishes to govern what one believes is just as problematic from an epistemic perspective as allowing one's racial prejudice to govern what one believes about the moral worth of members of other races. Hence, if a racist is not openly justified in adhering to her racist convictions in virtue of their being compromised by her prejudice against African Americans, Jerry is not openly justified in adhering to his religious beliefs, and in particular his belief that the Bible is a privileged source of information by virtue of his beliefs being the product of wish fulfillment. Thus, if Freud is correct about religion, Jerry's religious belief system is corrupted by the distorting effects of wishful thinking and, if Gaus is correct about justification, we may rely on knowledge of Freud's explanation of religion in determining what Jerry is justified in believing. We should conclude, if Freud's theory of religion is correct, that Jerry is *not* justified in adhering to any of his religious convictions and thus to the claim that the Bible is a reliable source of knowledge. We could easily make a parallel point showing that Jerry's beliefs about relevant evidence might be compromised by ignorance of what he takes to be relevant evidence.

It seems clear, then, that beliefs about what counts as relevant evidence enjoy no special exemption from the cognitive vicissitudes that afflict beliefs about particular bits of evidence. Since, according to Gaus, the fact that an agent's beliefs are compromised by prejudice or ignorance is sufficient for idealizing away from those beliefs, Gaus's unwillingness to idealize away from beliefs about what counts as relevant evidence is arbitrary.[13]

Ad (2): We may generalize this argument. No matter what type of belief Gaus wishes to exempt from idealization, we will have the same reason to idealize away from that type of belief as we have from those about which Gaus is willing to idealize. Otherwise put, no matter what residually populist elements Gaus integrates into his theory of epistemic justification, we have the same reason to idealize away from those elements as we have to idealize away from the types of belief about which Gaus is not a populist. Why? Unless we accept a strong version of foundationalism—a position Gaus explicitly rejects—we have no reason to believe that any type of belief is exempt from compromise by prejudice and limited information.[14] And, as I have been interpreting Gaus, that a given belief is compromised by prejudice or ignorance is sufficient for idealization. So the whole project of dividing up our beliefs into those from which we may idealize and those from which we may not seems doomed from the start: any such division will arbitrarily exempt one class of beliefs from the effects of ignorance and prejudice. The conclusion that this difficulty forces us to accept is that *any* of an agent's convictions are subject to the vicissitudes that warrant us in idealizing away from an agent's convictions: so long as we are willing to idealize, we have no principled grounds for refusing to idealize away from any particular type of belief.

Ad (3): A further conclusion follows. Since none of Jerry's beliefs enjoys a special exemption from prejudice or ignorance, and since it is possible that Jerry is ensconced in such epistemically hostile conditions that *all* of his convictions *relevant to the truth of some claim C* are compromised by prejudice or ignorance, it seems that it is appropriate to idealize away from *all* of Jerry's convictions that bear on C when determining whether or not Jerry is justified in adhering to C. Thus, consider a central liberal commitment: that all citizens are of equal moral value. We may suppose that Jerry is socialized to believe that African Americans are inherently inferior to whites, one consequence of which is that Jerry's visceral reactions (in philosophical lingo, his "intuitions") militate against the prospect of African Americans holding authority over, socializing with, living in close proximity to, or criticizing whites. Suppose further that the unambiguous testimony of the moral authorities holding sway in Jerry's social environment underwrites the prejudice that African Americans are inferior to whites. Suppose again that Jerry's religious authorities have drummed into his consciousness (and subconscious) the conviction that whites are God's chosen race. In short, imagine a situation in which the dominant forces that mold a citizen's convictions and subjective experiences are directed in such a way that they render incredible for Jerry what liberals take to be a central moral truth. So Jerry finds himself well ensconced in epistemically hostile conditions—in conditions sufficiently corrupt that Jerry's evidential set provides him with no reason to accept a moral claim fundamental to liberalism and plenty of reason to reject that moral claim. If we should idealize away from *some* of Jerry's beliefs when they are compromised by ignorance or prejudice, on what grounds may we refuse to idealize away from *all* of them, given that *all* of his beliefs that are relevant to the truth of the claim that all citizens have equal moral value are compromised in those very respects? In order to avoid arbitrariness, there must be some respect in which the beliefs from which we are permitted to idealize are relevantly different than those from which we may not idealize. But, in Jerry's unfortunate condition, there are no such differences—all of Jerry's convictions relevant to the claim that African Americans and whites have equal value are compromised by the very factors that motivate Gaus's proposal that we idealize.

Given the systemic corruption of Jerry's noetic structure regarding the claim that all human persons are equally valuable, we seem to have only two alternatives. Either we refuse to idealize away from any of Jerry's convictions that bear on the claim that African Americans and whites are of equal value or we idealize away not from some but from all of Jerry's beliefs relevant to the matter of the equality of African Americans and whites. In the first case, Jerry does not have good reason to accept that liberal tenet. In the second case, Gaus's proposal that we idealize only moderately goes by the boards. Since the first alternative is a dead end for Liberalism, Gaus has little option but to pursue the second. And this seems to be the inevitable result of Gaus's idealizing strategy: so long as we are willing to idealize away from some of an agent's convictions in determining whether or not she is justified in adhering to a given claim, then consistency requires us to idealize away from all of that agent's convictions so long as she is enmeshed in epistemic conditions that are systematically hostile to that claim.

Let me emphasize that I claim only that Jerry's beliefs relevant to a particular claim might be systematically misleading, not that *all* of Jerry's beliefs might be false. Perhaps there are limits, as Gaus argues, to the extent to which we can impute falsehood to others. But there is no reason to believe that we cannot intelligibly attribute systematic falsehood *regarding specific claims* to other people, and that is all my argument requires.

The implications of this argument for Gaus's theory of public justification are direct. As we saw, the defining feature of Gaus's conception of open justification, namely, its moderate idealization, translate directly to his theory of public justification. And the moderate idealization of Gaus's theory of public justification is of utmost importance: it allows Gaus to avoid the dead end of justificatory populism while at the same time allowing him to defend the claim that a proper public justification must articulate in some meaningful way with the actual beliefs of the members of the public. But the untenability of Gaus's moderately idealizing conception of public justification should impel him to embrace a radically idealizing conception of public justification.

Radical Idealization

In this section, I will briefly articulate one version of the type of theory of public justification to which Gaus is forced as a consequence of the criticism I presented in the prior section, and then I will indicate why that theory is no more promising than Gaus's original proposal. This will provide the necessary background for a central claim of this essay, namely, that there are no alternative theories open to Gaus that are free of troublesome objections. In order to evaluate the radically idealizing theory of public justification I have in mind, it will be helpful to have a (more or less) concrete formulation of that position in front of us. Here is one such proposal: a citizen may support a given policy if and only if each adequately informed and fully rational citizen would, upon consideration, find that policy acceptable.[15] As with Gaus's original theory of public justification, the theory under consideration requires that we idealize: we impute to citizens awareness of information of which they are not in fact aware. But the idealization involved is no longer moderate; it is radical. Why? Since an agent might be systematically misinformed about a given policy, it is possible that there is no overlap between the grounds she actually has to go on and the grounds she would have to go on if she were adequately informed about that policy. If that possibility is actualized in an agent's case, then the policy in question might be publicly justified even though nothing she actually has to go on provides her with good reason to support that policy.

What should we make of this theory of public justification? Recall that the Liberal wants to forbid citizens from supporting policies for which they lack an appropriate rationale—a public justification. The central component of any adequate conception of public justification is that it provide a criterion by which citizens can filter out of their political deliberations any rationale on the basis of which it is inappropriate for them to support a given policy. A criterion for identifying the sorts of rationale regarding which citizens should exercise such restraint that is too weak to exclude paradigmatically unacceptable grounds fails to achieve its appointed purpose. I will argue that the radically idealizing theory of public justification currently under consideration is too weak to exclude one sort of paradigmatically unacceptable ground according to Liberals, specifically, religious convictions.

Suppose that Elijah is fully committed to obeying the radically idealized theory of public justification under consideration. Suppose that Elijah also believes that God has a preference for the poor and that this conviction plays an essential evidential role in Elijah's commitment to radical income redistribution. So Elijah wonders: would an adequately informed citizen accept the claim that God has a preference for the poor? Well, Elijah's conviction that God has a preference for the poor is based on his conviction that the Bible is a reliable source of information regarding God's will and nature. So would an adequately informed citizen accept the claim that the Bible is reliable?

It is true, of course, that many of Elijah's compatriots *disagree* with his belief that the Bible is reliable. But, obviously, their disagreement with his belief does not settle the issue of whether the Bible is reliable. What would settle the issue is if his compatriots were to find his belief that the Bible is reliable acceptable *and* they were fully rational and adequately informed. So would such counterfactual citizens accept the claim that the Bible is reliable? What conclusion is it reasonable for *Elijah* to reach on the matter? (He is, after all, supposed to obey Liberal strictures on reasons and thus must arrive at some reasoned conclusion as to what the appropriately idealized citizens would think and thus must be able to apply the target conception of public justification to the issue at hand.)

It seems eminently reasonable for Elijah to conclude that his compatriots would be aware that the Bible is divinely inspired. Why? The following argument in support of that conclusion seems compelling to me.

1. If it is permissible for Elijah to determine, by employing his religious convictions, what adequately informed, rational citizens would find acceptable, then

it is appropriate for Elijah to conclude that adequately informed and fully rational citizens would regard the Bible as reliable.

2. It is permissible for Elijah to determine, by employing his religious convictions, what adequately informed, rational citizens would find acceptable.

3. Hence, it is appropriate for Elijah to conclude that adequately informed and fully rational citizens would regard the Bible as reliable.

Ad (1): The theory of public justification under consideration requires that a citizen who intends to respect her compatriots determine the truth of a particular counterfactual claim C: if her compatriots were adequately informed and fully rational, would they find her rationale for a given coercive law acceptable? Presumably, each citizen ought to make that determination *rationally.* Whether it is rational for a citizen to accept C is determined, in crucial part, by the total set of evidence in light of which she evaluates C. Since different agents will invariably evaluate C in light of different evidential sets, it will often be rational for different agents to reach differing and incompatible conclusions regarding C. There is every reason to believe that the conclusions citizens reach regarding the relevant counterfactual claim will vary in the expected way: since different agents rely on different evidential sets, they will arrive rationally at different conclusions regarding what suitably idealized citizens would find acceptable. And the conclusions a given citizen reaches regarding what her appropriately idealized compatriots would find acceptable will vary in accord with differences in the evidential set she employs in arriving at these conclusions. Otherwise put, the conclusions that a citizen draws regarding what her adequately informed and fully rational compatriots would find acceptable is a function of the information she relies on in making that determination.

For example, Liberals sometimes claim that citizens who are adequately informed about some coercive law will evaluate that law in light of whatever well-established scientific theories that bear on that law. Their confidence in the reliability of science is not imposed by transcendental necessity; rather, it is based on what they take to be adequate evidence that science provides us with an accurate understanding of reality. Those who lack that evidence, of course, will not be so willing to impute awareness of well-established scientific theories to adequately informed citizens. A primitive tribesman, if the Liberal could induce him to adhere to the theory of public justification under consideration, would reasonably conclude that adequately informed and fully rational citizens are aware, say, that the reading of chicken entrails is a reliable way of forming beliefs. The tribesman would not, we may assume, impute awareness of well-corroborated scientific theories to adequately informed and fully rational citizens. The difference in the convictions the Liberal and the tribesman impute to idealized citizens is a function of differences between the parochial convictions on the basis of which they attempt to determine what the appropriately idealized citizens would believe.

Similarly for religious citizens such as Elijah. Since Elijah believes that the Bible is a reliable source of information about God's will and nature, it is natural for him to conclude that an adequately informed and fully rational citizen will be aware of that fact. He has the same reason to impute the conviction that the Bible is divinely inspired to adequately informed and fully rational citizens that the Liberal has to impute the conviction that science is reliable to adequately informed and fully rational citizens. After all, how can Elijah's compatriots be *adequately* informed about his proposal if they are ignorant of one of the most important facts about that proposal, namely, that it follows from God's—an omniscient moral authority—express moral commitments?[16] Elijah claims that nonbelievers think otherwise because they are *inadequately informed*, just as justificatory liberals are free to the claim that a primitive tribesman who immigrates to the United States and who rejects the claim that science is reliable is inadequately informed.

Ad (2): It seems clear that, *if* Elijah is permitted to employ his religious convictions to determine what adequately informed and fully rational citizens would believe, he will read his parochial religious convictions into his understanding of what such idealized citizens would believe. So, if the Liberal is to achieve her purposes—articulating a conception of public justification powerful enough to forbid citizens from supporting laws that depend entirely on religious grounds— she must show that it is inappropriate for Elijah to employ his religious convictions to determine what adequately informed and fully rational citizens would believe. That is, she must articulate some principled reason why Elijah may not employ his religious commitments in determining whether adequately informed and fully rational citizens would be aware that the Bible is divinely inspired. But there is no such principled reason, so far as I'm aware.

Note first that the Liberal has no option but to permit Elijah to determine what adequately informed persons have good reason to believe *by relying on his own parochial commitments.* The argument in support of this claim takes the form of a dilemma. Either Elijah may determine what adequately informed and fully rational citizens would find acceptable by relying on some rendering of what adequately informed and fully rational citizens would find acceptable, or it is not the case that he may determine what adequately informed and fully rational citizens would find acceptable by relying on some rendering of what adequately informed and fully rational citizens would find acceptable. By hypothesis, Elijah does not yet know what an adequately informed and fully rationale citizen would believe about the Bible: we are imagining him in the throes of determining what the appropriately idealized citizens would find acceptable. Hence, he cannot determine what such citizens would find acceptable by relying on some rendering of what adequately informed and fully rational citizens would find acceptable. Consequently, in determining what an adequately informed and fully rational person would believe, Elijah must rely on *someone's* parochial convictions regarding reliable belief-forming practices, well-corroborated scientific theories, moral truths, and the like. He could, of course, rely on someone *else's* convictions in determining what idealized citizens would find acceptable, but that seems arbitrary: given that the content of "adequate information" is going to be filled out by *someone's* parochial convictions, why someone else's and not his own? It seems, then, that if Elijah is going to apply the radically idealizing theory of public justification in his actual circumstances, he has no option but to rely on *his own* parochial commitments. As is the case with each and every one of us, Elijah's judgment regarding what *ideally circumstanced* citizens would believe about the reliability of the Bible will be parasitic on judgments he has formed in his, alas, less than ideal circumstances.

Of course, that Elijah may rely on his parochial commitments in determining what radically idealized citizens would believe does not imply that he is permitted to rely on *all* of his parochial commitments. Certainly, he may rely on some of his commitments—otherwise he has no basis on which to make the relevant determination—but perhaps not all. And if not all, then perhaps he can rely on *none* of his religious commitments. So here is the question: if Elijah is permitted to rely on *some* of his parochial commitments in determining what radically idealized citizens would find acceptable, then why can't he rely on his religious convictions in making that determination? If he can rely on his scientific, perceptual, moral, and introspective commitments in determining what sufficiently idealized citizens would find acceptable, then why not religious commitments as well? We need some reason to single out religious commitments for special treatment.

Religious commitments are, of course, widely contested. But dissensus regarding religious convictions provides no good reason to prohibit Elijah from employing his religious commitments to determine what adequately informed and fully rational citizens would find acceptable. After all, the move to an idealizing conception of public justification is motivated by the fact that fully reasonable and rational citizens in modern, pluralistic democracies disagree with one another about so much; more particularly, just as many citizens will reject the claim that an adequately informed citizen will be aware that the Bible is reliable, many will reject the claim that an adequately informed citizen will be *un*aware that the Bible is reliable. Since it seems likely that citizens in a modern liberal democracy will disagree with one another about reliable sources of information just about as violently as they will disagree about anything else, to repair back to populism at this point would be to admit defeat. But in that case, what other options are there?

So long as Elijah's goal is to determine what adequately informed and fully rational citizens would find acceptable, it seems to me that there is no plausible alternative open to the Liberal other than that Elijah should make his determination on the basis of whatever information he rationally and conscientiously regards as reliable. Since Elijah, we may assume, rationally and conscientiously regards the Bible as reliable, it seems that it is appropriate for him to conclude that adequately informed and fully rational citizens would be aware that the Bible is reliable. It follows, further, that the radically idealizing theory of public justification under discussion provides no basis for the conclusion that citizens should withhold support from any policy for which they enjoy only a religious rationale. But this constitutes a *reductio* of that theory.

V. A General Argument against Public Justification

As I have already noted, it is essential to the Liberal project that its advocates provide concrete criteria that enable citizens to determine whether or not they may rely on a particular rationale for a given policy. If Liberals cannot provide those criteria, then their insistence that citizens refrain from relying on "inappropriate" grounds idles. I have attempted to show that Gaus fails to provide those criteria. I have also attempted to show that a natural modification of his original proposal fails to net Gaus the requisite criteria. I conclude that the Liberal project lacks an essential desideratum, but I realize that I have not provided anything close to the sort of argumentation required to justify that conclusion. Doing so would require that I articulate and criticize each of the extant, if not the possible, alternatives to which Gaus might avail himself. Since limitations of space render that task impossible, I'll complete my case against Gaus's theory of public justification by articulating some general grounds for skepticism regarding the existence of the sort of criteria he requires.

Any given theory of public justification may be placed somewhere along a continuum that is constituted by criteria that identify the sorts of reasons citizens must enjoy for a given policy in order for that policy to be publicly justified. That continuum runs from *populist* theories at one extreme to *idealizing* theories at the other extreme. Theories located at the populist end of the continuum require that, in order for some policy to be publicly justified, each citizen, taken as she is with her existing convictions—epistemic pockmarks and doxastic defects—supports that policy. (At the extreme of this end of the continuum, I would assume, is the proposal that, in order for some policy to be publicly justified, each citizen, taken as she is, would support that policy on the basis of exactly the same rationale as does each of her compatriots, taken as they are.) Theories located at the idealizing end of the continuum require that, in order for some policy to enjoy public justification, each citizen would have good reason to accept that policy if she were free of certain epistemic defects. (At the extreme of this end of the continuum, I would assume, is the proposal that, in order for some policy to be publicly justified, that policy is entailed by grounds that would be accepted by an Ideal Observer, that is, a being with no epistemic defects or limitations.) Between the extremes, pretty obviously, is a great deal of room for proposals that combine populist and idealizing elements.

Populist theories are attractive to the Liberal for the following reason: if she adopts a populist theory, then that theory provides her with principled grounds for denying that citizens may support their favored policies solely on the basis of allegedly inappropriate grounds—for example, religious grounds. Since religious convictions are widely contested, populist theories prohibit citizens from supporting policies solely on the basis of their religious convictions. Liberals who accept a populist theory may make short work as well of another paradigmatically unacceptable sort of ground, namely, conceptions of the good. As with religious convictions, conceptions of the good are widely contested and, as a consequence, are clearly ruled out of bounds by actualizing theories. So populist theories are attractive because they get the right results in certain central cases.

Nevertheless, Gaus has exposed with gusto the weaknesses of populist theories of public justification. Gaus's verdict on Rawls's fairly moderate populist theory of public justification strikes me as compelling:

> Rawls's theory . . . is indicative of the problems of embracing the commitment to justify while at the same time forgoing epistemological commitments. Political liberalism is driven to a sort of populist consensualism because it deprives itself of the resources on which to ground the claim that liberal principles are justified in the face of sustained dissent by reasonable people. Any reasonable person who does not accept its claims becomes a counter-example. Pushed by its populism, [Rawls's theory] moves to modify and weaken its liberal commitments in search of an ever wider and thinner consensus. Ultimately, I think, it loses its character as a liberal doctrine, for little, if anything, is the object of consensus among reasonable people. The project of securing a consensus of all reasonable people leads to the undermining of [Rawls's] liberalism, which is to say that it leads to self-destruction. (*JL*, 293)

If we move from one end of the spectrum to the other, it turns out that idealizing theories invert the merits and demerits of populist theories. On the one hand, such theories are attractive to Liberals because they make plausible the claim that idealized citizens (unlike actual citizens) agree on enough to insure that some policies enjoy public justification. If we assume that many of the disagreements between citizens result from imperfections in their epistemic circumstances, and if we idealize away from those imperfections, then it is plausible to assume that idealized citizens will agree with one another a great deal more than do actual citizens. Indeed, if we idealize sufficiently (the Ideal Observer model), we make plausible the claim that citizens will agree on enough to insure that they can arrive at a mutually agreeable resolution to any given political disagreement with which they are faced. (The Liberal's contention, of course, is that idealized citizens would agree on the propriety of characteristic liberal commitments.)

On the other hand, idealizing theories provide us with no reason to deny that religious convictions and conceptions of the good count as public justifications even though that is precisely the work Liberals want their favored conception of public justification to do. As we idealize further away from the cognitive imperfections that generate the dissensus that scuttles populist theories, we ipso facto idealize away from the imperfections that generate the dissensus regarding religious convictions and conceptions of the good. But in that case, why ought we refrain from supporting coercive laws on the basis of religious convictions and conceptions of the good?

So theories of public justification at the populist extreme rule out the right sorts of grounds, but leave intact dissensus. Theories of public justification at the idealizing extreme remove dissensus, but fail to rule out the right sorts of grounds. Neither extreme is, therefore, acceptable to the Liberal. A defensible theory of public justification must lie somewhere between the extremes. Gaus has attempted to articulate one such theory, but I believe that it is unstable—and a resolution of that instability forces Gaus in the direction of the extremes. Perhaps there is another mediating position, one better able to withstand criticism than Gaus's. But I think it unlikely that the Liberal will succeed in articulating a defensible mediating position.

My reasons for this last claim are as follows. Assume that Gaus's criticism of populist theories is basically accurate: since we disagree so much, to make actual consensus regarding a given policy a necessary condition of its enjoying public justification implies that no policies are publicly justified. As a consequence, we must accept a theory of public justification that idealizes somewhat: we must reduce the disagreement among citizens by idealizing away from the cognitive imperfections that generate disagreement. Realistically, we must adopt a theory that idealizes in fairly powerful respects: were we to hold the actual convictions of citizens constant and idealize *only* in the respect that we impute to them a cognitive endowment free of explicitly contradictory beliefs, we would have no better reason to expect consensus than were we not to idealize at all.

It seems to me that mixed theories are vulnerable to the same sort of objection to which idealizing theories are vulnerable. As we idealize more powerfully, and thus make more plausible the claim that idealized citizens would agree sufficiently to arrive at counterfactual consensus regarding the grounds Liberals take to be appropriate bases for political deliberation, we have every reason to believe that the relevant consensus would include the claim that religious grounds are appropriate bases for political deliberation. But if that is the case, why forbid citizens from relying on their religious convictions and conceptions of the good to determine which policies they should support?

The only alternative open to the Liberal at this point, so far as I can tell, is to deny that idealizing in the respects required to generate counterfactual consensus regarding the appropriate grounds is to idealize in respects that also generate counterfactual consensus regarding inappropriate grounds. Otherwise put, any moderately idealizing theory must satisfy two criteria: it must render plausible the claim that idealized citizens would reach consensus regarding the grounds that Liberals regard as contributors to public justification, but it must also render plausible the claim that idealized citizens would remain divided over religious convictions, conceptions of the good, and other grounds regarding which Liberals characteristically deny the status of public justification. I know of no plausible proposal that satisfies both of those criteria. Nor can I imagine any such proposal. The only option at this point is to throw down the gauntlet to the Liberal. Time will tell whether Liberals are up to the challenge.

NOTES

I thank Terence Cuneo and Gerald Gaus for very helpful feedback on this essay. I regret that I have been unable to address all of the concerns that Professor Gaus has articulated about my argument, but am grateful for his valiant efforts to set me straight!

1. For this characterization of mere liberalism, I rely on John Rawls, *Political Liberalism* (New York: Columbia University Press, 1993), 6. Of course, not all mere liberals accept this characterization.

2. For a sampling, see Charles Larmore, *Patterns of Moral Complexity* (Cambridge: Cambridge University Press, 1987), 40–68; John Rawls, *A Theory of Justice* (Cambridge, Mass.: The Belknap Press, 1971), 337–38; Stephen Macedo, *Liberal Virtues* (Oxford: Clarendon Press, 1990), 47, 249; Paul Weithman, "The Liberalism of Reasoned Respect," in *Re-*

ligion and Contemporary Liberalism, ed. Paul Weithman (Notre Dame, Ind.: University of Notre Dame Press, 1997), 6; Robert Audi, "The Place of Religious Argument in a Free and Democratic Society," *San Diego Law Review* 30 (Fall 1993): 701; Lawrence Solum, "Faith and Justice," *DePaul Law Review* 39 (1990): 1095; Kai Nielson, "Liberal Reasonability," *Dialogue* 37, no. 4 (Fall 1998): 750; and Colin Bird, "Mutual Respect and Public Justification," *Ethics* (October 1996): 62–96.

3. For explication and criticism of this argument, see Christopher J. Eberle, *Religious Conviction in Liberal Politics* (Cambridge: Cambridge University Press, 2002), 109–51.

4. I will focus on Gaus's position as explicated in *Justificatory Liberalism: An Essay on Epistemology and Political Theory* (Oxford: Oxford University Press, 1996), hereafter cited as *JL*.

5. Gaus allows that the set of occurrent (actual) beliefs that determine what counts as closedly justified for some agent is composed not only of those to which she consciously assents, but also of those she is disposed to accept and those she tacitly accepts (*JL,* 35–38).

6. Gaus does not deny that the closed conception captures an epistemically important conception of justification; what he denies is that the closed conception provides an adequate account of what is required to justify interpersonal moral demands (personal communication from Gerald Gaus).

7. Surprisingly, given its centrality to his argument, Gaus does not explicate in detail what he means by information that an agent's system of beliefs "acknowledges as relevant," but I take it that he means that agents adhere to claims regarding reliable sources of information, as distinct from claims regarding particular bits of information generated by putatively reliable belief-forming practices. Thus, an agent believes that sense perception is reliable and, on the basis of engaging in the sense-perceptual belief-forming practice, she forms the belief that there is a computer on the desk. The first is a claim about relevant information—about the kind of evidence to which an agent is willing to accord probative weight, and the second is about a particular bit of information. The information an agent's system of beliefs "acknowledges as relevant," I surmise, is a function of the first, but not the second, kind of belief.

8. This identification might not capture Gaus's intention exactly, but nothing essential to my objection to Gaus depends upon an exact match.

9. Gaus acknowledges the counterfactual test implicit in his conception of open justification in the following passage: "The core idea of open justification is that, at any given time, a justified belief system is, ideally, stable in the face of acute and sustained criticism by others and of new information. Full explication of the idea of open justification would thus require a counterfactual test, and once again, we would meet all the difficulties that idea poses" (*JL,* 31).

10. Although I will attempt to clarify this intuitive formulation in the rest of this section, one point merits immediate clarification. The rationale for a publicly justified policy will invariably be constituted by a *set* of arguments none of the elements of which need to be accepted by all citizens, so long as at least one argument in that set is openly justifiable to each citizen. See *JL,* 146. Although this is an important component of Gaus's theory of public justification, I will, for ease of exposition, suppress it in the ensuing discussion.

11. *JL,* 147. See also Gerald Gaus, "Public Reason and the Rule of Law," in *The Rule of Law,* ed. Ian Shapiro, *Nomos* 36 (New York: New York University Press, 1994), 338.

12. Gaus is willing, for example, to grant that a citizen can be openly justified in adhering to the Catholic doctrine of transubstantiation, so he should have no problem granting that Jerry can be openly justified in believing that the Bible is reliable. See *JL*, 52.

13. Perhaps, though, Gaus would respond that he is willing to idealize away from an agent's claim C only if she regards compromise by prejudice or ignorance as epistemically problematic such that, were she *not* to regard compromise by prejudice or ignorance as epistemically problematic, then idealization in the relevant respects would be inappropriate. So it is only the fact that a given agent regards compromise by prejudice as unreliable that warrants us to idealize in that respect. So far as I can tell, this understanding of the conditions in which idealization is appropriate avoids incoherence but at the steep price of veering sharply in the direction of justificatory populism. Given Gaus's conviction that respect requires that all citizens be provided with good reason for government restrictions, and given an unwillingness to idealize away from the convictions of those citizens who do not regard compromise by prejudice as epistemically troubling, it seems that Gaus is committed to the proposition that the most (epistemically) perverse among us exercise veto power over the moral propriety of our support for government restrictions. We disrespect *them* if we insist on supporting restrictions that they reject, but solely because they are untroubled by prejudices that lead them to reject those restrictions. This seems morally wrong: why should the policies that it is reasonable and respectful for *me* to support be held hostage to the predilections of the most perverse and prejudiced among us?

14. Well, okay. Perhaps some truths of logic and some kinds of introspective claims are exempt from compromise by prejudice and ignorance.

15. Robert Audi seems to accept some such account.

> According to this view, coercing a person, S, for reason P, to perform an action A, in circumstances C, is fully justified if and only if at least the following three conditions hold in C: (a) S morally ought to A in C, for example to abstain from stealing from others (perhaps someone has a right, in the circumstances, against S that S A—certainly a feature of most cases in which a liberal democracy can reasonably coerce its citizens); (b) if fully rational and adequately informed about the situation, S would see that (a) holds and would, for reason R (say a sense of how theft creates mistrust and chaos, or for some essentially related reason), perform A, or at least tend to A; (c) A is both an "important" kind of action (as opposed to breaking a casual promise to meet for lunch at the usual place) and one that may be reasonably believed to affect someone else (and perhaps not of a highly personal kind at all). ("The Place of Religious Argument in a Free and Democratic Society," 689)

16. God is, Elijah assumes, an omniscient being and so cannot be wrong in God's moral commitments. Hence, to be unaware of a source of information about an omniscient being's moral commitments is to be desperately ignorant.

9 RELIGIOUS CONVICTIONS AND PUBLIC DISCOURSE

RICHARD J. MOUW

In 1996 the Roman Catholic ethicist Bryan Hehir reported a shift that had been taking place in his thinking about the role of explicitly theological language in addressing the issues of public life:

> My own long-term posture, undoubtedly shaped by Catholic reliance on natural law, has been to support John Courtney Murray's position that when speaking to the state, the church must use a language the state can comprehend. I remain persuaded of the wisdom of this position, but in surveying the principally social policy debates of the 1990s, I am also struck by the limits of the ethical, that is to say the failure of purely moral argument to address underlying dimensions of our public policy disputes and decisions.[1]

Hehir wasn't ready simply to dispense with a reliance on the "purely moral" in Christian efforts to foster a healthy public debate. But he had come to see more clearly, he confessed, the importance of some key "premoral convictions that must be addressed to confront the societal questions we face today." And Hehir went on to suggest that when it comes to connecting these convictions to important public policy matters, "the comparative advantage is with communities that are convinced of the kind of theological truths the Christian community takes for granted. These are embedded convictions—capable of being articulated, so not unintelligible for public discourse."[2]

This willingness, albeit a guarded one, to introduce theologically explicit language into public discourse may signal only a modest shift within Hehir's own personal perspective in recent years. Even so, it is not an isolated case—it fits into a larger pattern of change that has occurred within Roman Catholic thought during the past several decades. This can be seen already, for example, in the "peace pastoral" issued by the U.S. Catholic bishops in 1983. In announcing that they meant to address their call to peacemaking to both "the Catholic faithful" and "the wider civil community, a more pluralistic audience,"[3] the bishops stated clearly that they saw no alternative but to ground their appeal "solidly in the biblical vision of the kingdom of God"[4]:

> We believe the religious vision has an objective basis and is capable of progressive realization. Christ is our peace, for he has "made us both one, and has broken down the dividing wall of hostility . . . that he might make in himself one new man in the place of the two, so making peace, and might reconcile us both to God" (Eph. 2:14–16). We also know that this peace will be achieved fully only in the kingdom of God.[5]

To be sure, the bishops did not only employ biblical language. In making their case—an effort in which Hehir played a key role as an active advisor to the bishops—they acknowledged the importance of using "two complementary styles of teaching": one for those who share their faith convictions and the other for those who are not Christian believers, but who are nonetheless "equally bound by certain key moral principles."[6] But it is also obvious that their peacemaking message relied much more extensively on explicitly biblical themes than was the case in previous Catholic documents of this sort.

I. Criticizing "Thinness"

The kind of approach exemplified in the bishops' document—wherein biblical and "purely moral" languages are taken to be "complementary"—has been subjected to sustained criticism in recent decades. The charge against a heavy reliance by Christians on a "thin" language of public discourse[7] has been led by Stanley

Hauerwas, who rejects the notion that terms like "justice" and "peace" have core meanings that are understandable from a variety of perspectives. How can Christians give meaning to such terms, Hauerwas asks, "apart from the life and death of Jesus of Nazareth"? It is the biblical narrative regarding Jesus' mission that "gives content to our faith, judges any institutional embodiment of our faith, and teaches us to be suspicious of any political slogan that does not need God to make itself credible."[8]

Hauerwas's views on these matters have had an important impact on contemporary debates, including Catholic ones, over the appropriate patterns of Christian involvement in public life. Michael Baxter, a self-described "Catholic radicalist," has used Hauerwas's perspective specifically to criticize what he sees as some dangerous tendencies in Catholic social thought. Baxter is especially concerned about the way in which "Catholic social ethics today continues to posit a separation between theology and social theory," and he argues that this separation is traceable to two prominent influences. One is the understanding of the relationship of religion to practical politics that was set forth in the nineteenth century by Max Weber: according to this view, religion posits "a lofty vision of ultimate ends," in which certain ideals are set forth, as in the Sermon on the Mount, that are considered unrealizable in this present life; and while the Weberians concede that it is good to be inspired by these ideals, they still want practical politics to be pursued "within the domain of the state to ensure that the ethical means be appropriate to real-life circumstances."[9]

Baxter sees this "Weberian paradigm" as having been firmly wedded in recent Catholic thought to a second pernicious influence, namely, "John Courtney Murray's project of providing the nation with a 'public philosophy' (or now, a 'public theology') to which all in a pluralistic society can appeal."[10] He acknowledges that "Murray was more ready and able than his predecessors to import theological terms and categories into his social theory"; nonetheless, Baxter argues, Murray's overall approach was such "that his theology effaced itself as it moved into the realm of the natural and the social."[11] Murray's theological appeals function mainly "to reinforce the premise of the primacy of the spiritual order, a premise that serves to reinforce the existence of another order set aside solely for temporal affairs—the affairs of politics, the state, civil law, public discourse—wherein the language of faith yields to the language of reason and natural law."[12] The net result, then, is that "references to Christ, the sacraments, scripture, the saints, and other tradition-specific theological terms and categories" are segregated off so that they "do not easily conform to the discursive protocols of the modern liberal state."[13]

While Baxter does not single out either Hehir's writings or the American bishops' declarations on social policy issues for explicit criticism, there is no reason to think that he sees them as a serious improvement on Murray's approach. Their approach clearly does not honor what Baxter's "Catholic radicalism" treats as a fundamental assumption for faithful Christian social witness, specifically, "that Christian discipleship entails a form of life that is embedded in the beliefs and practices of the Church and therefore cannot serve as the basis for universal, supra-ecclesial ethical principles that are then applied in making public policy."[14]

Baxter does acknowledge in passing that there is an increased interest these days among Christian scholars, including the sorts of Catholic thinkers who are sympathetic to the overall patterns of Christian social thought established by John Courtney Murray, in developing a "public theology." At first glance it may seem odd that Baxter does not give more sympathetic attention to this phenomenon as at least a step in the right direction, given his insistence that theological categories should have primacy over—possibly even eliminating the need for—purely philosophical ones in addressing questions of public life. But Baxter does not take the references to "theology" in "public theology" discussions at face value. "Public theology," he insists, must be "unmasked" as an "ideology" that bestows its blessing on the workings of "the modern nation-state" and the "capitalist culture" that it sustains.[15]

The use of the word "public" in these discussions, says Baxter, simply hides the fact that

> the mechanisms of the state have never really been "public" for much of the population—the ones who live in shelters and S.R.O.'s, who work the fields or sweep the floors at McDonald's, who live a pay check away from eviction, who are not counted in the census, who live in constant economic depression. Similar criticisms could be made of notions like "freedom," "justice," "the common good," "civil society," and "the limited state," words or phrases that conceal the dehumanizing world of those who live on the bottom fifth of "our society." Public theologians, of course, respond that this is the situation that they seek to reform, which would seem to be a worthy task; but this kind of reformist agenda only serves to reinforce the assumption that the only effective mechanism for implementing justice in the modern world is the modern state.[16]

It would be difficult to fault Baxter for calling attention to the needs of the seriously disadvantaged, and for asking whether those scholars who are commending this or that approach to public policy issues are paying adequate attention to those needs. Beyond that, though, his brief treatment of public theology discussions is seriously misleading, especially when he contends that those discussions are based on the premise that the state is "the only effective mechanism for implementing justice." Actually, the emergence of "public theology" as a way of exploring justice issues has been explicitly linked by its advocates to an insistence that any Christian approach will be inadequate if it concentrates too narrowly on "official" political processes. By choosing to focus broadly on "public" life, the public theologians have insisted that there is a vast and complex territory that lies between the individual and the state. They want to emphasize the importance of those contexts for human association that extend beyond the realm of kinship but are not yet—or at least they ought *not* to be—swallowed up by the "political." And they are especially interested in how the Christian community can effectively address this broader public agenda.

There is much in this public theology discussion, then, that should be encouraging to Michael Baxter and other "Catholic radicalists." The Christian promotion of strong voluntary associations would seem to be an important strategy for defending the concerns of the marginalized groups that Baxter mentions in his critique of the standard liberal democratic definitions of "public." Public theology discussions have not encouraged the notion that we can rely on statist programs alone for eliminating poverty, economic depression, or social disadvantages. Nor have they inspired many sermons proclaiming individual initiative as a solution. Instead, they have made much of strengthening families, neighborhoods, churches, and service organizations—all of which, presumably, would fit well with the goals of Catholic radicalism.

But, while it seems obvious that Baxter's rejection of public theology as mere ideology is much too sweeping, it is likely that he would still have serious objections to some of the themes that are advocated by public theologians, even if he were to engage their views with a more generous spirit. Indeed, one point of disagreement seems certain, namely, the willingness of many Christian social theorists to appeal to what he describes as "universal, supra-ecclesial ethical principles" when addressing questions of public policy.

Keeping in mind these important matters that have been debated in recent Catholic thought, I will look now in some detail at the Calvinist perspective that Nicholas Wolterstorff has defended throughout his career. Wolterstorff has given much attention to how Christians can address issues of public policy, both in his popular writings and in his more technical philosophical explorations. His overall perspective provides, as I will show, a kind of mediating position between Baxter's position and the views of those Catholic thinkers whom Baxter criticizes. My main reason for wanting to lay out the basic contours of Wolterstorff's view is that I am convinced that it has distinct advantages over the positions defended by Baxter and his opponents. But I will also point to a few matters where I think Wolterstorff's views about public discourse need some further amplification.

II. Working "within the Structures"

Wolterstorff addressed a position very much like Baxter's in the late 1970s. Earlier in that decade a new interest in social activism had emerged within evangelical Protestantism. While this particular expression of social concern was united in its focus on poverty, militarism, and racial justice—unlike the agenda of the "Christian Right" movement that was to gain considerable attention a decade later—it soon became clear that there were also some important theological differences at play. Some of the most prominent disagreements were between Jim Wallis and the other editors of *Sojourners* magazine, who looked for inspiration to the Anabaptist tradition—especially as it had been recently reformulated for the contemporary context in John Howard Yoder's influential book *The Politics of Jesus*[17]—and the Calvinist perspective set forth in the pages of *The Reformed Journal,* where Wolterstorff served as an editor.

In the October 1977 issue of *The Reformed Journal,* Wolterstorff laid out some of the key elements in his Reformed perspective, in response to the ways in which the differences between Calvinists and Anabaptists had been depicted in a recent *Sojourners* editorial (likely written by Jim Wallis). Among other things, Wolterstorff provided a Reformed reading of the Pauline understanding of the role of the state, as set forth in Romans 13, arguing that while obedience to civil authority was not simply "a matter of ultimate prudence, but of *right,*" this does not require obedience under all circumstances, since "[t]here are times when disobedience is not only allowed but demanded."[18]

Wolterstorff also questioned the ways in which Anabaptists and others often attempt to ground Christian social involvement in the *imitatio Christi.* While the call to imitate Christ is certainly a "dominant theme in the New Testament epistles," he observed, there is "no way of understanding the significance of Jesus Christ except to see in him God working effectively for the renewal of his creation." If we see that "the renewal of creation [is] the purpose of redemption . . . then the fact that Jesus never ran for political office does not become an objection to running for political office, any more than the fact that he never heard a piano concerto becomes an objection to listening to piano concertos."[19]

But Wolterstorff was obviously most vexed by the charge, in the words he quoted from the *Sojourners* editorial, that *The Reformed Journal's* stance . . . is one of moderate to liberal reform of existing structures, using a "realistic" approach which accepts the fundamental values and the basic framework of the American system of economics and politics. Thus, beneath all the doctrinal assertions, what one finds is the theological version of traditional Western liberalism.[20]

This kind of attack on "realism" and "strategic effectiveness," Wolterstorff reported, "seems to me to exhibit a crucial confusion." Unless we are willing to work for "total revolution," what alternative do we have but to work for justice within the existing political and economic structures of American life? It certainly doesn't follow, he argued, from an advocacy of working within the present system "that we accept the structure of American politics and economics as fundamentally right." Indeed

[t]he *Sojourners* community, living as it does in Washington, D.C., likewise makes all its decisions within the basic framework of American society, using the American system of communications, the American system of food production and distribution, the American system of transportation, and so forth. That does not entail that they *accept* all those structures, or regard them all as basically the way things should be, needing only a bit of tinkering here and there. Not at all. To work within a structure to alleviate the evils it causes and to change it wherever one can for the better is not to accept that structure as fundamentally good.[21]

III. Christianity and the Liberal State

It is not difficult to extrapolate from Wolterstorff's response to the *Sojourners* editorial what he would say to Michael Baxter's insistence that the "Weberian paradigm" has no place in a Christian body of social teaching. Baxter thinks that there is something deeply misguided about saying as Christians that the Bible sets forth "ideals" that are unattainable in a "real" world where politics typically means looking for practical ways of achieving limited goals. Wolterstorff's assessment of that kind of attack on "realism" is summarized in this blunt comment in his 1977 article: "The fact that the politics of earth is not the harmony of heaven renders neither irrelevant nor illegitimate our engagement in that politics."[22]

But Wolterstorff would actually have considerable sympathy for the second element in Baxter's criticism—his worries about the tendency in John Courtney Murray and other Catholic thinkers to believe that "the language of faith yields to the language of reason and natural law" when it comes time to abide by "the discursive protocols of the modern liberal state."[23] For the fact is that Wolterstorff himself has serious questions about the protocols that modern liberalism often attempts to impose upon Christians in the public arena.

For example, in an essay in which he exposits and defends Abraham Kuyper's perspective on pluralistic democracy, Wolterstorff contrasts Kuyper's views with what he sets forth as seven key theses of "political liberalism." One of the liberal theses that he spends considerable time discussing is the one he labels the "'independent basis' thesis," which implies that

> [c]itizens must be prepared to conduct their public debates concerning the scheme of constitutional and legal rights, and to make their decisions concerning that scheme, on the basis of deliverances of some source of relevant principles which is not only independent of all the comprehensive religious and philosophical perspectives to be found in society, but is one to which all normal adult citizens (or prospective citizens, in the case of constitutional debates) can rightly be required to appeal for this purpose.[24]

Wolterstorff notes that this independent basis has been defended in a variety of ways: Locke, for example, appealed to rational standards to which, he was convinced, all humans have access, while Rawls and other contemporaries, having become skeptical about appeals to a universal Reason, propose that we can extract the necessary principles from a Hegelian-type "governing Idea of one's extant liberal society."[25]

The fundamental error underlying all such proposed bases for positing the independent basis, Wolterstorff argues, is the assumption that in dealing with important issues of human life, "religion is an add-on, in principle if not always in practice." This means that while

> citizens, in their public debates and their decisions concerning issues of constitutionality and basic justice, may, if they wish, use arguments drawn from their comprehensive religious or philosophical perspectives, they must [still] always be prepared to offer arguments drawn from the independent source. Religious arguments, though not disallowed, may only function as dispensable add-ons.[26]

Wolterstorff continues his critique of liberalism in his book-length debate with Robert Audi over the propriety of employing religious discourse in the public arena. While he acknowledges here that he endorses "the Idea of liberal democracy" as a way of structuring political life, he refuses to accept "the liberal thesis" that is often considered to be necessitated by the acceptance of liberal democratic patterns, namely, "that the role of citizen in a liberal democracy includes a restraint on the use of reasons, derived from one's religion, for one's decisions and discussions on political issues, and a requirement that citizens instead use an independent source."[27]

IV. The Independent Source Requirement

Wolterstorff's critique of the liberal thesis, and his exposition of his own alternative perspective, covers considerable territory. For my purposes here, I will briefly list some key considerations he raises in his critique of the independent source requirement of liberalism.

First, Wolterstorff firmly rejects the independent source requirement on epistemological grounds. From the perspective of the "Reformed epistemology" developed in recent years by Wolterstorff and others,[28] it is not the case that a person is entitled to hold a belief only if that belief would be accepted by all rational persons who consult an independent source. Entitlement to a belief is, the Reformed epistemologists hold, a more complicated business than that. When considering whether a person is entitled to hold to a specific belief, we must also take into account information about the person who is holding the belief, as well as that person's situatedness.[29] While this is not meant to encourage a relativistic understanding of human disagreement, it does emphasize the ways in which our beliefs have to be seen as immersed in the complexities of our specific circumstances. This means that the liberal hope of finding a common rational space in which we each are stripped of our particularities is not only impossible, but also such that we should not even *regret* the fact that it is unattainable.

Second, even if there were an independent source that was in principle available to all citizens, regardless of their substantive views about the basic issues of life, it is not clear that it would play the role in decision making that the liberal theorists want it to. It is a fact of human life that we are influenced by our deepest individual convictions about what life is all about. It is impossible for us simply to "leap out of our perspectives" on reality.[30] The liberal search for "a politics that is the politics of a community with a shared perspective" is, says Wolterstorff, "hopeless and misguided. We must learn to live with a politics of multiple communities."[31] Given this state of affairs, the best course is to encourage citizens to articulate the *actual* reasons that shape their views about public life, rather than to engage in an artificial—and misleading—thinning-out of them.

And, third, even if such a thinning-out could be accomplished on a fairly regular basis, what reason do we have to believe that this would be *beneficial* for our life together as people representing a variety of perspectives on the basic issues of life? "We need," Wolterstorff insists, "a politics that not only honors us in our similarity as free and equal, but in our particularities. For our particularities—some of them—are constitutive of who we are, constitutive of our narrative identities." And this honoring of particularities will actually serve to "enrich our common life," as we are encouraged to explain to each other how we view the issues of public concern from within our own perspectives.[32]

The advantages of Wolterstorff's position over the kind advocated by Baxter are, I think, relatively easy to demonstrate. While Baxter's basic position on the need for thick language—like that of both Hauerwas and the *Sojourners* community—is quite compatible with the analysis of entitled basic beliefs offered by Reformed epistemology, he pays little attention to the larger question of societal pluralism. The public theologians whom Baxter criticizes are attempting to make a case for a healthy pluralism. Rather than taking seriously their efforts to foster a variety of voluntary associations in the context of which the development of diverse thick discourses would be able to flourish, however, he simply dismisses their project as nothing but an ideological reinforcement of the liberal state.

Like Baxter, Wolterstorff wants the Christian community to employ the thick discourse of Christian particularity in addressing public issues. But like the public theologians, and unlike Baxter, Wolterstorff also insists that this address can happen properly only within the framework of societal pluralism. He sees the encouragement of diverse communities of thick particularity as crucial for healthy public order. And although in the writings I have cited he regularly uses the term "public" as if its range of application is coextensive with "political," there can be no mistaking his conviction that political well-being requires a flourishing public life that extends far beyond politics narrowly understood. Furthermore, in his sustained critique of both Lockean and Rawlsian conceptions of the independent source, as well as in the careful way he distinguishes between a posture of governmental neutrality toward religious diversity (a stance that he thinks is not really possible) and one of governmental impartiality (which he defends), Wolterstorff goes well beyond the recent writings on public theology in making a detailed case for a flourishing public order.

Wolterstorff's position also has important advantages over the contemporary versions of the Catholic natural law perspective. His critique of liberalism's independent source notion, for example, obviously applies also to Bryan Hehir's continuing fondness for appealing to the "purely moral" in public debates. But Wolterstorff does share with the present-day followers of John Courtney Murray a strong desire to speak effectively to the issues of public life, and in doing so to engage people of other perspectives in a genuine dialogue about issues of common concern. It is important, then, that we are clear about the real differences between his position and the Catholic public philosophers.

V. A Not-So-Thick Discourse?

In his contribution to a 1979 symposium on the relative merits of Catholic public philosophy and theology in shaping the Christian address to public policy questions, Hehir conceded a number of key points to the defenders of a public theology approach. But he still insisted on an important continuing role for a Murray-type public philosophy, not only as a proper answer to "the epistemological question of how we speak intelligently in a pluralistic setting," but also because of "the need for mediating language which can move between the richness of biblical symbolism or theological affirmation and the empirical density of the complex technical issues" which have to be addressed in contemporary public life.[33] Hehir does not provide illustrations of mediating language here, but it is not difficult to think of what he has in mind. The sorts of Roman Catholic policy documents that he has long been involved in formulating provide clear examples. On the one hand, there is the thick language of the Bible by which Christ's disciples are called to be peacemakers. On the other hand, there are the technical descriptions of currently available military weaponry. In order to make the connections between the thick call to peacemaking and concrete recommendations regarding the use of specific military technology, one must employ the language of, say, Just War doctrine: we must avoid strategies that directly target civilian populations; the means that we use must be proportionate to the ends that we seek; the ends themselves must be evaluated with respect to whether they conform to principles of justice and are designed to restore peaceful conditions; and so on.

Hehir is obviously pointing to an important concern, one that must also be addressed from the perspective that Wolterstorff defends. It does not strike me that the notion of a "mediating language" in any way violates the principles of Reformed epistemology. But if it does, something else in the neighborhood should be explored, since there does seem to be a need, in dealing with issues of public policy, to employ a vocabulary that is not quite as thick as that which characterizes our ordinary religious conversations.

Indeed, Wolterstorff himself regularly employs this not-quite-so-thick language in talking about the patterns of public life. And what he says when he is employing this discourse is often not very different from things that are said by thinkers with whom he obviously disagrees on the level of thick convictions. For example, when Wolterstorff makes his case for pluralism, what he says is not all that different from how John Stuart Mill argues for respecting diverse particularities in our societal life. Here is Mill:

> It is not by wearing down into uniformity all that is individual in themselves, but by cultivating it and calling it forth, within the limits imposed by the rights and limits of others, that human beings become a noble and beautiful object of contemplation; and as the works partake the character of those who do them, by the same process human life also becomes rich, diversified, and animating, furnishing more abundant aliment to high thoughts and elevating feelings, and strengthening the tie which binds every individual to the race, by making the race infinitely better worth belonging to.[34]

Of course, Mill and Wolterstorff are arguing out of very different worldviews—indeed Mill offers this particular formulation in a context where he also renders a harsh verdict on the Calvinist understanding of human nature![35] But in spelling out his somewhat different grounds for encouraging diversity, Wolterstorff still uses language that is not explicitly Christian and is quite similar to Mill's. Like Mill, for example, he insists that this diversity must be fostered "within the limits imposed by the rights and limits of others." Wolterstorff spells out his own view of these limits by delineating three kinds of restraints that are necessary for "the citizen of a liberal democracy": we must all "show respect for the other person" in the ways in which we make our case on any given topic; our "debates, except in extreme circumstances, are to be conducted and resolved in accord with the rules provided by the laws of the land and the provisions of the Constitution"; and in making our case we must aim at achieving justice rather than merely a balance of diverse interests.[36]

All of this seems to be taking place in the "mediating language" territory. Of course, when we begin to ask how these restraint descriptions are grounded, we do need to look at the basic convictions that are at work. For example, Wolterstorff refuses to see them as requiring a commitment to "the Idea of liberal democracy." Grounding them in that Idea cannot be accomplished, he says, "without controversy": while some liberals think that the taming of competing interests is the primary goal of political debate, he observes, others insist that the political process should be "governed only by respect for the freedom and equality of citizens." The differences here will not be settled simply by appealing to the liberal

Idea. In dealing with such matters, Wolterstorff insists, "we cannot leap out of our perspectives."[37]

Fair enough. But disagreements about the point of the political process show up in the Christian community as well. Wolterstorff's contention that justice—and not a mere taming of competing interests—is the proper aim of political debate is certainly not without controversy within the Christian tradition. Indeed, it is not without controversy within the *Calvinist* tradition, where the taming of competing interests has often been taken to be the proper and sole aim of the political process. The view of the Calvinist philosopher Gordon Clark is an especially poignant case in this regard, since Clark seems simply to *equate* justice with the taming of diverse interests: God introduced political authority into human affairs, says Clark, only because of the need to control "a large number of evil people working at cross purposes."[38]

How would Wolterstorff respond to Gordon Clark? I have no doubt that he could marshal impressive arguments drawing on biblical sources. But I also have no doubt that Clark would remain unconvinced, since he would understand the biblical references to justice cited by Wolterstorff in rather negative and remedial terms—for Clark, doing justice primarily consists in seeing to it that evildoers are punished and that orderly patterns of societal life are maintained.

Here is what I think is actually going on when Wolterstorff argues with a fellow Calvinist like Gordon Clark. It seems obvious to me that Clark is combining certain Calvinist emphases—original sin, the teaching in Romans 13 about the "ordaining" of the government's use of the sword—with a Hobbesian kind of view about the role of government and an Adam Smith-type perspective on economics, with the result that he interprets the biblical call to justice primarily in remedial and "taming" terms. In responding to that brand of Calvinism, Wolterstorff wants to emphasize themes in his reading of the biblical justice passages that echo those long associated with liberal social thought, with its positive respect for all persons and for the promotion of basic human rights.

As a Reformed epistemologist, of course, Wolterstorff does not accept the ways in which liberal thinkers attempt to *ground* these convictions. And so he explores the biblical and theological resources available to him to find ways of articulating a case for a conception of justice that features respect for human dignity and an advocacy on behalf of the poor and the oppressed. In doing so, though, he is working with philosophical clues that he has received from a larger intellectual conversation, which are different from the philosophical clues that have influenced Clark. And that seems to me a good thing. Many of the confusions of a Clark-type version of Calvinism are philosophical ones that have been critiqued in helpful ways by non-Christian philosophers in their arguments with each other. From those conversations Christians can learn of things that we need to place on our own agenda, so that we can find uniquely Christian ways of articulating the case for taking such things seriously. And in this process it is beneficial for us to engage in conversations where we employ a less-than-fully-thick "mediating" discourse.

VI. Explaining Commonalities

Wolterstorff does not give explicit attention to this Calvinist emphasis on commonalities in his discussions of public discourse. But he clearly does not mean to depict a state of affairs where each of us is held captive in our own perspectival ghetto, with little capacity for engaging in intelligent conversations across the boundaries established by our deepest convictions. He does encourage Christians to listen carefully in the public arena to people of other religions, even allowing ourselves to be "enriched" by what we hear.[39]

But for the most part Wolterstorff concentrates on differences rather than commonalities. And it is easy to see why. He has taken on the very important task of countering the bias, deeply entrenched especially among cultural elites, against the appeal to religious particularities in public policy debates. He has made an impressive—indeed, I think compelling—case for encouraging thick discourse in the public square.

His focus on differences is nicely exemplified in his response to Robert Audi's attempt to look for Christian reasons to posit a moral framework that both believers and nonbelievers can take for granted. Like many other Christian thinkers who have looked more kindly than Wolterstorff does on the epistemology that has undergirded political liberalism, Audi emphasizes the need for Christians to find common ground with their non-Christian fellow citizens. What is wrong with thinking, Audi asks, that perhaps God made an independent source available to all human beings, so that together we can discern important moral truths that can facilitate our common life?

Wolterstorff responds by pointing to the reality of sin. The problem with Audi's proposal, he says, is that it is put

> exclusively in terms of creation, not at all in terms of fallenness. We do not exist in a pristine state. We all live east of Eden. We, one and all, are all mucked up, not only in our actions but in our beliefs on moral mat-

ters. Though God may indeed have provided paths, we have all, like sheep, gone astray.[40]

Wolterstorff makes a predictable—and laudable—Calvinist move here. Reformed Christians have placed a strong emphasis on what has traditionally been called "the noetic effects of sin." Human fallenness has affected the totality of our being, so that there is no aspect of our humanness that escapes the corrupting power of sin. In the Kuyperian tradition from which Wolterstorff takes many of his clues, this has been expressed in an emphasis on "the antithesis" between Christian and non-Christian thought: the regenerate person who seeks to understand all of reality in the light of divine revelation will inevitably think about the important issues of life in ways that run counter to how reality is seen from other basic perspectives.[41] Wolterstorff has rightly wanted to do justice to this emphasis, not only in his epistemological explorations but in his views about public life. Christians must approach the public square, he has insisted, with the expectation that they will encounter there very different belief systems, and must therefore advocate a framework of societal pluralism in which we all—as much as possible—are allowed to live out our fundamental convictions.

Again, this emphasis on diversity is an important one. But there is more that must be said from a Reformed perspective. It is one thing to insist, as Wolterstorff does in responding to Audi, that we not view human beings "exclusively in terms of creation," thereby disregarding the diversity that emerges out of our religious and other differences. But it is another simply to emphasize human sinfulness in a way that ignores the possibility of discovering commonalities—including the possibility of shared understandings of our common life.

John Calvin himself found it necessary to account for both difference and commonality. He certainly was often quite harsh in his comments about the unregenerate person's capacity for discovering truth. The sinful mind, he says, is typically "choked with dense ignorance, so that it cannot come forth effectively"; plagued by a spiritual "dullness," it "cannot hold to the right path, but wanders through various errors and stumbles repeatedly, as if it were groping in the darkness. . . . Thus it betrays how incapable it is of seeking and finding truth."[42]

But Calvin is not always so pessimistic about the "natural mind." He held some of the ancient Roman writers in high regard, and it was probably with their contributions in mind that he acknowledged "a universal apprehension of reason and understanding [that] is by nature implanted in men," which, "because it is bestowed indiscriminately upon pious and impious, it is rightly counted among natural gifts"; indeed, he insists, every human being ought to recognize this implanted rational nature as a "peculiar grace of God."[43] And when we do observe this gift at work in "secular writers," Calvin urges Christians to

> let that admirable light of truth shining in them teach us that the mind of man, though fallen and perverted from its wholeness, is nevertheless clothed and ornamented with God's excellent gifts. If we regard the Spirit of God as the sole fountain of truth, we shall neither reject the truth itself, nor despise it where it shall appear, unless we wish to dishonor the Spirit of God. . . . Those men whom Scripture [1 Cor. 2:14] calls "natural men" were, indeed, sharp and penetrating in their investigation of inferior things. Let us, accordingly, learn by their example how many gifts the Lord left to human nature even after it was despoiled of its true good.[44]

Abraham Kuyper also put considerable weight on commonalities between Christians and non-Christians, even to the point of insisting that in moral matters all human beings are accountable to a common set of norms. There is, he said, a "firm moral world-order" that "remains just what it was from the beginning. It lays full claim, not only to the believer (as though less were required from the unbeliever), but to every human being and to all human relationships."[45]

VII. The Larger Calvinist Picture

While it is understandable that this emphasis on commonalities does not get much play in Wolterstorff's discussions of public life, it does mean that one does not get the whole Reformed picture from what he discusses. And the rest of the picture is important for our present context, especially the emphasis on commonality.

One reason is simply the horrible record of Christians in the past of exploiting the fact of differences to reinforce religious intolerance. Christians have often been unspeakably cruel to other people—including other Christians—in the public square. And Reformed Christians loom large in the gallery of mean-spirited religious types. As Jeffrey Stoutly has rightly observed, the growth of liberal institutions in the West has been necessitated in large part by "the manifold failure of religious groups of various sorts to establish rational agreement on their competing detailed visions of the good."[46] Because of the past sins committed by people who took religious differences with utmost seriousness, Christians today have a special obligation to contribute to the search for commonalities, even as we explore the legitimate role of diversity in contemporary pluralistic societies.

Furthermore, our actual practice shows more of a reliance on commonalities than we sometimes acknowledge in our theorizing. The fact is that people with different fundamental convictions do actually manage to communicate quite effectively with each other in the public square—a little better, certainly, than some Reformed views might suggest. Yes, we have, all of us, gone astray like lost sheep— and we have strayed along different paths in our diverse moral and religious wanderings. For all of that, however, we do succeed in understanding each other on a regular basis when we talk about important issues. Again, Jeffrey Stout:

> Don't we in fact muddle through much of the time, quite reasonably, by appealing to areas of agreement with our fellow citizens, by practicing immanent criticism on our opponents or on ourselves, by coming to terms with unfamiliar vocabularies in conversation, by using our creative powers, by confronting the moral imagination with instances of injustice and suffering, and by, in countless other ways, exploiting a culture too rich and complicated to be confined to a canon?[47]

And it is a good thing that we can find these "areas of agreement with our fellow citizens," given some of the urgent matters we must address together. June O'Connor makes this case nicely in her discussion of a decade of United Nations *Human Development Reports*. These studies contain, she observes, obvious "points of connection and shared values," not only with "the religious vocabulary of the Christian common good tradition" but also with the teachings "promoted by many religions: the dignity of the person both female and male, the good of the community, the importance of attention to and engagement of the poor and powerless in the life of the society, the significance of using the earth's resources appreciatively and wisely in gratitude and as a legacy to future generations."[48] In espousing these things, the UN perspective "appeals to the moral sensibilities of persons and communities which do not share metaphysical or theological worldviews but which do share common value commitments to the dignity and freedom of the human person, and to social justice and stewardship of the earth's resources."[49]

Calvinists will likely struggle a little more than O'Connor is inclined to do in exploring the possibility of finding "common value commitments" on such matters. But we cannot *care* any less about a quest that has such important stakes for the human community.

VIII. Humility and Hope

In the July 2002 issue of *Harper's Magazine*, Stanley Fish responded at length to critics who had been arguing in opinion pieces in various popular media that the destruction of September 11, 2001, had finally exposed the superficiality of the views attributed to the "postmodernists." He was particularly exercised by the charge that he and others had been teaching that it is impossible to say whether one person's views on important matters are "truer" than another's.

Fish responds to this characterization with the insistence that he does indeed believe in an objective truth. "The problem is not that there is no universal," he says; "the universal, the absolutely true, exists, and I know what it is. The problem is that you know it, too, and that we know different things." This leaves us in a predicament where we are both "armed with universal judgments that are irreconcilable, all dressed up with nowhere to go for an authoritative adjudication." We are "finite situated human beings," Fish reminds his readers, and so

> [w]e have to live with the knowledge of two things: that we are absolutely right and that there is no generally accepted measure by which our rightness can be independently validated. That's just the way it is, and we should just get on with it, acting in accordance with our true beliefs (what else could we do!) without expecting that some God will descend, like the duck in the old Groucho Marx TV show, and tell us that we have uttered the true and secret word.[50]

A good part of what Fish sets forth in these brief remarks is also the stuff of Reformed epistemology. We are finite. We do believe in the truth of what we affirm—and in the falsity of the claims made by people with whom we disagree. And there is no independent source available to us that will allow us decisively to adjudicate our disagreements.

Christian philosophers, however, will want to think very seriously about the implications of what for Fish is a throwaway line: his lighthearted reference to God. We believe that there really is a God, and this God does have access to all that is necessary to decide between competing interpretations of reality. This acknowledgment sheds important light on what Christians mean when they criticize the idea of an independent source. Strictly speaking, what we must reject is a specific *understanding* of the independent source, namely, the notion that human beings can arrive—by stripping ourselves of the particularities of our thick situatedness—at a perspective that will allow all of us together to form uncontestable assessments of the truth of things.

This is not possible for the very reason that Fish insists upon: we are finite, situated human beings. But God, as the omniscient and omnipresent One, is neither finite nor situated. And so we can get on with it—just as Fish encourages us to do—but with the deep conviction that there is Someone who has the answers, and that though we presently "see in a mirror, dimly," we will someday "see face to face" (1 Cor. 13:12).

Rousseau had the right sort of perspective in mind when he wrote this in *The Social Contract:*

The task of discovering the best laws, i.e., those that are most salutary for each nation, calls for a mind of the highest order. This mind would have insight into each and every human passion, and *yet* be affected by none. It would be superhuman, and *yet* understand human nature through and through. It would be willing to concern itself with our happiness, but would seek its own outside us. It would be content with fame far off in the future; i.e., it would be capable of laboring in one century and reaping its reward in the next.

And, then, lest we miss the theological lesson, he immediately made it explicit: "Law-giving is a task for gods not men."[51]

The belief in the existence of an all-knowing, all-wise God is what undergirds Wolterstorff's prescriptions regarding the proper patterns of public discourse. It is precisely because we are finite beings—and if that were not bad enough, fallen ones as well—that we must take a rather modest approach to human knowing. God alone knows all things. We humans are mere creatures of God, limited, both individually and collectively, to our finite places in the larger scheme of things. As Arthur Holmes has put it, the appropriate posture for people who see things in this way is *epistemic humility.* But Holmes further observes that because we look forward to a Final Accounting, we can also cultivate *epistemic hope,* so that "[h]umility and hope thus combine in a creational view to avoid both the dogma of the rationalist and the pessimism of the relativist."[52] And in the meantime we learn to live with multiple perspectives, multiple public discourses.

The fact that we do look forward to something more in our epistemic quest should actually give us some sympathies for the defenders of an independent source, as they reach for a point of view that transcends our finite ways of seeing and thinking. Their error does not lie in their refusal to accept our limited vision as all that is available in the universe. Rather, they go wrong in thinking that if we just make the right cognitive moves we can gain access to the requisite independent source. This is a vain hope. It is to grasp for that which only God possesses.

While those who want to eliminate our present perspectival multiplicity by seeking out an independent source are looking for the wrong sort of thing, the underlying yearnings that motivate their quest are not completely wrongheaded. Or perhaps it is better to say, taking our clue from Augustine's well-known prayer, that their yearnings are not completely wrong*hearted:* for our hearts—including our public-minded hearts—are indeed restless until they rest in the One whose knowledge is too wonderful for the likes of us.

NOTES

1. J. Bryan Hehir, "Personal Faith, the Public Church, and the Role of Theology," *Harvard Divinity Bulletin* 26, no. 1 (1996): 5.

2. Ibid.

3. National Conference of Catholic Bishops, *The Challenge of Peace: God's Promise and Our Response,* parts 1 and 2, *Catholic Social Teaching* (1983), http://www.osjspm.org/cst/cp.htm, sec. 1, para. 16.

4. Ibid., sec. 1, para. 25.

5. Ibid., sec. 1, para. 20.

6. Ibid., sec. 1, para. 17.

7. The terms "thick" and "thin" as applied to public discourse have been popularized by John Rawls, Michael Walzer, and others. The distinction is borrowed, however, from ethnographic studies, especially from Clifford Geertz; see his "Thick Description: Toward an Interpretive Theory of Culture," in *The Interpretation of Cultures* (New York: Basic Books, 1973), 3–30—although Geertz confesses to have borrowed it in turn from the philosopher Gilbert Ryle.

8. Stanley Hauerwas and William Willimon, *Resident Aliens: Life in the Christian Colony* (Nashville, Tenn.: Abingdon Press, 1989), 23. Hauerwas himself has been criticized recently, however, by writers who see him as still conceding too much to the possibility of a thin public language. For example, Robert Brimlow cites some instances where Hauerwas allows for some sort of "translation" of particularistic Christian language into terms that make sense to non-Christians. See Robert W. Brimlow, "Solomon's Porch: The Church as Sectarian Ghetto," in *The Church as Counterculture,* ed. Michael L. Budde and Robert W. Brimlow (Albany: State University of New York Press, 2000), 115.

9. Michael J. Baxter, C.S.C., " 'Blowing the Dynamite of the Church': Catholic Radicalism from a Catholic Radicalist Perspective," in *The Church as Counterculture,* 203.

10. Ibid.

11. Ibid., 198.

12. Ibid., 199.

13. Ibid.

14. Ibid., 205.

15. Ibid., 206–8.

16. Ibid., 207.

17. John Howard Yoder, *The Politics of Jesus* (Grand Rapids, Mich.: Eerdmans, 1972).

18. Nicholas P. Wolterstorff, "How Does Grand Rapids Reply to Washington?" *The Reformed Journal*.27, no. 10 (October 1977): 10.

19. Ibid., 13.

20. Quoted by Wolterstorff, ibid.

21. Ibid.

22. Ibid.

23. Baxter, " 'Blowing the Dynamite of the Church,' " 199.

24. Nicholas Wolterstorff, "Abraham Kuyper's Model of Democratic Polity for Societies with a Religiously Diverse Citizenry," in *Kuyper Reconsidered: Aspects of His Life and Work,* ed. Cornelis van der Kooi and Jan de Bruijn (Amsterdam: VU Uitgeverij, 1999), 191.

25. Ibid., 193.

26. Ibid., 196.

27. Robert Audi and Nicholas Wolterstorff, *Religion in the Public Square: The Place of Religious Convictions in Public Debate* (Lanham, Md.: Rowman and Littlefield, 1997), 81.

28. In this discussion, Wolterstorff does not develop the case for Reformed epistemology; he refers the reader to *Faith and Rationality,* ed. Alvin Plantinga and Nicholas Wolterstorff (Notre Dame, Ind.: University of Notre Dame Press, 1983).

29. Wolterstorff, *Religion in the Public Square,* 87.

30. Wolterstorff, Ibid., 113.

31. Wolterstorff, Ibid., 109.

32. Wolterstorff, Ibid., 111.

33. J. Bryan Hehir, "The Perennial Need for Philosophical Discourse," *Theological Studies* 40 (1979): 712, n. 27.

34. John Stuart Mill, *On Liberty* (Arlington Heights, Ill.: AHM Publishing Corporation, 1947), 62–63.

35. Ibid., 57, 61.

36. Wolterstorff, *Religion in the Public Square,* 112–13.

37. Ibid., 113.

38. Gordon Clark, *A Christian View of Men and Things* (Grand Rapids, Mich.: Eerdmans, 1952), 146.

39. See Wolterstorff, *Religion in the Public Square,* 111.

40. Ibid., 164.

41. For a detailed discussion of the concept of "the antithesis," see Henry Stob, "Observations on the Concept of the Antithesis," in *Perspectives on the Christian Reformed Church: Studies in Its History, Theology, and Ecumenicity,* ed. Peter De Klerk and Richard R. De Ridder (Grand Rapids, Mich.: Baker Book House, 1983).

42. John Calvin, *Institutes of the Christian Religion,* ed. John T. McNeill, trans. Ford Lewis Battles, Vol. II (Philadelphia: Westminster Press, 1960), II, 2.12.270–71.

43. Calvin, Ibid., II, 2.14.273.

44. Calvin, Ibid., II, 2.15.273–75.

45. Abraham Kuyper, *Lectures on Calvinism* (Grand Rapids, Mich.: Eerdmans, 1931), 71–72.

46. Jeffrey Stout, *Ethics after Babel: The Languages of Morals and Their Discontents* (Boston: Beacon Press, 1988), 212.

47. Ibid., 217.

48. June O'Connor, "Making a Case for the Common Good in a Global Economy: The United Nations Human Development Reports (1990–2001)," *Journal of Religious Ethics* 30 (Spring 2002): 169.

49. Ibid., 169–70.

50. Stanley Fish, "Postmodern Warfare: The Ignorance of Our Warrior Intellectuals," *Harper's Magazine* 305, no. 1826 (July 2002): 37–38.

51. Jean Jacques Rousseau, *The Social Contract*, trans. Willmore Kendall (Chicago: Henry Regnery Co., 1954), 41.

52. Arthur F. Holmes, *Contours of a World View* (Grand Rapids, Mich: Eerdmans, 1983), 128.

10   RELIGION AND THE PUBLIC SCHOOL TEACHER

KENT GREENAWALT

In recent decades, political philosophers have debated the grounds on which liberal democracies should make political decisions, particularly coercive ones. To oversimplify, the basic question is whether citizens and officials should rely freely on their own religious or other comprehensive views about reality and human life or should limit themselves to grounds that are in some sense shared by citizens in general. More particularly, the "excluded" grounds might not be rationally based, might not enjoy a consensus, might take a position about the good life, or might rest on comprehensive views. The fundamental arguments that people should exercise self-restraint are that fairness and considerations of political stability require that citizens not be coerced on the basis of reasons that cannot be expected to appeal to them. Against what we may call the "exclusive" position, others have urged an inclusive position: citizens should be able to rely on whatever grounds are convincing to them, at least so long as those grounds are not directly at odds with premises of liberal democracy (as a belief in racial hierarchy would be). In an illuminating exchange with Robert Audi, Nicholas Wolterstorff has eloquently defended an inclusive position.[1] No principle, he says, bars the use of religious grounds in politics.

Some scholars have argued for various intermediate positions. Among these, the best known is that of John Rawls, who argues that people should not rely on comprehensive views when they resolve constitutional issues and issues about basic economic justice, but they may rely on those views for ordinary political issues.[2] I have suggested that this position has serious flaws and defended a different intermediate position. Here are its central elements.[3]

Many judgments about what grounds officials and citizens appropriately use cannot be reached about liberal democracies in general; they need to be contextualized according to society's culture and history.[4] In the United States in the early twenty-first century, ordinary citizens should feel free to rely on religious and other comprehensive grounds as they address discrete political issues and elections. Asking someone not to rely on the grounds they find most persuasive—say, religious authority—is a significant restraint on his or her liberty, and most citizens are unable to distinguish what they believe for religious reasons from what they believe for other reasons. Officials, however, should exercise self-restraint. Legislators and chief executives should rely on shared public grounds when they announce the reasons for their positions, and, although they may silently rely to some extent on religious grounds, they should give a kind of priority to shared reasons in reliance as well as in public defense. (The restraints on judges are greater; except in rare instances, they should not self-consciously rely on religious grounds.)

Although this is only the crudest sketch of competing positions, it sets the background for this essay's subject: the responsibilities of public school teachers. A teacher is a special kind of public official; she works for the government but is neither a political official nor an executive officer merely carrying out tasks set by others. How should religion figure in public school teaching? I hope to show that the problem is severe, partly by summarizing some earlier writings of Nicholas Wolterstorff. I survey some possible resolutions, opting for what strikes me as the best of imperfect alternatives.

I begin by outlining what Wolterstorff says about the responsibilities of public schools in respect to religion. I then turn to his perspectives on Christian scholars, which provide insight about how we might view teachers who are committed to various religious perspectives. From there I go on to the hard work of analyzing competing approaches.

I. Public Schools and Affirmative Impartiality

In a 1967 essay entitled "Neutrality and Impartiality,"[5] supplemented later by a shorter encyclopedia piece entitled "Religion in the Public Schools,"[6] Wolterstorff considers what a public school should aim at with respect to religion. Accepting for this purpose the Supreme Court's declaration that the Free Exercise Clause protects irreligion as well as religion, Wolterstorff begins: "No matter what a man's *Weltanschauung,* no matter what his world and life view, whether it is religious or irreligious, the state is not to act so as to prevent him from implementing or exercising it. The state is not to do anything, the purpose or avoidable effect of which is to put restraint, constraint, coercion, or compulsion on some man's attempt to implement his way and view of life as he sees fit."[7] The way in which this principle applies to public schools is crucially affected by their being the one kind of school that receives public tax money, although the school's "officers and personnel are not, in any very strict sense, officials or employees of the state."[8]

In a subsequent essay, "The Schools We Deserve,"[9] Wolterstorff suggests that the Supreme Court should move away from a no-support approach to an equal-support approach, under which tax funds could be spent for religious schools. Since that essay, the Supreme Court has taken small steps in that direction, and in June of 2002, a 5–4 majority accepted the idea that substantial tax monies may go to parochial schools as well as to other private schools.[10] Nevertheless, this change in constitutional principle should not alter most of what Wolterstorff says about public schools. The Supreme Court has not suggested that states must spend as much for private schools as for public ones. Many states and localities will continue not to provide significant financial help for private education; thus, many parents of different religious persuasions will continue to have strong financial incentives to rely on public schools; and even where public support of parochial schools is generous, many parents will not have a school in the geographical area that fits their religious inclinations. Support for parochial education can diminish the practical magnitude of the tensions Wolterstorff discusses, but it will not eliminate them.

Public schools are supposed to be impartial among religions and between religion and irreligion, but, for Wolterstorff, arriving at the right sense of "impartial" is not easy. Some parents, as a matter of conscience, want schools to engage in religious practices and set their educational program in the context of some worldview. Other parents, as a matter of conscience, want schools to be free of religious practices and do not want the education set in the context of any particular worldview. No educational program can satisfy all these parents. Indulging in a bit of hyperbole, Wolterstorff writes that the public school cannot act in full accord with the Constitution.[11]

Schools must aim for "affirmative impartiality," which a person displays "if nothing he says or does manifests preference for the religion or irreligion of one person over that of the other."[12] What is impossible for schools is what

Wolterstorff calls "full impartiality," which requires, in addition, that "there is nothing such that . . . not doing or saying it manifests a preference for the religion or irreligion of one person over another."[13] This is unattainable because, if the schools remain silent about religion, that manifests a preference for parents who want silence as compared with parents who want schools to take an active religious stance.

Given a tradition in which religious differences are muffled in public schools, they should strive for affirmative impartiality.[14] Schools guided by affirmative impartiality can take no position on the nature and existence of God or on possibilities of immortality. But traditional religions go far beyond propositions about these subjects. What schools that undertake moral education say may be compatible or incompatible with particular religious views. Having noted that much of what schools teach agrees with the principles of many religions, such as "murder is wrong" and "people should care for each other," Wolterstorff considers a possible directive: "*Nothing that the public school says or does shall manifest disagreement with a tenet of some citizen's religion or irreligion.*" But this approach also fails, because teaching germ theory, the heliocentric view of the solar system, the justification of American involvement in World War II, and the norm of racial equality will all conflict with the tenets of some religions.

To meet this problem, Wolterstorff offers a reformulation: "*Nothing that the public school says or does shall have as its purpose or as an avoidable effect of its manner of achieving its purpose, the manifesting of approval or disapproval of any citizen's religion or irreligion.*"[15] So the school cannot set out to manifest approval or disapproval of a religious view, and if two ways of achieving a purpose are open, the school should choose the one that does not indicate approval or disapproval.[16] According to Wolterstorff, a school can be affirmatively impartial even though not "neutral in the sense we have given to the word 'neutral.'"[17] Mentioning the theory of evolution, the nature of human beings in psychology courses, and the causes of the Reformation, Wolterstorff concludes that, "On many significant issues, the public school, in our religiously diverse society, may either have to be silent or shift from teaching that such and such is the case to teaching that certain people *believe* that such and such is the case."[18]

Under Wolterstorff's general directive, schools may teach a good deal about religion and authoritative scriptures, but they must do so without taking a position about religious truth. Although believing that such education will increase knowledge and mutual understanding, Wolterstorff is doubtful, as are many parents, that it will improve the moral lives of students and increase the likelihood of their becoming religious.[19]

When Wolterstorff discusses courses about religion, he indulges assumptions about how they will actually be taught, but early on he distinguishes the stance of schools per se from the stance of individual teachers. The teacher, like the president, may be openly partial as an individual, but the distinction between what an institution and its personnel may do "is especially difficult to apply in the schools."[20] Remarking that most discussions have "overlooked and confused" the distinction between schools and teachers, Wolterstorff leaves it to others to focus on the work of individual teachers.[21]

II. Christian Scholarship

We need not look far to see why Wolterstorff regards the responsibilities of individual teachers as such a serious issue. Someone who believes religion is a contained, separate domain of life, or that people of diverse religious views share a strata of secular knowledge, might easily adopt the view that individual teachers should not express positions on religious issues. But for Wolterstorff, who sees authentic religious commitment as pervasive in a person's life, the problem is much more difficult. I could draw on much of his scholarship to make this point, but I shall concentrate on his short book *Reason within the Bounds of Religion* because its focus on Christian scholars has a bearing on the perspectives of Christian, and other religious, teachers.[22]

The heart of his thesis is that everyone has commitments that affect what they believe over a wide range of subjects. It was such "control beliefs" that led the Roman Catholic Church to reject a heliocentric view of the world,[23] that led Cartesians to reject Newtonian theory, and that led Ernst Mach to reject prevailing atomic theory.[24] When people consider theories, they bring along "the whole complex" of their beliefs.[25] The commitment of an authentic Christian will affect how he weighs and devises theories,[26] for example, leading him to reject behaviorism and Freudianism, which deny Christian assumptions about human freedom and responsibility.[27] A person with authentic Christian commitment "cannot take for granted that the data, beliefs, and theories of contemporary scientists are true" because scientists disagree among themselves and "experts" practice science with their own control beliefs.[28] When Christian scholars face incompatibilities between scientific conclusions and religious ones, they can revise their scientific views or their sense of what a Christian commitment entails.[29] Christians have typically chosen the latter course, and often that has been the right choice, as with their abandonment of the geocentric view of the universe.[30] Still, Wolterstorff indicates that there is much work to be done on such issues and closes with an expression of strong regret that qualified Christian scholars have not done more to devise their own scientific theories.[31]

III. Christian Teachers

What has Wolterstorff's account of scholarship to do with teaching in elementary and secondary schools? The vast majority of school teachers are not researchers, but they, like everyone else, will bring to bear all they believe in assessing theoretical claims *and* in evaluating what they believe is worth teaching.[32] The biology teacher who believes that God has intervened actively in the history of the universe will be *more likely* to doubt that neo-Darwinian evolutionary theory provides a full explanation of life's development on earth than a committed atheist will. And, to take a more modest illustration, how will a science teacher respond to a recent study of women seeking assistance to become pregnant that suggests the success of intercessory prayer by strangers?[33] A committed atheist will dismiss such results or may attribute them to a form of not-yet-understood mental telepathy; he will almost certainly not take class time to teach the study. A committed Christian might see the study as having far greater importance, worth examining for its possible evidence of a supernatural power that responds to prayer. It is not that she would proselytize in class; but acquainting the students with the study's surprising result and spending a few moments on possible explanations would seem worthwhile. In short, we do not need much imagination to see how Wolterstorff's thesis about the control beliefs of scholars could apply to public school teachers. Were teachers completely unconstrained, enjoying the kind of freedom of parents who homeschool their children, their religious commitments would affect what exactly they teach and how they teach it.

IV. Teachers and Schools

This brings us to the hard question: how is what teachers should do affected by the constraints under which public schools fall? Taking Wolterstorff's idea of affirmative impartiality as capturing well the constraint on schools and, perhaps unlike Wolterstorff, regarding that ideal as one of constitutional principle, as well as tradition, how should we understand the responsibilities of individual teachers?

Before I engage that inquiry, I want to revert for a moment to implications of the principle of affirmative impartiality for schools themselves. How does it affect the subjects schools teach and what schools say about the likely truth of facts and theories? When I mention the prayer experiment to people, it evokes interest, and, for what it is worth, *The New York Times* published two articles about it. Could a school board decide to have it taught, because the members judge its significance in light of their Christian commitments? A school board decision to teach a topic legitimately within the domain of the discipline does not involve teachers directly in violating the principle of affirmative impartiality; no one need say anything inside the school that manifests agreement with anyone's religion or irreligion. Yet, in a sense, the *board's* decision does manifest a particular religious view; and *if* the basis for the board's decision is understood by others, this message will be communicated to a broader public, including many students.

We *may* reach a similar equivocal conclusion about a board decision about whether to teach theories as highly confirmed or not. Let us imagine that the issue is the centrality of natural selection as the explanation for the evolutionary development of life, and let us suppose (which may be contrary to fact) that scientists reasonably disagree. The school board is choosing between two biology texts. One, reflecting the dominant view of scientists, treats the centrality of natural selection as firmly established fact. The other, reflecting a respectable minority view, asserts that other, yet undiscovered, elements of natural biological processes may put natural selection in a less central place than it enjoys in neo-Darwinian theory. The board members, remembering Wolterstorff's caution that experts have their own sets of control beliefs, and possessed of religious views that disincline them to accept natural selection as central, decide to adopt the second text. Again, the text itself manifests no view about religious questions in the ordinary sense, but the decision to use the text does so.

I am not sure how Wolterstorff would treat these examples.[34] Our own conclusions depend on what we think school board members are capable of. If we think of scientific judgment as independent, with religious opinions layered on top, we could ask the school board to stick to scientific premises for these decisions. But if we think religious views permeate all evaluation, we could not expect that, and we might think it unwise to ask the board members to try.[35] We can see at play here exactly the kinds of questions that figure in debate about whether citizens and officials should rely on their comprehensive views in political life.

Although the implications of affirmative impartiality for what the school board requires to be taught and for its choice of texts are not completely clear, we do know that some things are barred: the school itself cannot teach any religious propositions as true and it cannot choose to teach other material as true *in order* to promote some religious position.[36] In regard to individual teachers, we can sketch two alternative models. According to the first, the teacher is the spokesperson for the school. Insofar as possible, teachers, while in school, should observe the same constraints as would schools themselves.[37] According to the second model, the teacher is free to express her individual opinions, but she must make it clear that these do not represent the official views of the school.

Most people, on reflection, will probably find that the appeal of each model depends on the stage of education. Professors at state universities may declare their own beliefs and develop arguments that reflect those beliefs (although they may not actively proselytize in class). Kindergarten teachers represent the school, and five-year-olds cannot easily distinguish what the teacher asserts from the policy of the school. What is true for kindergarten teachers is probably true for most elementary school teachers. We can regard the main contested terrain as junior high school and high school.

Some of the central issues about what a teacher teaches are well posed by Warren A. Nord, who outlines eight ways in which texts, teachers, and courses might deal with religiously controversial subjects:

1. Religion might be ignored. . . .
2. Religion (or religious views of a contested issue) might be discussed, but only *reductively.* That is, religion is interpreted in terms of some worldview hostile to religion. This might happen if Freudian categories are used to explain religion in a psychology class or text or if a historian explains why certain events happened in fully secular terms. . . .
3. Religion might receive *bare mention,* in which case it is neither ignored nor explained reductively, but it is still not taken seriously (from the inside, as a contender for truth). The text or teacher might mention some fairly straight-forward facts relating to religion (that the ancient Hebrews were monotheists or that Christian fundamentalists reject evolution, for example) but if students are given little, if any, sense of why this is the case, and the text or the teacher uses a secular worldview to explain the subject at hand, then neutrality is violated. . . .
4. The text or teacher might convey to students an understanding of religion(s) *from the inside.*
5. The text or teacher might consider religious ways of understanding the world as live contenders for the truth, to be argued about and critically assessed . . . [but without] drawing conclusions. . . .
6. A teacher might offer his or her own *personal conclusion* about the truth or significance of religious claims, perhaps in response to a student's question, but not argue for it, and certainly not insist that students accept it as an official conclusion of the course. For example, a teacher might say at the begin-

ning of the text or course: "This is my (religious) bias, or perspective, and while I shall try to be fair, you should be aware of where I am coming from in sorting out the controversial material we will be discussing."

7. The teacher or textbook author might actively argue for particular conclusions after all the relevant views have been taken seriously but stop short of making them the official view. In effect, the teacher's voice is added to the conversation. This is certainly more than the expression of a personal view: it is the argument of someone with some authority in the subject, citing evidence and building a coherent case. . . .

8. The teacher or textbook author might consider all points of view fairly, argue for the truth of a particular point of view, and make that the final and *official conclusion* of the course or text.[38]

In explaining these eight possibilities, we are interested in what teachers in class may permissibly do that schools officially cannot do. We can dispose of four possibilities fairly quickly; three of these would be consistent with "affirmative impartiality" as outlined by Wolterstorff; one definitely is not, and the implications for individual teachers are obvious.

Although Nord believes that *ignoring* religion violates appropriate neutrality and fairness, and Wolterstorff believes that, on balance, some aspects of religion (say, the history of the Reformation) should definitely be covered, Wolterstorff remarks on some of the dangers of teaching religion as a cultural phenomenon and he does not think schools legally must treat religion. For a school or individual teacher to omit topics that are controversial religiously would not violate Wolterstorff's principle of affirmative impartiality.

The same conclusion holds for possibility (3); if the teacher limits herself to mentioning some basic facts about religion, without exploring them in depth, that is consistent with Wolterstorff's principle. One might respond that "bare mention" tests the limits between saying and not saying. If I, as a teacher, develop the views of Plato, Aristotle, and the Stoics in great depth and hardly mention Augustine, Aquinas, Luther, and Calvin, do I not imply that the former group is the much more important, and is this not manifesting a preference for their worldviews over Christian worldviews? This is a troublesome point, but a teacher can take much of the sting out of "bare mention" by indicating her (or the school's) view that deeper treatment is not desirable in the public school.

Possibility (4) is relatively uncontroversial, so long as it does not slide into (2), (5), (6), or (7). Teachers may present religious views from the "inside," using some primary sources and, for example, trying to elucidate just how the early Puritans viewed the Massachusetts Bay Colony in religious terms.

Nord's eighth possibility is definitely barred. Without doubt, the school cannot present a particular point of view about a dominantly religious issue as being the official conclusion. It is a short step, one I am sure Wolterstorff would take, to assuming that a teacher cannot say that a point of view is the official conclusion of her course, whatever that might mean.

The interesting possibilities are (2), (5), (6), and (7); and at least three of these sharply pose the possible difference between teachers and schools. Of these, I think (6) is the easiest. A school may not have a conviction about religious truth.[39] Especially if students ask, it would be unhealthy for spontaneous and candid interchange for teachers to refuse to reveal their religious inclinations, a restraint that applies to no other official and would be practically pointless in communities where students or their parents witness the teacher's religious practice outside school.

Possibility (7) is perhaps the crucial one for what a teacher might do that a school cannot. A school could not issue a publication arguing that unitarianism is more plausible than trinitarianism, or that Luther was fully justified in breaking away from the Catholic Church, even if the school noted that its position did not represent official state policy. For the school to argue for religious conclusions would violate Wolterstorff's principle of affirmative impartiality. But may the teacher do so?

Nord thinks yes, and it might be said that different teachers will make different arguments, thus challenging students to think for themselves. But in many school districts, the teachers will not be very diverse, and it takes a courageous schoolteacher to argue directly in an overwhelmingly Catholic community that Luther was fully justified. The net result of allowing individual teachers to argue for religious points of view might well be to reinforce prevailing religious notions.

I think the significance of the public school rests less on tax money than Wolterstorff assumes. The state puts the public school teacher in a position of great authority and influence, with at least a temporary monopoly power. I believe this a sufficient reason for teachers to exercise restraint. For teachers to argue vigorously for points of view on religiously controversial issues is too close to an outright violation of affirmative impartiality by the school to be desirable. Constitutional permissibility is a harder issue. If, in context, a school can persuade a court that students are mature enough to handle such expressions of view without being unduly influenced, the practice may not overstep constitutional bounds.

Possibility (2), in one of its aspects, turns out to be a variation on possibility (7). The teacher who adopts a worldview hostile to religion, as he teaches about religion, is taking a position on controversial religious issues. So long as he makes clear that the position is not official, and his arguments are openly made, this is not different in principle from arguing for positive religious views.[40] A perspective that is hardly acknowledged and is treated as self-evident can be more insidious than one that is recognized and openly argued for. *In any event,* teachers who are presenting and defending their own positions must make clear what the are alternatives are and sketch what might be said in their favor.

In discussing possibility (2), Nord equates teaching Freudian categories to explain religion in a psychology class and explaining historical events in wholly secular terms. Whatever he had exactly in mind, an explanation that rejects the validity of religious claims is critically different from one that takes no position about them. A typical Freudian explanation treats traditional religion as a kind of illusion, having no ontological truth. A secular historical explanation *need not* deny the validity of a religious explanation of the same events. For example, a secular historical analysis of the spread of Christianity need take no position on whether Christianity is "true"—although it does tend to rebut the position that the religion's spread can only be explained as a miracle. Insofar as a teacher makes clear—as some professors in departments of religion do—that he or she is not addressing whether truth claims within a religion are valid, a "secular" approach is more a matter of ignoring or barely mentioning than of rejecting. As such, it fits the principle of affirmative impartiality.

Possibility (5) involves student discussion and critical analysis of controversial religious issues, with the teacher withholding judgment, in the manner of a so-called Socratic dialogue, in which law professors withhold their own views. This possibility raises serious concerns about peer pressure and class tensions, but so long as the teacher indicates neither an official position nor defends any particular view she can attempt to adhere to affirmative impartiality. After all, an expression of a view by an individual student is a long way from the school or the teacher adopting a position that is approving or disapproving of a religious perspective. And no student enjoys the monopoly that is the teacher's. Nevertheless, in areas where one or two religious positions dominate, the predictable effect of a wide-open student discussion about religious issues will be the dominance of one or two points of view. And there is always the risk that the way a teacher poses questions or leads the discussion will be perceived, rightly or wrongly, as reflecting a particular point of view. It is debatable whether a student or teacher that sets such predictable partial effects in motion should be regarded as striving for affirmative impartiality.

The main point of this comment on Wolterstorff's insightful and challenging writings on public schools is to explore the tension between his model of affirmative impartiality for the schools, their avoidance of manifestations of approval or disapproval of religious views, and his belief that those who consider theories in a wide realm of subjects bring to bear control beliefs derived from their religious or other worldviews. The crucial question is how far public school teachers should teach their full understanding of a subject, as influenced by their religious views, and how far they should exemplify the school's aspiration to affirmative impartiality.

Our analysis of this problem indicated two important questions about affirmative impartiality that go beyond what is *said* about religion: does affirmative impartiality restrict the grounds for school decisions about what topics to teach? And does it restrict what is said about degrees of confirmed truth? We have identified the central question about the possible difference between teachers and schools as whether teachers should freely argue for particular positions on religious topics, making clear they are speaking only for themselves. Warren Nord's approval of such an approach might appeal to Wolterstorff's sense that the teacher, as a whole person addressing her subject matter, should not have to self-censor her own notions of truth. For most circumstances, I reach a different conclusion. The teacher's dominant role in the classroom, where she has been placed by the state, should lead to a more circumscribed sense of what she should say to students on religious subjects.

NOTES

1. Robert Audi and Nicholas Wolterstorff, *Religion in the Public Square: The Place of Religious Convictions in Political Debate* (Lanham, Md.: Rowman and Littlefield, 1997), 67–120, 145–65.

2. John Rawls, *Political Liberalism* (New York: Columbia University Press, 1993).

3. Kent Greenawalt, *Private Consciences and Public Reasons* (New York: Oxford University Press, 1995), and *Religious Convictions and Political Choice* (New York: Oxford University Press, 1988).

4. On this point Wolterstorff agrees, in *Religion in the Public Square*, 79–80.

5. Nicholas Wolterstorff, "Neutrality and Impartiality," in *Religion and Public Education*, ed. Theodore Sizer (Boston: Houghton Mifflin, 1967), 3–21.

6. Nicholas Wolterstorff, "Religion in the Public Schools," in *Encyclopedia of Education*, vol. 7, ed. Lee C. Deighton (New York: Macmillan Company, 1971), 464–69.

7. "Neutrality and Impartiality," 4. I think Wolterstorff oversimplifies in assuming that, for all purposes, nonreligious ways of life must be treated equally with religious ways of life, but the needed qualification would not affect the central topic of his essays or mine.

8. Ibid., 5–6.

9. Nicholas Wolterstorff, "The Schools We Deserve," in *Schooling Christians*, ed. Stanley Hauerwas and John Westerhoff (Grand Rapids, Mich.: Eerdmans, 1992), 3–28.

Reprinted as chap. 13 of *Educating for Life*, ed. Gloria Goris Stronks and Clarence W. Joldersma (Grand Rapids, Mich.: Baker Academic, 2002).

10. *Zelman v. Superintendent of Public Instruction*, 2002 U.S. Lexis 4885 (decided June 27, 2002).

11. This is hyperbole because the Constitution is not interpreted, and should not reasonably be interpreted, to demand what is impossible.

12. "Neutrality and Impartiality," 9.

13. Ibid.

14. Wolterstorff concludes that the Constitution cannot be used to justify affirmative impartiality because the Supreme Court has mistakenly assumed that affirmative impartiality equates with full impartiality. But, even if he is right about the Court's misconception, his conclusion does not follow. If full impartiality is impossible, as Wolterstorff rightly assumes, it is entirely plausible that the Constitution is better interpreted to require affirmative impartiality than any other alternative.

15. "Neutrality and Impartiality," 16.

16. Wolterstorff does not discuss an important nuance, related to "avoidable effect." Suppose the school has a legitimate purpose. The way it can be achieved best will involve manifesting approval; the school can avoid approval but at some sacrifice of its purpose. I assume that such situations call for a weighing of loss and benefit.

17. "Neutrality and Impartiality," 16. In fact, he does not in this essay provide an elaboration of what neutrality entails, but I believe we are to equate it with the impossible-to-achieve full impartiality.

18. Ibid, 17. In "Religion in the Public Schools," 467, he remarks in passing that "schools are not legally required to treat religion in their educational programs."

19. "Religion in the Public Schools," 468.

20. "Neutrality and Impartiality," 6.

21. Ibid., 7.

22. Nicholas Wolterstorff, *Reason within the Bounds of Religion* (Grand Rapids, Mich: Eerdmans, 1976).

23. Ibid., 7–13.

24. Ibid., 14–15.

25. Ibid., 62.

26. Ibid., 72.

27. Ibid., 73.

28. Ibid., 78.

29. Ibid., 88.

30. Ibid., 89–90. Wolterstorff makes the subtle point, p. 96, that although many Christian thinkers have harmonized their ideas of authentic commitment with elements of evolutionary theory, it is very unlikely ("an historical impossibility") that Christian scholars of the day would themselves have developed evolutionary theory in its Darwinian form.

31. Ibid., 102. He suggests that they should "devise theories that lead to promising, interesting, fruitful, challenging lines of research."

32. We would do well at the outset to recognize that the impact of religious control beliefs is likely to vary widely among subject matters. What one thinks and says about math does not depend very much on one's religious premises. What one thinks and says about morality will depend a great deal. Natural science and history lie in between, with most of natural science now falling closer than history to the math end of the spectrum.

33. See Jim Holt, "Prayer Works," *New York Times,* December 9, 2001, sec. 6, p. 92.

34. Conceivably, he would say about the second example that taking any definitive position on the centrality of natural selection would have an "avoidable effect" of disapproving someone's religion. See text accompanying n. 15 above. But he clearly thinks that scientific theories can be taught as highly confirmed, such as the heliocentric view of the solar system, although some religions may disagree. If so, there is a threshold of scientific evidence, or minuteness of religious opposition, that allows schools to offer assertions about confirmation. See my related comment in n. 17 above.

35. Conceivably, one might ask the board members to rely on their perception of some amalgam of the diversity of views throughout the state or country, but that seems a strained and impossible exercise.

36. The choice to teach the prayer study might come close to this, but it could be defended as opening students' minds to a range of possibilities.

37. One evident limit to this possibility involves a teacher's response to a student's question whether she is a practicing Christian. The teacher must either answer honestly, say it is not the student's business, or explain that standards about schools and religion preclude her answering. But the latter two responses seem almost ridiculous, and they are particularly ridiculous in small communities in which a particular teacher's religious practice is likely to be widely known.

38. Warren A. Nord, *Religion and American Education* (Chapel Hill: University of North Carolina Press, 1995), 249–50.

39. One may say a school may not have a conviction about anything, but it can be the official policy of the school that liberal democracy and racial equality are good.

40. One might distinguish a Marxist presentation of religious subjects from argument for religious positions on the basis that a perspective that pervades the entire course is more troublesome than arguments on discrete subjects. This seems a distinction without a difference. A teacher who expresses herself on a range of religious subjects is likely to reflect some consistent religious view, even if it is less coherent and well labeled than Marxism.

11

SHAME AS
A POLITICAL VIRTUE

MEROLD WESTPHAL

I

I was standing in the checkout line at Blockbuster Video and couldn't help but notice two young boys running wild nearby. One of them ran beside a shelf with toys on it with his arm extended so as to knock them onto the floor. The other had found a small bag with toys or candy or something in it and was using it as a hammer to pound on the shelf from which it had been taken. Unable to restrain himself any longer, a gentlemen standing nearby rebuked the boy, informing him not only that the bag was not his, but also that it was not a pounding toy in any case. The mother, who up to this time had been totally oblivious, suddenly became alert. And angry. "You mustn't scold him," she said. "He'll feel bad."

I found myself thinking that he ought to feel bad, for both boys were old enough to know better than what they were doing; and I thought to myself, "The cult of self-esteem run amok," wondering what happened to that school to which all parents used to be sent. That they were all trained at the same school is the only plausible explanation for the uniformity of the lines they had ready for every occasion: "What? You think that money grows on trees?" "If I've told you once, I've told you a thousand times . . . !" And, most relevantly to the present situation, "Shame on you! You ought to be ashamed of yourself!"

This incident reminded me of another. I was giving my undergraduate course in Chinese philosophy. An Asian American student was excited about a course that would put him in touch with some of his roots to which he had not previously been introduced. But at a certain point—I don't remember if we were still doing Confucianism or had gone on to Taoism—he came to me and announced, "The more of this stuff we do the clearer it is to me that I'm really an American." We had encountered a number of not-very-American motifs, and he did not indicate which ones made him uncomfortable. But I would be surprised if they did not include the Confucian notion, to which I called explicit attention, that a healthy society requires a basis in shame and that, by contrast, a shameless society is a sick society. I had left it to them to reflect on the growing shamelessness of the culture in which they lived and of the not-uncommon link between shamelessness and celebrity.

Confucius (Kongzi) teaches, "Lead the people with governmental measures and regulate them by law and punishment, and they will avoid wrong-doing but will have no sense of honor and shame. Lead them with virtue and regulate them by the rules of propriety (*li*),[1] and they will have a sense of shame, and, moreover, set themselves right."[2]

Chad Hansen gives a most interesting interpretation of Confucius's reasoning:

> He [Confucius] accepts the proposition that legal motivations *will work.* People will avoid wrongdoing. He objects that, in working, coercive regulation subverts the innate inclination to absorb social programming. The more we regulate behavior by fear [of punishment], the less people will develop spontaneous social practices such as *li.* Our potential for conventional social intercourse depends on our having a sense of shame—the inclination to conformity. We can explain Confucius' rationale by two assumptions: (1) humans have inclinations both to social conformity and to self-interested calculation and (2) exercise of an inclination strengthens it. Regulating coercively exercises the people's inclination to prudence or self-interest, since avoiding punishment is in our self-interest. Coercion requires this self-regarding disposition, the disposition to prudence. Punitive regulation strengthens the tendency to egoism and correspondingly weakens, by inattention, our natural social instincts. Law undermines our tendency to ritual conformity and emulation of models. It thus endangers the very root of the *natural* social order.[3]

An important corollary of Confucius's view is that a shameless society will be a litigious society. Legal coercion will produce a measure of social conformity, but by fostering self-interested calculation it simultaneously encourages legal sophistry in the service of getting what one wants and avoiding punishment.[4]

The shame motif is a recurring one in Confucian thought. Confucius himself teaches, "The superior man is ashamed that his words exceed his deeds."[5] In arguing that humans are naturally good, Mencius (Mengzi) traces four cardinal virtues to four innate feelings.

> If you let people follow their feelings (original nature), they will be able to do good. This is what is meant by saying that human nature is good. If man does evil, it is not the fault of his natural endowment. The feeling of commiseration is found in all men; the feeling of shame and dislike is found in all men; the feeling of respect and reverence is found in all men; and the feeling of right and wrong is found in all men. The feeling of commiseration is what we call humanity; the feeling of shame and dislike is what we call righteousness; the feeling of respect and reverence is what we call propriety (*li*); and the feeling of right and wrong is what we call wisdom. [These] are not drilled into us from outside. We originally have them with us.[6]

The Doctrine of the Mean quotes Confucius as teaching, "To know to be shameful is akin to courage." Courage, along with humanity and wisdom, are presented as the three universal virtues of personal life, each of which is necessary to the good ruler. [7]

But it should be clear that for classic Confucianism shame is a political virtue in a more inclusive sense. Regardless of one's place in the hierarchy of authority, it provides motivation for cooperative participation in society on the basis of right and wrong rather than on the basis of calculative self-interest. If shame is an especially important characteristic in the ruler that is because the ruler's task is more that of an exemplar than an expert.

In the West, shame has not been a very popular virtue; it has rather struggled to be a virtue at all. But shame is, I shall suggest, an important trait insofar as it is a habit or disposition of character we ought to have vis-à-vis our habitual failure to welcome the other, human and divine, as we should. This virtue is, moreover, an eschatological, political virtue, one that cannot be institutionalized or rendered routine, but which can break in with disruptive force to the politics of calculated self-interest and the ontology of war to which it is linked. Indeed, I will suggest later in discussing Levinas's views that it is a virtue to which Christian political theorists have good reason to pay attention. Why, however, has this trait been nearly universally neglected by Western philosophers? A selective historical tour will enable us to consider the case(s) against it, beginning with Aristotle.

II

There would seem to be a certain natural affinity between Aristotle and the Confucian tradition that can be expressed by the phrase "the politics of virtue without metaphysics." As to virtue, for Aristotle politics is concerned with the structure of institutions, but before constitution comes character, without which the former is fruitless. In the Confucian tradition, concern for character all but drowns out questions of constitution. For neither the Aristotelian nor the Confucian tradition are there political virtues in addition to or distinct from moral virtues. Ethics belongs essentially to politics and the virtues are political because they are seen as indispensable to a healthy society.[8] As to metaphysics, these traditions appeal, to be sure, respectively, to Reason and to Heaven, but in neither case are these given the kind of ontological and epistemic independence of historical social reality that would give them the kind of bite they have in traditions we could call either Platonic or prophetic.

But the affinity between the two traditions generates no agreement on the subject of shame. Aristotle's brief discussion concludes book 4 of the *Nichomachean Ethics* (1128b10–35).[9] We should not consider shame to be a virtue or an excellence, we are told, "for it resembles an emotion more than a characteristic." But this is not a compelling argument. At most it shows that merely to feel ashamed is not as such a virtue nor even the sure sign of a virtue. But Aristotle has been telling us all along that moral virtue, which is political because the health of the polis depends on it, concerns the rational mean in relation to both actions *and* emotions. From this it would seem to follow that there is a virtue related to shame, the habit or disposition of feeling this emotion in accordance with reason.

This line of thinking is confirmed when Aristotle immediately continues, "At any rate, [shame] is defined as a kind of fear of disrepute, and the effect it produces is very much like that produced by fear of danger: people blush when they feel ashamed and turn pale when they fear death." To be sure, fear is not a virtue, but courage as the habit of fearing "the right things, for the right motive, in the right manner, and at the right time" (1115b17–18) is a paradigmatic virtue. Correspondingly, one would think, to be ashamed "of the right things, for the right motive, in the right manner, and at the right time" would also be a virtue. At most, Aristotle's first argument shows that it would be dangerous to name such a virtue "shame" because we would then run the risk of confusing merely having the emotion with the virtue of habitually having it in accordance with right reason. "Fear" is not the name for the virtue related to fear. But Aristotle is fully aware that ordinary language is not in neat and natural conformity with his theory, that we do not have names for some of the virtues or some of the extremes between which they are the mean. A more careful Aristotle would have concluded that a proper sense of shame is a political virtue, even if ordinary language has no neat way of distinguishing the virtue from the raw emotion.

Aristotle's second argument against shame presupposes that there is a seemly shame, and thus a virtue, which in desperation we might call shame$_v$, but he insists that it is only for kids, not for adults.

> The emotion of shame does not befit every stage of life but only youth. For we think that . . . living by their emotions as they do, they often go wrong and then shame inhibits them. We praise young people who have a sense of shame, but no one would praise an elderly man for being bashful [having a sense of disgrace; Oxford translation], for we think he ought not to do anything that will bring him shame. In fact, shame is not the mark of a decent man at all, since it is a consequence of base actions . . . they ought not to be performed, and as a result, a man ought not to be ashamed. . . . It is absurd for a man to believe himself actually to be decent because he is the kind of person who would be ashamed if he performed some such act.

Really? Is this not an argument from the moral complacency[10] of "the best and the brightest"? Is it not true with young people, whom we praise for having a sense of shame, that shameful acts ought not to be performed? What is the basis for the distinction between children and adults if not the arrogant assumption that socialization is sanctity and that, at least for respectable citizens, the transition from adolescence to adulthood signifies the completion of the process? If it is true that "no decent man will ever voluntarily do what is base," it is tautologically true as a definition of decency. But a politics based on this tautology would be a politics for (unfallen) angels. One need not be a Calvinist to come to such a conclusion. One need only observe the shameful behavior of various religious, business, and political leaders (including priests, presidents, and CEOs), to say nothing of the celebrities of our sports and entertainment industries.

Even Aristotle seems to recognize this, and he acknowledges that "a decent man will feel ashamed if he were to [voluntarily do what is base]." The tautology is gone and with it the moral complacency that required it. But Aristotle stubbornly tries to keep shame off his list of virtues. The "if" in the above concession makes shame "conditionally good . . . but there is nothing conditional about the virtues." But this is a third bad argument. Virtues are typically conditional in the required sense. The *habitus* is not conditional, but its exercise is. I can exercise generosity only if I have the appropriate resources, and I can exercise courage only if I am in danger. Similarly, I can be virtuously ashamed only if I have done something shameful. No doubt Aristotle knows I can be courageous only if I am in danger and that courage is conditional in this sense. His real objection is to a condition of a particular sort, namely, personal fault, whether one calls this weakness of will or, in a biblical frame of reference, sin. But he has carelessly overstated his objection so as to exclude virtues he wants to acknowledge and in doing so has failed to give any reason for rejecting as virtues those whose condition is fault.

At the very end of his brief discussion, Aristotle seems to concede the case by admitting that shamelessness is base. It would seem to follow that there is a virtue, which is the mean between the extremes of shamelessness, and what we might call false shame.[11] But Aristotle seeks to avoid this conclusion by insisting that "it does not follow that it is decent for a man to act this way and then feel ashamed of it." But this is not the conclusion he needs to deny if he is to keep shame off his list of virtues. It is rather the conclusion that it is decent, if someone has acted shamefully, to feel appropriately ashamed of it; but this he has already conceded.

I think it is fair to conclude that, in spite of himself, Aristotle points us toward shame as a political virtue. Perhaps the same can be said of Spinoza. He gives us a physics or a physical chemistry of the emotions, anticipating Hume's attempt in the next century "to introduce the experimental method of reasoning into moral subjects."[12] Then he gives us a therapeutics of the emotions, anticipating Freud. He calls this an ethics, and in the larger context of his work it is a politics as well, for it is about living in accord with reason, which is as important to our common life as to our private lives.

The conceptual context for Spinoza's reflections is quite different from that for Aristotle, but he will be no more favorable toward shame (*pudor*) than Aristotle. He distinguishes it from repentance (*paenitentia*). Both are modes of hatred, namely, self-hatred or painful self-regard. The difference is that shame has an external cause, the belief that one is blamed by others, while repentance has an internal cause (30).[13] "Shame is pain accompanied by the idea of some action of ours that we think that others censure" (D31). "Repentance is pain accompanied by the idea of some deed which we believe we have done from free decision of the mind" (D27).

I have argued elsewhere that this distinction, more familiar to us as the distinction between shame and guilt,[14] does not sustain phenomenological investigation. The evidence shows, it seems to me, that both when we speak of shame and when we speak of guilt we are pointing to a dialectically complex event of self-relation and other-relation, that the self-relation is one in which I disapprove of myself and the other-relation is one of awareness of disapproval directed toward me by the other. I would not feel shame if I did not disapprove of myself in the face of others' disapproval; nor would I feel guilt if I did not feel that others either do disapprove of me or would *and should* if only they knew what I know. The structure in which the two moments of self-relation and other-relation are united can be expressed by saying that in guilt or shame, which are not essentially different, I approve of the other's disapproval of me.[15] So I shall include Spinoza's discussion of repentance as part of the discussion of shame, remembering that it signifies pain rather than change of heart and is better expressed by 'guilt' (as a feeling as distinct from a moral or legal status) and perhaps by 'penitence'.

One needn't be a genius at the "geometrical" method Spinoza employs to draw the obvious conclusion from the preceding claims. Like pity, both shame and repentance are pains and as such are bad. They can hardly be recommended as virtues. Thus, "Repentance is not a virtue, i.e., it does not arise from reason; he who repents of his action is doubly unhappy or weak. . . . For the subject suffers himself to be overcome first by a wicked desire (*cupiditas*),[16] and then by pain" (IV, 54 and 54P).

But Spinoza cannot quite contain his utopianism. In the previous proposition he had similarly argued that humility, being a pain, cannot be a virtue. Now with reference to both propositions, he makes a major concession, calling attention in the process to the political character of his ethics.

> As men seldom live according to the dictates of reason, these two emotions, humility and repentance . . . bring more advantage than harm; and thus, if sin we must, it is better to sin in their direction. For if men of weak spirit should all equally be subject to pride and should be ashamed of nothing and afraid of nothing, by what bonds could they be held together and bound? The mob is fearsome, if it does not fear. So it is not surprising that the prophets, who had regard for the good of the whole community, and not of the few, have been so zealous in commending humility, repentance, and reverence. (IV, 54S)[17]

Humility and repentance, and, by easy extension, shame, are desirable character traits, if not for the few, at least for the many, the mob. Here Plato's hoi polloi take the place of Aristotle's youths; humility, repentance, and shame are political virtues for "them," but "we" are exempt. But of course if "we" are not as different from "them" as "we" would like to think, then these will be, our protests to the contrary notwithstanding, political virtues for us as well.

The result is similar when Spinoza speaks specifically about shame. Like pity, it is not a virtue but "can be good in so far as it is an indication that the man who feels ashamed has a desire to live honourably. . . . Therefore, although the man who is ashamed of some deed is in fact pained, he is nearer perfection than the shameless man who has no desire to live honourably" (IV, 58S). As with Aristotle, it is the thought of shamelessness that deconstructs, if you will, the attempt to exclude shame from the catalog of virtues. How timely!

Nietzsche feels a great kinship with Spinoza, and in a letter to Overbeck says that "in five main points of his doctrine I recognize myself; this most unusual and loneliest thinker is closest to me precisely in these matters: he denies the freedom of the will, teleology, the moral world order, the unegoistic, and evil."[18] In the attempt, not entirely successful by his own admission, to break free from a moral world order which condemns the self-centered life as evil and categorically commands the virtues of altruism,[19] Spinoza's *conatus essendi* becomes the will to power, and shame is once again made to be, so far as possible, ashamed to show its face. Thus Nietzsche concludes book 3 of *The Gay Science* with a little dialogue on the subject:

> *Whom do you call bad?*—Those who always want to put to shame.
> *What do you consider more humane?*—To spare someone shame.
> *What is the seal of liberation?*—No longer being ashamed in front of oneself.[20]

By themselves, the first two colloquies do not take us where Nietzsche wants to go. They are the flip side of the notion that there is false shame, shame that is not appropriate. They call attention to the ways in which shame can be hypocritically (dare one say shamefully?) induced as a means of manipulation. Ever the "master of suspicion,"[21] Nietzsche suspects that what goes on under the banner of high moral seriousness is but a (thinly) disguised exercise of the will to power that is unwilling to be honest about itself. These lines are of a piece with Zarathustra's warning in "On the Tarantulas": "Mistrust all in whom the impulse to punish is powerful . . . the hangman and the bloodhound look out of their faces. Mistrust all who talk much of their justice . . . they would be pharisees, if only they had—power."[22]

Such critiques are quite compatible with the notion that proper shame is a virtue and that there is such a thing as justice in terms of which punishment can be, well, just. It is the last brief exchange that makes it clear that Nietzsche's target is not false shame but shame as such. Already at the conclusion of book 2, he had written, "We should be *able* to stand *above* morality. . . . And as long as you are in any way *ashamed* before yourselves, you do not yet belong with us."[23] Later he will find more cheerful "the days when mankind was not yet ashamed of its cruelty. . . . The darkening of the sky above mankind has deepened in step with the increase in man's feeling of shame *at man*." This pessimism, "the icy No of disgust with life," he describes as the "swamp weeds" that flourish when "the animal 'man' finally learns to be ashamed of all his instincts."[24] Or again, it turns out that Nietzsche's beloved deity, Dionysus, is also a philosopher. "One guesses: this type of deity and philosopher is perhaps lacking in shame?" Yes, indeed, and this is only one reason that "all of the gods could learn from us humans. We humans are—more humane."[25]

If my claim that guilt and shame are fundamentally of a piece is sound, then Nietzsche's more extensive critique of guilt is but another facet of the same attempt to go "beyond good and evil," to escape from the moral worldview taken over in the West from Moses, and Jesus, and Paul, and Plato, whom Nietzsche sees, in the words of Spiro Agnew, as the "nattering nabobs of negativity," saying "no" to the only life there is, here on earth and now in time, for the sake of an illusory life in heaven and in eternity.

And yet, like Aristotle and Spinoza before him, he cannot quite break with shame. In a passage that highlights its political significance, he writes

> Within a community in which all regard themselves as equivalent there exist *disgrace* [*Schande,* often and appropriately translated as "shame"] and *punishment* as measures against transgressions. . . . In this way the transgressor is *reminded* that through his act he has *excluded* himself from the community and its moral *advantages:* the community treats him as one who is not equivalent, as one of the weak standing outside it; that is why punishment is not only retribution but contains something *more,* something of the *harshness of the state of nature:* it is precisely *this* that it wants to *recall.*[26]

In the context of social contract theory, we are pointed to the social utility of shame along with punishment.[27]

It might well be objected (1) that this is an early text not expressive of the mature Nietzsche, and (2) that it is merely descriptive of a certain type of society of which Nietzsche does not necessarily approve. Fair enough. But two considerations make possible a different reading according to which Nietzsche values shame precisely for its social utility. First, Nietzsche is speaking of a society of equals, one "in which all regard themselves as equivalent," not a hierarchical society or a society of paper equality (such as a formal democracy in which the principle of one person/one vote is a pious platitude without descriptive probity); and insofar as he envisages a community of free spirits and *Übermenschen*, it is such a community. Second, in the immediately following section, entitled "Have the adherents of the theory of free-will the right to punish?", he carries on his assault on free will by giving a negative answer to his own question. So we might read the two sections together as saying something like this: shame is a political virtue by virtue of its social utility, but this very natural fact provides no basis for generating a nonnatural metaphysics of free will (and all that goes with it, as in God, freedom, and immortality).

Another hint that Nietzsche, too, finds it necessary to affirm shame comes from the indisputably mature Nietzsche. "In men who are hard, intimacy involves shame—and is precious."[28] Gnomic utterances like this are notoriously nebulous. But it might mean something like this: wherever there is society, community, even friendship, there are shared values (not necessarily those of Platonic-Christian morality), and wherever there are shared values shame is at hand, for if I violate those values, without disowning them altogether, my comrades will disapprove of my having done so and I will inevitably approve their disapproval. Moreover, in light of the previous passage, this is not merely a psychosocial fact but a good thing, for it helps to sustain our life together.[29] Where there are shared values and those values are violated, there will be shame; and there should be, for it can be avoided, or, more likely repressed, only at the price of honesty.

If Nietzsche is a great admirer of Spinoza, Sartre is in important respects a Nietzschean, and surely a major philosopher of shame.[30] One of Nietzsche's comments on shame points us directly to Sartre: "The feeling 'I am the mid-point of the world!' arises very strongly if one is suddenly overcome with shame; one then . . . feels dazzled as though by a great eye which gazes upon us and through us from all sides."[31] For it is in Sartre's analysis of the Look and its consequences that he gives us his phenomenology of shame, the feeling of oneself "as thrown in the arena beneath millions of looks."[32]

Sartre's view is that I am aware of the Other as another subject not through intending an object, which I somehow construe as another subject, but through the awareness of being the object of another subject's gaze. It is the Other's look that gives the Other to me as such. My responses to that look, on Sartre's account, are three: fear, pride, and shame. But by far the greatest attention is given to shame, and this is not an accident. Fear is too general. I can be afraid of anthrax spores, of a downed power line, or of a rabid dog on the loose. Of course, since we both have bodies, I can be afraid of the Other as well, but fear has no special ties to the Look, as pride and shame do.

I like to read Sartre as anticipating Levinas's claim that "the face speaks."[33] I experience pride or shame uniquely in the presence of a look from a coparticipant in a language game. I leave to other discussions the question of whether a dog with its tail between its legs is experiencing shame or whether animals, or ecosystems, or the earth have faces that speak to us and in doing so put claims on us. By appealing to linguistic competence in its most immediate, dare I say "literal," sense, I give Sartre a good reason for mentioning and then all but ignoring fear.

But why the same for pride? Here he gives us his reasons himself. I am, on his account, the desire to be God. I want to be the subject before whom all else is object.[34] I want to be the center of the world, not in the Nietzschean sense of being looked at, but as the one who does the looking. I want to be the master before whom the others are the slaves who know they must lower their gaze. Above all, I want to be able to define myself. Of course, if the look of the Other is the occasion for pride, I welcome it so far forth. But such a look is a wolf in sheep's clothing, a welcome content in an unwelcome form. For it remains the case that "the Other teaches me who I am" (274). Not only can I not define the Other, I cannot even define myself. The Look as such is my "fall," my "alienation" (263). Before it, regardless of its content, I am slave and not master (265, 267). So it makes sense to focus on shame, in which I experience both the form and the content of the Look as a threat to my project. Accordingly, the paradigm of the Look is the famous scene in which I am peeping through a keyhole and hear footsteps in the hall; I know I've been seen and I experience myself in shame (259–61).

I spoke above of Sartre's analysis of the Look *and its consequences* (not consequences of his analysis but of the Look on his analysis). This comes in part 3, chapter 3 of *Being and Nothingness*, entitled "Concrete Relations with Others." I always hope for a bright, sunny day when I teach this section because it is so depressing. It is on the basis of these descriptions of our behavior as those whose project is to be God that I add Sartre's name to those of Marx, Nietzsche, and Freud as the great secular theologians of original sin. What he gives is a phenomenological sermon on the Spinozistic text, "Shame is pain." Accordingly, we do everything we can to neutralize the Look of the Other. We adopt one of two strategies: either to deny the Other's subjectivity—to transcend the Other's transcendence by making the Other into an Object—or by seeking to possess, to incorporate, to assimilate the Other's subjectivity by making it my own (263). The first of these works itself out in indifference, desire, hate, and sadism (379–412). The second shows itself as the love, which is the demand to be loved, as seductive language, and as masochism (364–79). In this context sadism and masochism as forms of sexual violence are extended to become metaphors for relations that are not literally either sexual or violent. "Each attempt is the death of the other," or perhaps, each is the attempted death of the other, and "the failure of the one motivates the adoption of the other" (363).

This is a descriptive phenomenology, not an ethics. In a frighteningly impassive footnote at the end of these descriptions, Sartre writes, "These considerations do not exclude the possibility of an ethics of deliverance and salvation. But this can be achieved only after a radical conversion which we cannot discuss here" (412).[35] So we cannot expect any direct discussion of the possibility of shame as a political virtue.

Nevertheless, Sartre makes two important contributions to our investigation. First, he adds to our diagnosis of the shamelessness of our society. From Aristotle and Spinoza arises the suggestion that shamelessness results from moral complacency. From Nietzsche, the more radical suggestion is that it results from the desire to step outside the realm of moral obligation into a natural world in which values are but expressions of our will to power. Now, from Sartre comes the suggestion that the will to power is not Spinoza's *conatus essendi* but more nearly Lucifer's "I will make myself like the Most High" (Isa. 14:14). On our historical journey, the closer we get to the present the farther we get from a site in which shame could be a virtue of any sort, including a political virtue.

Second, out of this diagnosis emerges a sense of just how radical a conversion would be required for shame to get a legitimate foothold. Beyond overcoming the moral complacency of respectable adults signified by Aristotle, and beyond overcoming the amoral naturalism of Spinoza and Nietzsche, it will be necessary to overcome original sin, the pride that wishes to be God, which lies at the basis of the seemingly less serious obstacles.

It is Levinas who provides an opening in this direction. He might be described as what you get when you link Sartre to Moses and the prophets rather than to Nietzsche. The Look or the face of the other, which is also the voice of the other, is utterly fundamental to my identity. Moreover, it puts me in question and calls me to responsibility in ways I do not automatically welcome. So the Sartrean response is always possible.

But if one is thinking with Moses rather than Nietzsche there are two differences that point in a different direction. First, ontologically speaking, we are not the atomic substances Washington and Jefferson imagined the republic to be. We cannot, as individual selves, avoid "permanent" and "entangling" alliances with others, for they belong to our very being and we are permanently entangled with them whether we like it, or even acknowledge it, or not. As members of families, as citizens of states, and as participants in communities and cultures of shared values, our relations with others are internal and not external relations, to use the language of the British Hegelians.

Second, morality is not reducible to the morality of mores, the laws and customs of my family, my state, my community (Hegel's *Sittlichkeit*). Empirically speaking, the claims of the other on me may not be valid, whether the other be an individual or a community. But in and through these, especially in and through the face of the widow, the stranger, and the orphan, I am addressed by a claim that is not in essence their *conatus essendi* or will to power over against mine, as Sartre à la Nietzsche would have it.[36] I am rather addressed by the Glory of the Most High with a claim whose unconditionality and asymmetry rob me of all pretensions to autonomy while at the same time calling me to my truest self.

So there is a very Sartrean sound to Levinas's claim, "My arbitrary freedom reads its shame in the eyes that look at me."[37] What is different is the legitimacy, the moral authority expressed in the face and voice of the other. In a passage that describes this authority in the language of height, Master, transcendence, infinity, exteriority, and teaching,[38] Levinas writes, "In this commerce with the infinity of exteriority or of height the naïveté of the direct impulse, the naïveté of the being exercising itself as a force on the move, is ashamed of its naïveté."[39] As with Sartre, the look and voice of the other interrupt my solipsistic sovereignty, but not in the same way. "The other is not opposed to me as a freedom other than, but similar to my own, and consequently hostile to my own. . . . His alterity is manifested in a mastery that does not conquer, but teaches. Teaching is not a species of a genus called domination, a hegemony at work within a totality,[40] but is the presence of infinity breaking the closed circle of totality" (171). Epistemically speaking, it is truth breaking in on me beyond and against my being the condition of its possibility. The Platonic soul that recollects a truth already within, the Cartesian subject whose clear and distinct ideas are the measure of truth, and the Husserlian subject whose intentional acts constitute its intentional objects are interrupted and invaded by a truth over which they do not preside.

Working backwards in the text, we should not be surprised to find Levinas's most extensive discussion of shame in a section entitled "Truth and Justice," in which he gives his own version of Kant's primacy of practical reason thesis. Justice is the foundation of truth rather than vice versa. In other words, "The freedom that can be ashamed of itself founds truth" (83). This is because "measuring oneself against the perfection of infinity is not a theoretical consideration; it is accomplished as shame, where freedom discovers itself murderous in its very exercise. . . . Shame does not have the structure of consciousness and clarity. It is oriented in the inverse direction; its subject is exterior to me" (84).

What does it mean to say that when I experience shame the subject is outside me? To begin with, perfection is about goodness rather than power, and infinity is an ethical rather than an ontic category. Thus the primacy of the practical. Second, I experience shame not as a Platonic soul recollecting the truth within, nor as a Cartesian/Husserlian subject intending various intentional objects.[41] I am the object looked at rather than the subject doing the looking. That is why Levinas sees the ethical relation as grounded "intentionality of a wholly different type" (23). We might call it inverse intentionality, one in which the intentional arrows are directed toward me as a moral claim rather than emanating from me as a theoretical judgment. The other is the subject, and my awareness of the other and of myself is precisely as the object of the other's gaze and address. Such experience is, for Levinas, the ground of language and truth. The bearer of Gyges's ring, who sees without being seen, is the wish-fulfilling fantasy of much of the Western tradition. The Sartrean self, totally vulnerable to the look of the other, as the realization that this wish is pure fantasy, is the proper starting point for philosophical reflection. And since that look will always be the bearer (among other things, to be sure) of a disapproval of which I cannot but approve, shame is properly basic to human experience.

All of these themes are complex and call for more attention than can be given here. What is immediately clear, however, is that shame is a virtue for Levinas. "Conscience welcomes the Other. . . . To welcome the Other is to put in question my freedom. . . . The welcoming of the Other is ipso facto the consciousness of my own injustice—the shame that freedom feels for itself. If philosophy consists in knowing critically, that is, in seeking a foundation for its freedom, in justifying it, it begins with conscience" (84–86). Conscience, welcoming the Other, shame: these are inextricably intertwined. Shame is not just *a* virtue, but is utterly integral to the moral life.

But is shame a political virtue? What we need to remember is the political context in which Levinas places his account of the ethical relation right from the start. The opening sentence of *Totality and Infinity* wonders "whether we are not duped by morality." The standpoint from which this worry arises is that of politics. "Politics is opposed to morality, as philosophy to naïveté." In other words, over against the sentimental idealism of morality, politics purports to be realistically rational. Thus, although politics is associated with war and violence, it presents itself as reason and philosophy, and Levinas will describe the mainstream of the Western tradition (to which he acknowledges exceptions) as "the ontology of war" (21–22).

In accepting this antithesis between politics and morality, Levinas does not treat morality as a retreat into the private as opposed to the public domain.

"Morality will oppose politics *in history*" (22, emphasis added), for two reasons. First, Levinas rejects the identification of morality with uncritical immediacy, the naïveté that politics takes it to be. The ethical relation to the other is what puts me radically in question and thus gives birth for the first time to critical reflection. As we saw above, "If philosophy consists in knowing critically, that is, in seeking a foundation for its freedom, in justifying it, it begins with conscience" (86).

Second, morality is operative in history by virtue of its eschatological character. "The moral consciousness can sustain the mocking gaze of the political man only if the certitude of peace dominates the evidence of war." But this certitude is not that of philosophical evidence, which looks to the present for its warrants; it belongs rather to "the eschatology of messianic peace." This standpoint rests on a faith and a hope that cannot be reduced to the evidences of philosophy, which it insists on finding in the now. But—and here the Bible wins out over Plato most decisively—Levinas refuses to equate this faith with mere opinion (22).

This eschatology takes us beyond the totality of history, which philosophy purports to comprehend. But if the morality of peace is not a private inwardness, it is not an otherworldly future, either. "This 'beyond' the totality and objective experience is, however, not to be described in a purely negative fashion. It is reflected *within* the totality and history, *within* experience. The eschatological, as the 'beyond' of history, draws beings out of the jurisdiction of history and the future; it arouses them in and calls them forth to their full responsibility" (23). In other words, the conscience that is capable of shame is the one historical agent that can be politically significant as the only challenge to the politics of war and violence.

In presenting morality as the "eschatology of messianic peace," Levinas agrees with the Confucian tradition that a shameless society cannot be a healthy society. But there is a definitive difference. The Confucian classics have a distinctly conservative nature to them. They tie shame quite tightly to a particular *Sittlichkeit*, to a historically particular and contingent set of traditions.[42] By virtue of their eschatological character, Levinasian morality and shame, which is its sine qua non, are not tied to any particular language game. They can be utopian and not merely ideological. As the face and voice of the other break into history from "beyond" history, it is not only the individual who is called into question but those totalities of institutions, practices, and traditions that were just referred to as language games. This is why shame has a religious as well as a political character for Levinas.

To the religious character of Levinas's reflections on shame, the Christian political theorist is likely to offer both a "yes" and "no." On the one hand, Christian thinking will agree with Levinas that shame has its roots in the failure to welcome properly the other who is integral to my own being precisely as having the right to be welcomed. And Christian thinking will also agree that the biblical concept of sin provides protection against the bourgeois moral complacency of the Confucian and Aristotelian traditions and against the attempt to naturalize evil as conatus or will to power in Spinoza and Nietzsche. Even Sartre's account of the desire to be God, which underlies my attempt to neutralize the look of the other, can be seen as naturalizing evil insofar as this desire is but a desire to be against the background of nothingness (as opposed to nature in Spinoza and Nietzsche), rather than being understood as rebellion against God.

But whereas Levinas makes the other first and foremost to be the human other, and attributes to the widow, the orphan, and the stranger such tradition-ally divine predicates as Glory and Revelation, and, in the process, tends toward a reduction of religion to ethics, Christian thinking will find the glory that lights the face of the widow and orphan and the teaching that resounds in the voice of the stranger to be but reflections and echoes of their divine original. Levinas will say the same, but for him the movement is always from ethics to religion, and there is nothing of God, either in the order of being or the order of knowing, other than what is to be found in the face of the neighbor. For the Christian (as for the biblical Jew and the Koranic Muslim), neither the being nor our knowl-edge of God is restricted to this ethical analogue of natural theology. God has a being independent of the widow and orphan and is knowable other than through the voice of the stranger. The movement will be from religion to ethics. The first commandment is to love God, the second to love the neighbor.

There is a substantial and growing philosophical literature on shame. For the most part, so far as I can tell, it belongs to the domain of moral psychology. This essay is a plea for the inclusion of such reflection in political theory with an eye to giving healthy shame a place of honor in political and educational practice. Robert F. Drinan, S.J., gives eloquent testimony to such a possibility in the title of his book about the struggle for internationally recognized human rights in the aftermath of World War II. Borrowing a phrase from an Amnesty International document, he calls it simply *The Mobilization of Shame*.[43]

NOTES

1. *Li* originally referred to rituals or rites, but its meaning extended to behavior gov-erned by manners or etiquette and eventually to behavior governed by custom as distinct from law.

2. *Analects* 2:3, in *A Sourcebook in Chinese Philosophy,* trans. Wing-Tsit Chan (Prince-ton: Princeton University Press, 1963), 22.

3. Chad Hansen, *A Daoist Theory of Chinese Thought* (New York: Oxford University Press, 1992), 64.

4. See Hansen, *A Daoist Theory*, 65. Cf. also Plato's notion that a healthy society is one that minimizes litigation, in *Republic* 464 d–e and *Laws* 743 c–d.

5. *Analects* 14:29, 42.

6. *The Book of Mencius* 6A:6, in *A Sourcebook in Chinese Philosophy*, 54. Cf. also 2A:6, in *A Sourcebook*, 65: "we see that a man without the feeling of commiseration is not a man; a man without the feeling of shame and dislike is not a man; a man without the feeling of deference and compliance is not a man; and a man without the feeling of right and wrong is not a man."

7. *A Sourcebook*, 105.

8. The modern, liberal division of society into public and private realms would have seemed more than strange to both the Confucians and to Aristotle. In such a context the distinction between moral and political virtues is possible, but the unfortunate result has all too often been to restrict the notion of virtue to the private realm and leave the public realm to calculative reason.

9. I am using the Ostwald translation, *Nichomachean Ethics* (Indianapolis: Bobbs-Merrill, 1962).

10. In Pauline/Augustinian/Calvinist perspective, "complacency" would represent a serious understatement of the problem.

11. The possibility of false shame is implicit in the above acknowledgment that it is not necessarily virtuous merely to feel shame as soon as one allows that the distinction between isolated acts and the corresponding habit is not the only basis for such a claim. One might feel ashamed (even habitually) but not for "the right things, for the right motive, in the right manner, and at the right time."

12. The quoted phrase is from the subtitle to Hume's *A Treatise of Human Nature*. All quotations from Spinoza are from *The Ethics*, trans. Samuel Shirley (Indianapolis: Hackett, 1982). Unless otherwise indicated they are from part 3. Propositions are cited by simple numbers, dropping the italics in which they are customarily given. S = Scholium, C = Corollary, P = Proof, D = Definition of the Emotions. For Spinoza's account of his physics of the emotions, see the preface to part 3.

13. The corresponding opposites are honor (*gloria*) and self-contentment (*acquiescentia in se ipso*).

14. Thus Robert Solomon writes, "Guilt (not causal or legal guilt, but the feeling of guilt) is a highly individualistic emotion, a matter of self-scrutiny and self-condemnation. Shame, by contrast, is a highly social emotion. . . . Like guilt, it is self-accusatory, but it is so through the eyes of others, as an inextricable member of a group or community" ("Shame," in *The Oxford Companion to Philosophy*, ed. Ted Honderich [New York: Oxford University Press, 1995], 825).

15. For the argument to support this conclusion, see my *God, Guilt, and Death: An Existential Phenomenology of Religion* (Bloomington: Indiana University Press, 1984), chap. 4. Of course, if the disapproval is not moral disapproval, the shame (we are not likely to speak of guilt in this context) will not be moral shame. See Rawls's distinction between "natural" and "moral" shame, *A Theory of Justice* (Cambridge, Mass.: Harvard University Press, 1971), 444. On the next page Rawls distinguishes between guilt and shame, but not in the "standard" way (à la Spinoza and Solomon). We feel guilty, he says, when we

have acted against our sense of right and justice, and ashamed because we have failed to achieve some good. Whatever the merits of this attempt to distinguish the two in terms of the difference between the right and the good, it should be noted that on this account guilt and shame might well share the structure of being my approval of others' disapproval of me, and Rawls's own account of both guilt and shame supports this notion of a self-relation that is simultaneously and essentially an other-relation (see 442–45).

16. In this context it's not clear that "wicked" can mean anything other than "stupid."

17. In commending both fear and shame for the mob, Spinoza ignores the difference, so important to the Confucian tradition, between legal sanctions by which the state punishes and the "punishment" of social disapproval.

18. *The Portable Nietzsche,* ed. and trans. Walter Kaufmann (New York: Viking Press, 1954), 92.

19. In speaking of the moral world order Nietzsche reminds us that the biblical traditions, Jewish and Christian, along with the Platonic and Kantian traditions in ethics, are united in the claim that the values they affirm are not merely what Hegel calls *Sittlichkeit*— the laws and customs of one's people—but are grounded in a God, or a Good, or a Reason that is never identical with nor reducible to any *Sittlichkeit.* In denying that the laws can ever be identified with justice, Derrida sides with the tradition against Hegel and Nietzsche. See Jacques Derrida, "Force of Law: The 'Mystical Foundation of Authority,'" in *Deconstruction and the Possibility of Justice,* ed. Drucilla Cornell, Michel Rosenfeld, and David Gray Carlson (New York: Routledge, 1992), and my own "Derrida as Natural Law Theorist," in *Overcoming Onto-Theology* (New York: Fordham University Press, 2001).

20. *The Gay Science,* trans. Walter Kaufmann (New York: Random House, 1974), 220.

21. See Paul Ricoeur, *Freud and Philosophy: An Essay on Interpretation,* trans. Denis Savage (New Haven: Yale University Press, 1970), 32.

22. *Thus Spoke Zarathustra,* in *The Portable Nietzsche,* 212.

23. *Gay Science,* 164.

24. *The Genealogy of Morals* (with *Ecce Homo*), trans. Walter Kaufmann and R. J. Hollingdale (New York: Random House, 1967), 67.

25. *Beyond Good and Evil,* trans. Walter Kaufmann (New York: Random House, 1966), 236.

26. *Human, All Too Human: A Book for Free Spirits,* trans. R. J. Hollingdale (New York: Cambridge University Press, 1986), 312.

27. Like Spinoza and unlike the Confucian tradition, Nietzsche does not treat shame and punishment as significantly different. See note 17 above.

28. *Beyond Good and Evil,* 92.

29. The Nietzsche I envisage here is willing to endure loneliness for the sake of his values, but does not seek it as an end in itself. It is not as such one of his values.

30. On the Sartre-Nietzsche connection, see especially Walter Kaufmann, "Nietzsche between Homer and Sartre: Five Treatments of the Orestes Story," *Revue Internationale de Philosophie,* no. 67 (1964): 50–73, and *Philosophy and Tragedy* (Garden City, N.Y.: Doubleday and Co., 1968), especially chap. 8.

31. *Daybreak: Thoughts on the Prejudices of Morality,* trans. R. J. Hollingdale (New York: Cambridge University Press, 1982), 166.

32. *Being and Nothingness,* trans. Hazel Barnes (New York: Philosophical Library, 1956), 281. Between Nietzsche and Sartre the difference between one great dazzling eye and millions of looks is merely rhetorical.

33. *Totality and Infinity: An Essay on Exteriority,* trans. Alphonso Lingis (Pittsburgh: Duquesne University Press, 1969), 66.

34. What theology has he been reading? Marcion, perhaps?

35. Cf. the similar footnote in relation to bad faith on p. 70.

36. Levinas can be read as the natural law tradition presented in the language of Sartre's analysis of the Look.

37. *Totality and Infinity,* 252. Subsequent references in the text to Levinas are to this text.

38. Levinas strongly repudiates the Socratic notions of the maieutic and recollection in his insistence that the other actually teaches me, gives me what I cannot produce from myself. See 43, 51, 61, 126, 180, and 204; also see Norman Wirzba, "From Maieutics to Metanoia: Levinas's Understanding of the Philosophical Task," *Man and World* 28 (1995): 129–44, and "Teaching as Propaedeutic to Religion: The Contribution of Levinas and Kierkegaard," *International Journal for Philosophy of Religion* 39 (April 1996): 77–94; finally, see my own "Levinas and the Immediacy of the Face," *Faith and Philosophy* 9 (1993): 486–502.

39. In *Otherwise Than Being or Beyond Essence,* Levinas often uses Spinoza's term, *conatus,* to refer to what he here calls "arbitrary freedom," "direct impulse," and "being exercising itself as a force on the move."

40. We might call this a zero sum game concerned with the distribution of power.

41. In both cases I am the ground of the truth I discover, the condition for its possibility. Levinas thinks that ethics requires abandoning these dominant models of knowing in the Western tradition, which make me the seer and protect me (in theory if not in fact) from being seen.

42. For a reading of Confucius as a traditionalist, see Philip J. Ivanhoe, *Ethics in the Confucian Tradition* (Indianapolis: Hackett, 2002). But perhaps there are what might be called eschatological openings in this tradition. See Wm. Theodore DeBary, *Asian Values and Human Rights: A Confucian Communitarian Perspective* (Cambridge, Mass.: Harvard University Press, 1998). See note 36 above, linking Levinas to the natural law tradition.

43. Robert F. Drinan, S.J., *The Mobilization of Shame* (New Haven: Yale University Press, 2001).

BIBLIOGRAPHY

I am grateful to Daniel McWhorter for help compiling the bibliography.

Adams, Robert. *Finite and Infinite Goods.* Oxford: Oxford University Press, 1999.

———. "A Modified Divine Command Theory of Ethical Wrongness." In *The Virtue of Faith and Other Essays in Philosophical Theology.* Oxford: Oxford University Press, 1987.

Aquinas, Thomas. *Summa Theologica.* Translated by Fathers of the Dominican Providence. Westminster, Md.: Christian Classics, 1981.

Aquinas, Thomas. *Truth (Quaestiones Disputatae de Veritate).* Chicago: Henry Regnery Co., 1952.

Aristotle. *Nicomachean Ethics.* Translated by Terence Irwin. Indianapolis: Hackett, 2000.

Arnhart, Larry. "Evolutionary Ethics in the Twentieth Century." In *Biology and the Foundations of Ethics.* Edited by Jane Maienschein and Michael Ruse. Cambridge: Cambridge University Press, 1999.

———. *Darwinian Natural Right.* Albany: State University of New York Press, 1998.

Audi, Robert. *Religious Commitment and Secular Reason.* Cambridge: Cambridge University Press, 2000.

———. "The Place of Religious Argument in a Free and Democratic Society." *San Diego Law Review* 39 (1993): 677–702.

Audi, Robert, and Nicholas Wolterstorff. *Religion in the Public Square: The Place of Religious Convictions in Political Debate.* Lanham, Md.: Rowman and Littlefield, 1997.

Baier, Annette C. "Claims, Rights, Responsibilities." In *Prospects for a Common Morality.* Edited by Gene Outka and John Reeder. Princeton: Princeton University Press, 1993.

Barth, Carl. *Church Dogmatics.* Vol. 3, bk. 2. Translated by Harold Knight, G. W. Bromiley, J. K. S. Reid, and R. H. Fuller. Edinburgh: T. and T. Clark, 1960.

Batson, C. D., J. Fulz, P. A. Schoenrade, and A. Paduano. "Critical Self-Reflection and Self-Perceived Altruism: When Self-Reward Fails." *Journal of Personality and Social Psychology* 53 (1987): 594–602.

Baxter, Michael J., C.S.C. " 'Blowing the Dynamite of the Church': Catholic Radicalism from a Catholic Radicalist Perspective." In *The Church as Counterculture.* Edited by

Michael L. Budde and Robert W. Brimlow. Albany: State University of New York Press, 2000.

Bayertz, Kurt. "Human Dignity: Philosophical Origin and Scientific Erosion of the Idea." In *Sanctity of Life and Human Dignity*. Edited by Kurt Bayertz. Boston: Kluwer Academic Press, 1996.

Benhabib, Seyla. *Situating the Self: Gender, Community, and Postmodernism in Contemporary Ethics*. New York: Routledge, 1992.

Bird, Colin. "Mutual Respect and Public Justification." *Ethics* 107 (October 1996): 62–96.

Blackburn, Simon. "The Flight to Reality." In *Virtues and Reasons*. Edited by Rosalind Hursthouse, Gavin Lawrence, and Warren Quinn. Oxford: Clarendon Press, 1995.

———. *Essays in Quasi-Realism*. Oxford: Oxford University Press, 1993.

Boyd, Richard. "How to Be a Moral Realist." In *Essays on Moral Realism*. Edited by Geoffrey Sayre-McCord. Ithaca, N.Y.: Cornell University Press, 1988.

Brandom, Robert M. *Making It Explicit: Reasoning, Representing, and Discursive Commitment*. Cambridge, Mass.: Harvard University Press, 1994.

Brimlow, Robert. "Solomon's Porch: The Church as Sectarian Ghetto." In *The Church as Counterculture*. Edited by Michael L. Budde and Robert W. Brimlow. Albany: State University of New York Press, 2000.

Brink, David. *Moral Realism and the Foundations of Ethics*. Cambridge: Cambridge University Press, 1989.

Calvin, John. *Institutes of the Christian Religion*. Edited by John T. McNeill. Translated by Ford Lewis Battles. Philadelphia: Westminster Press, 1960.

Campbell, Donald T. "On the Conflicts between Biological and Social Evolution and between Psychology and Moral Tradition." *American Psychologist* 30 (1975): 1103–26.

Campbell, Donald T., and Judith C. Specht. "Altruism: Biology, Culture, and Religion." *Journal of Social and Clinical Psychology* 3 (1985): 33–42.

Carter, Stephen. *The Culture of Disbelief*. New York: Basic Books, 1993.

Chan, Wing-Tsit, trans. *A Sourcebook in Chinese Philosophy*. Princeton: Princeton University Press, 1963.

Childs, Brevard. *Old Testament Theology in a Canonical Context*. Philadelphia: Fortress Press, 1986.

Clark, Gordon. *A Christian View of Men and Things*. Grand Rapids, Mich.: Eerdmans, 1952.

Clark, R. D., and E. Hatfield. "Gender Differences in Receptivity to Sexual Offers." *Journal of Psychology and Human Sexuality* 2 (1989): 39–55.

Clines, David. "Humanity as the Image of God." In *On the Way to the Postmodern: Old Testament Essays, 1967–1998*. Sheffield, England: Sheffield Academic Press, 1998.

Coleman, John A. "Deprivatizing Religion and Revitalizing Citizenship." In *Religion and Contemporary Liberalism*. Edited by Paul Weithman. Notre Dame, Ind.: University of Notre Dame Press, 1997.

The Compact Edition of the Oxford English Dictionary. Oxford: Oxford University Press, 1971.

Curley, Edwin. "'I Durst Not Write So Boldly' or, How To Read Hobbes' Theological-Political Treatise." In *Hobbes e Spinoza, Scienza e Politica*. Edited by Daniela Bostrenghi. Naples: Bibliopolis, 1992.

De Waal, Frans. *Good Natured: The Origins of Right and Wrong in Humans and Other Animals*. Cambridge, Mass.: Harvard University Press, 1996.

DeBary, Wm. Theodore. *Asian Values and Human Rights: A Confucian Communitarian Perspective*. Cambridge, Mass.: Harvard University Press, 1998.

Derrida, Jacques. *The Gift of Death.* Translated by David Wills. Chicago: University of Chicago Press, 1995.

———. "Force of Law: The Mystical Foundation of Authority." In *Deconstruction and the Possibility of Justice.* Edited by Drucilla Cornell, Michel Rosenfeld, and David Gray Carlson. New York: Routledge, 1992.

Donagan, Alan. *The Theory of Morality.* Chicago: University of Chicago Press, 1977.

Doppelt, Gerald. "Rawls's System of Justice: A Critique from the Left." *Noûs* 15 (1981): 259–308.

Drinan, Robert F., S.J., *The Mobilization of Shame.* New Haven: Yale University Press, 2001.

Dworkin, Ronald. *Sovereign Virtue: The Theory and Practice of Equality.* Cambridge, Mass.: Harvard University Press, 2000.

———. *Freedom's Law: The Moral Reading of the American Constitution.* Cambridge, Mass.: Harvard University Press, 1996.

———. *Life's Dominion: An Argument about Abortion, Euthanasia, and Individual Freedom.* New York: Knopf, 1993.

Eberle, Christopher J. *Religious Convictions in Liberal Politics.* Cambridge: Cambridge University Press, 2002.

Feinberg, Joel. *Social Philosophy.* Englewood Cliffs, N.J.: Prentice-Hall, 1973.

Finnis, John. "Natural Law and Legal Reasoning." In *Natural Law Theory.* Edited by Robert George. Oxford: Oxford University Press, 1992.

———. *Natural Law and Natural Rights.* Oxford: Oxford University Press, 1980.

Fish, Stanley. "Postmodern Warfare: The Ignorance of Our Warrior Intellectuals." *Harper's Magazine* 305, no. 1826 (July 2002): 37–38.

Flanagan, Owen. *The Problem of the Soul: Two Visions of Mind and How to Reconcile Them.* New York: Basic Books, 2002.

Frank, R.H.T., T. Gilovich, and D. Regan. "Does Studying Economics Inhibit Cooperation?" *Journal of Economic Perspectives* 7 (1993): 159–71.

Gaus, Gerald. *Justificatory Liberalism: An Essay on Epistemology and Political Theory.* Oxford: Oxford University Press, 1996.

———. "Public Reason and the Rule of Law." In *The Rule of Law.* Edited by Ian Shapiro. *Nomos* 36. New York: New York University Press, 1994.

Gauthier, David. *Morals by Agreement.* Oxford: Clarendon Press, 1986.

Geertz, Clifford. *The Interpretation of Cultures.* New York: Basic Books, 1973.

George, Robert. "A Response." In *A Preserving Grace.* Edited by Michael Cromartie. Grand Rapids, Mich: Eerdmans, 1997.

———. *Making Men Moral: Civil Liberties and Public Morality.* Oxford: Oxford University Press, 1993.

———. "Recent Criticisms of Natural Law Theory." *University of Chicago Law Review* 55 (1988): 1371–429.

———. *Natural Law, Liberalism, and Morality.* Oxford: Oxford University Press, 1996.

Graham, Daniel. *Aristotle's Two Systems.* Oxford: Oxford University Press, 1987.

Greenawalt, Kent. *Private Consciences and Public Reasons.* Oxford: Oxford University Press, 1995.

———. *Religious Conviction and Political Choice.* Oxford: Oxford University Press, 1988.

Grisez, Germain, Joseph Boyle, and John Finnis. "Practical Principles, Moral Truth, and Ultimate Ends." *American Journal of Jurisprudence* 32 (1987): 99–151.

Hampton, Jean. "Should Political Philosophy Be Done without Metaphysics?" In *Liberalism and the Good*. Edited by R. Bruce Douglas, Gerald M. Mara, and Henry S. Richardson. New York: Routledge, 1990.

Hampton, Jean, and Jeffrie G. Murphy. *Forgiveness and Mercy*. Cambridge: Cambridge University Press, 1988.

Hansen, Chad. *A Daoist Theory of Chinese Thought*. New York: Oxford University Press, 1992.

Hare, John E. "Is There an Evolutionary Foundation for Human Morality?" In *Evolutionary Ethics: Human Morality in Biological and Religious Perspective*. Edited by Philip Clayton and Jeffrey Schloss. Grand Rapids, Mich.: Eerdmans, 2004.

———. "Christian Scholarship and Human Responsibility." In *Christian Scholarship . . . For What?* Edited by Susan Felch. Grand Rapids, Mich.: Calvin College, 2003.

———. *Why Bother Being Good?* Downers Grove, Ill.: InterVarsity Press, 2002.

———. *God's Call*. Grand Rapids, Mich.: Eerdmans, 2001.

———. *The Moral Gap*. Oxford: Clarendon Press, 1996.

Harrison, Jonathan. *Hume's Theory of Justice*. Oxford: Clarendon Press, 1981.

Hauerwas, Stanley. *Dispatches from the Front: Theological Engagements with the Secular*. Durham, N.C.: Duke University Press, 1994.

———. *After Christendom: How the Church Is to Behave if Freedom, Justice, and a Christian Nation Are Bad Ideas*. Nashville, Tenn.: Abingdon Press, 1991.

Hauerwas, Stanley, and William Willimon. *Resident Aliens*. Nashville, Tenn.: Abingdon Press, 1989.

Hefner, Philip. *The Human Factor*. Minneapolis: Fortress Press, 1993.

Hehir, J. Bryan. "Personal Faith, the Public Church, and the Role of Theology." *Harvard Divinity Bulletin* 26 (1996): 4–5.

———. "The Perennial Need for Philosophical Discourse." *Theological Studies* 40 (1979): 710–13.

Hobbes, Thomas. *Leviathan*. Edited by Edwin Curley. Indianapolis: Hackett, 1994.

Hollenbach, David. "Politically Active Churches: Some Empirical Prolegomena to a Normative Approach." In *Religion and Contemporary Liberalism*. Edited by Paul Weithman. Notre Dame, Ind.: University of Notre Dame Press, 1997.

Holmes, Arthur. *Contours of a World View*. Grand Rapids, Mich.: Eerdmans, 1983.

Holt, Jim. "Prayer Works." *New York Times*, December 9, 2001, sec. 6, p. 92.

Honderich, Ted, ed. *The Oxford Companion to Philosophy*. New York: Oxford University Press, 1995.

Hume, David. *Enquiry Concerning the Principles of Morals*. Edited by L. A. Selby-Bigge. Revised by P. H. Nidditch. Oxford: Oxford University Press, 1975.

Isaacson, Walter. *Benjamin Franklin: An American Life*. New York: Simon and Schuster, 2003.

Ivanhoe, Philip J. *Ethics in the Confucian Tradition*. Indianapolis: Hackett, 2002.

Jackson, Timothy. *The Priority of Love: Christian Charity and Social Justice*. Princeton: Princeton University Press, 2003.

———. "A House Divided, Again: Sanctity vs. Dignity in the Induced Death Debates." In *In Defense of Human Dignity*. Edited by Robert Kraynak and Glenn Tinder. Notre Dame, Ind.: University of Notre Dame Press, 2003.

———. "The Return of the Prodigal? Liberal Theory and Religious Pluralism." In *Religion and Contemporary Liberalism*. Edited by Paul Weithman. Notre Dame, Ind.: University of Notre Dame Press, 1997.

Kant, Immanuel. *Critique of Practical Reason.* In *Immanuel Kant: Practical Philosophy.* Translated by Mary J. Gregor. Cambridge: Cambridge University Press, 1996.

———. *Groundwork of the Metaphysics of Morals.* In *Immanuel Kant: Practical Philosophy.* Translated by Mary J. Gregor. Cambridge: Cambridge University Press, 1996.

Kaufmann, Walter. *Philosophy and Tragedy.* Garden City, N.Y.: Doubleday and Co., 1968.

———. "Nietzsche between Homer and Sartre: Five Treatments of the Orestes Story." *Revue Internationale de Philosophie* 67 (1964): 50–73.

Kaufmann, Walter, trans. and ed. *The Portable Nietzsche.* New York: Viking Press, 1954.

Keenan, James F. "The Concept of Sanctity of Life." In *Sanctity of Life and Human Dignity.* Edited by Kurt Bayertz. Boston: Kluwer Academic Press, 1996.

Kierkegaard, Søren. *The Concept of Anxiety.* Translated by Reidar Thomte. Princeton: Princeton University Press, 1998.

———. *The Sickness Unto Death.* Translated by Howard V. Hong and Edna H. Hong. Princeton: Princeton University Press, 1980.

Kuyper, Abraham. *Lectures on Calvinism.* Grand Rapids, Mich.: Eerdmans, 1931.

Larmore, Charles. *Patterns of Moral Complexity.* Cambridge: Cambridge University Press, 1987.

A Latin Dictionary. Compiled by Lewis and Short. Oxford: Clarendon Press, 1987.

Lear, Jonathan. *The Desire to Understand.* Cambridge: Cambridge University Press, 1988.

Levinas, Emmanuel. *Totality and Infinity: An Essay on Exteriority.* Translated by Alphonso Lingis. Pittsburgh: Duquesne University Press, 1969.

Lisska, Anthony. *Aquinas's Theory of Natural Law.* Oxford: Oxford University Press, 1998.

Lloyd, S. A. "Hobbes's Self-Effacing Natural Law Theory." *Pacific Philosophical Quarterly* 82 (2001): 285–308.

Macedo, Stephen. *Liberal Virtues: Citizenship, Virtue, and Community in Liberal Constitutionalism.* Oxford: Clarendon Press, 1990.

MacIntyre, Alasdair. "Theories of Natural Law in the Culture of Advanced Modernity." In *Common Truths: New Perspectives on Natural Law.* Edited by Edward McLean. Wilmington, Del.: ISI Books, 2000.

———. *Whose Justice? Which Rationality?* Notre Dame, Ind.: University of Notre Dame Press, 1988.

———. *After Virtue.* 2d ed. Notre Dame, Ind.: University of Notre Dame Press, 1984.

Mackie, J. L. *Ethics: Inventing Right and Wrong.* Harmondsworth, England: Penguin, 1977.

Martinich, A. P. *The Two Gods of Leviathan.* Cambridge: Cambridge University Press, 1992.

McDowell, John. "Values as Secondary Qualities." In *Morality and Objectivity.* Edited by Ted Honderich. London: Routledge and Kegan Paul, 1985.

Milbank, John. *Theology and Social Theory.* Oxford: Blackwell, 1993.

Mill, John Stuart. *On Liberty.* New York: Penguin, 1988.

Murdoch, Iris. *The Fire and the Sun.* Oxford: Oxford University Press, 1977.

Murdoch, Iris. *The Sovereignty of Good over Other Concepts.* Cambridge: Cambridge University Press, 1967.

Murphy, Mark C. *Natural Law and Practical Reasoning.* Cambridge: Cambridge University Press, 2001.

———. "Divine Command, Divine Will, and Moral Obligation." *Faith and Philosophy* 15 (January 1998): 3–27.

———. "Hobbes on Conscientious Disobedience." *Archiv für Geschichte der Philosophie* 77 (1995): 263–84.

Murphy, Mark C. "Theological Voluntarism." *The Stanford Encyclopedia of Philosophy* (Fall 2002 Edition). Edited by Edward N. Zalta. Available at http://plato.stanford.edu/archives/fall2002/entries/voluntarism-theological/.

National Conference of Catholic Bishops. *The Challenge of Peace: God's Promise and Our Response.* Parts 1 and 2. *Catholic Social Teaching* (1983). Available at http://www.osjspm.org/cst/cp.htm.

Neibuhr, Reinhold. *Christian Realism and Political Problems.* New York: Charles Scribner's Sons, 1953.

Nielson, Kai. "Liberal Reasonability a Critical Tool? Reflections after Rawls." *Dialogue* 37, no. 4 (Fall 1998): 734–54.

Nietzsche, Friedrich. *Daybreak: Thoughts on the Prejudices of Morality.* Translated by R. J. Hollingdale. New York: Cambridge University Press, 1982.

———. *The Gay Science.* Translated by Walter Kaufmann. New York: Random House, 1974.

———. *The Genealogy of Morals (with Ecce Homo).* Translated by Walter Kaufmann and R. J. Hollingdale. New York: Random House, 1967.

———. *Beyond Good and Evil.* Translated by Walter Kaufman. New York: Random House, 1966.

Nord, Warren A. *Religion and American Education.* Chapel Hill, N.C.: University of North Carolina Press, 1995.

Nussbaum, Martha C. *Women and Human Development: The Capabilities Approach.* Cambridge: Cambridge University Press, 2000.

———. *Sex and Social Justice.* Oxford: Oxford University Press, 1999.

———. "Non-Relative Virtues: An Aristotelian Approach." In *The Quality of Life.* Edited by Martha C. Nussbaum and Amartya Sen. Oxford: Clarendon Press, 1993.

O'Connor, June. "Making a Case for the Common Good in a Global Economy: The United Nations Human Development Reports (1990–2001)." *Journal of Religious Ethics* 30 (Spring 2002): 157–73.

O'Donovan, Joan Lockwood. "The Concept of Rights in Christian Moral Discourse." In *Preserving Grace.* Edited by Michael Cromartie. Grand Rapids, Mich.: Eerdmans, 1997.

O'Donovan, Oliver. *The Desire of the Nations.* Cambridge: Cambridge University Press, 1996.

The Oxford English Dictionary. Oxford: Oxford University Press, 1978.

Parfit, Derek. *Reasons and Persons.* Oxford: Oxford University Press, 1984.

Perry, Michael. *Love and Power.* Oxford: Oxford University Press, 1988.

Phelan, Gerald, trans. *St. Thomas Aquinas on Kingship.* Toronto: The Pontifical Institute of Mediaeval Studies, 1949.

Pinsky, Robert. *Democracy, Culture, and the Voice of Poetry.* Princeton: Princeton University Press, 2002.

Plato. *The Republic.* Translated by G. M. A. Grube. Indianapolis: Hackett, 1974.

———. *The Dialogues of Plato.* Translated with analysis by R. E. Allen. New Haven: Yale University Press, 1984.

Pollock, John. *Contemporary Theories of Knowledge.* Totowa, N.J.: Rowman Littlefield, 1986.

Quinn, Philip. "Religious Citizens within the Limits of Public Reason." *Modern Schoolman* 78 (January/March 2001): 105–24

———. "Divine Command Theory." In *The Blackwell Guide to Ethical Theory.* Edited by Hugh LaFollette. Oxford: Blackwell, 1999.

———. "Political Liberalisms and Their Exclusions of the Religious." In *Religion and Contemporary Liberalism.* Edited by Paul Weithman. Notre Dame, Ind.: University of Notre Dame Press, 1997.

———. "The Primacy of God's Will in Christian Ethics." In *Philosophical Perspectives,* Vol. 6, Ethics. Edited by James Tomberlin. Atascadero, Calif.: Ridgeview Publishing Company, 1992.

———. "An Argument for Divine Command Ethics." In *Christian Theism and the Problems of Philosophy.* Edited by Michael Beaty. Notre Dame, Ind.: University of Notre Dame Press, 1990.

———. *Divine Commands and Moral Requirements.* Oxford: Oxford University Press, 1978.

Rawls, John. "The Idea of Public Reason Revisited." *The University of Chicago Law Review* 63 (1997): 765–807.

———. *Political Liberalism.* New York: Columbia University Press, 1993; paperback ed., 1996.

———. *A Theory of Justice.* Cambridge, Mass.: The Belknap Press, 1971.

Richards, Robert J. "Darwin's Romantic Biology." In *Biology and the Foundations of Ethics.* Edited by Jane Maienschein and Michael Ruse. Cambridge: Cambridge University Press, 1999.

———. "A Defense of Evolutionary Ethics." *Biology and Philosophy* 1 (1986): 265–93.

Ricoeur, Paul. *Freud and Philosophy: An Essay on Interpretation.* Translated by Denis Savage. New Haven: Yale University Press, 1970.

Rorty, Richard. "Human Rights, Rationality, Sentimentality." In *On Human Rights: The 1993 Oxford Amnesty Lectures.* Edited by Susan Hurley and Stephen Shute. New York: Basic Books, 1993.

Rousseau, Jean-Jacques. *The Social Contract.* Translated by Willmore Kendall. Chicago: Henry Regnery Co., 1954.

Ruse, Michael. "Evolutionary Ethics in the Twentieth Century." In *Biology and the Foundations of Ethics.* Edited by Jane Maienschein and Michael Ruse. Cambridge: Cambridge University Press, 1999.

———. *Taking Darwinism Seriously.* Oxford: Blackwell, 1986.

Sartre, Jean-Paul. *Being and Nothingness.* Translated by Hazel Barnes. New York: Philosophical Library, 1956.

Scanlon, Thomas M. *What We Owe Each Other.* Cambridge, Mass.: Harvard University Press, 1996.

Schneewind, Jerome. *The Invention of Autonomy.* Cambridge: Cambridge University Press, 1998.

Sidgwick, Henry. *The Methods of Ethics.* 7th ed. Indianapolis: Hackett, 1981.

Simon, William, and Michael Novak. *Liberty and Justice for All: Report on the Final Draft of the U.S. Catholic Bishops' Pastoral Letter "Economic Justice for All."* Washington, D.C.: The Brownson Institute, 1986.

Singer, Peter. *Unsanctifying Human Life.* Edited by Helga Kuhse. Malden, Mass.: Blackwell Publishers, 2002.

Singer, Peter. "Dangerous Words." Interview by Kathryn Federici Greenwood. *Princeton Alumni Weekly,* January 26, 2000, p. 19.

———. *Rethinking Life and Death: The Collapse of Our Traditional Ethics.* Oxford: Oxford University Press, 1994.

———. *Practical Ethics.* Cambridge: Cambridge University Press, 1993.

Sober, Elliot, and David Sloan. *Unto Others: The Evolution and Psychology of Unselfish Be-havior.* Cambridge, Mass.: Harvard University Press, 1999.

Solum, Lawrence. "Faith and Justice." *DePaul Law Review* 39 (1990): 1083–106.

Spinoza, Baruch. *The Ethics.* Translated by Samuel Shirley. Indianapolis: Hackett, 1982.

Starobinski, Jean. *Jean-Jacques Rousseau: Transparency and Obstruction.* Translated by Arthur Goldhammer. Chicago: University of Chicago Press, 1971.

Stob, Henry. "Observations on the Concept of the Antithesis." In *Perspectives on the Christian Reformed Church: Studies in Its History, Theology, and Ecumenicity.* Edited by Peter De Klerk and Richard R. De Ridder. Grand Rapids, Mich.: Baker Book House, 1983.

Stout, Jeffrey. *Ethics after Babel: The Languages of Morals and Their Discontents.* Boston: Beacon Press, 1988.

Taylor, Charles. *The Ethics of Authenticity.* Cambridge, Mass.: Harvard University Press, 1991.

———. *Sources of the Self.* Cambridge, Mass.: Harvard University Press, 1989.

Tinder, Glenn. *The Political Meanings of Christianity.* San Francisco: Harper Collins, 1991.

Trible, Phyllis. "Eve and Adam: Genesis 2–3 Reread." In *Womanspirit Rising: A Feminist Reader in Religion.* Edited by Carol Christ and Judith Plaskow. San Francisco: Harper-SanFrancisco, 1979.

———. *God and the Rhetoric of Sexuality.* Philadelphia: Fortress Press, 1978.

Twain, Mark. *The Autobiography of Mark Twain.* New York: Harper Perennial, 1990.

Urmson, J. O. "Saints and Heroes." In *Moral Concepts.* Edited by Joel Feinberg. Oxford: Oxford University Press, 1969.

Van Inwagen, Peter. *Material Beings.* Ithaca, N.Y.: Cornell University Press, 1990.

Weithman, Paul. *Religion and the Obligations of Citizenship.* Cambridge: Cambridge University Press, 2002.

———. "The Liberalism of Reasoned Respect." In *Religion and Contemporary Liberalism.* Edited by Paul Weithman. Notre Dame, Ind.: University of Notre Dame Press, 1997.

———. "Liberalism and the Political Character of Political Philosophy." In *Liberalism and the Good.* Edited by R. Bruce Douglas, Gerald M. Mara, and Henry S. Richardson. New York: Routledge, 1990.

Weithman, Paul, ed. *Religion and Contemporary Liberalism.* Notre Dame, Ind.: University of Notre Dame Press, 1997.

Westphal, Merold. *Overcoming Onto-Theology.* New York: Fordham University Press, 2001.

———. "Levinas and the Immediacy of the Face." *Faith and Philosophy* 9 (1993): 486–502.

———. *God, Guilt, and Death: An Existential Phenomenology of Religion.* Bloomington, Ind.: Indiana University Press, 1984.

Wirzba, Norman. "Teaching as Propaeduetic to Religion: The Contribution of Levinas and Kierkegaard." *International Journal for Philosophy of Religion* 39 (April 1996): 77–94.

———. "From Maieutics to Metanoia: Levinas's Understanding of the Philosophical Task." *Man and World* 28 (1995): 129–44.

Witte, John, Jr. "Between Sanctity and Depravity: Human Dignity in Protestant Perspective." In *In Defense of Human Dignity.* Edited by Robert Kraynak and Glenn Tinder. Notre Dame, Ind.: University of Notre Dame Press, 2003.

Wittgenstein, Ludwig. *Philosophical Investigations.* Translated by G. E. M. Anscombe. Oxford: Blackwell, 1958.

Wolff, Robert Paul. *In Defense of Anarchism.* New York: Harper and Row, 1970.

Wolterstorff, Nicholas. *Educating for Life: Reflections on Christian Teaching and Learning.* Edited by Gloria Stronks and Clarence W. Joldersma. Grand Rapids, Mich.: Baker Book House, 2002.

———. "A Discussion of Oliver O'Donovan's *The Desire of the Nations.*" *Scottish Journal of Theology* 54 (2001): 87–109.

———. "A Religious Argument for the Civil Right to Freedom of Religious Exercise, Drawn from American History." *Wake Forest Law Review* 36 (Summer 2001): 535–56.

———. "Do Christians Have Good Reasons for Supporting Liberal Democracy?" *The Modern Schoolman* 78 (2001): 229–48.

———. "Abraham Kuyper's Model of Democratic Polity for Societies with a Religiously Diverse Citizenry." In *Kuyper Reconsidered: Aspects of His Life and Work.* Edited by Cornelis Van der Kooi and Jan de Bruijn. Amsterdam: VU Uitgeverij, 1999.

———. "The Contours of Justice: An Ancient Call for *Shalom.*" In *God and the Victim.* Edited by Lisa Barnes Lampman. Grand Rapids, Mich.: Eerdmans, 1999.

———. "Christian Political Reflection: Diognetian or Augustinian?" *The Princeton Seminary Bulletin* 20 (July 1999): 150–68.

———. "Why We Should Reject What Liberalism Tells Us about Speaking and Acting in Public for Religious Reasons." In *Religion and Contemporary Liberalism.* Edited by Paul Weithman. Notre Dame, Ind.: University of Notre Dame Press, 1997.

———. *Divine Discourse.* Cambridge: Cambridge University Press, 1995.

———. "Has the Cloak Become a Cage: Charity, Justice, and Economic Activity." In *Rethinking Materialism.* Edited by Robert Wuthnow. Grand Rapids, Mich.: Eerdmans, 1995.

———. "The Schools We Deserve." In *Schooling Christians.* Edited by Stanley Hauerwas and John Westerhoff. Grand Rapids, Mich.: Eerdmans, 1992. Reprinted in *Educating for Life: Reflections on Christian Teaching and Learning.* Edited by Gloria Stronks and Clarence W. Joldersma. Grand Rapids, Mich.: Baker Book House, 2002.

———. "Worship and Justice." In *Major Themes in the Reformed Tradition.* Edited by Donald McKim. Grand Rapids, Mich.: Eerdmans, 1992.

———. "Justice as a Condition of Authentic Liturgy." *Theology Today* 48 (1991): 6–21.

———. "The Moral Significance of Poverty." *Perspectives* 6 (February 1991): 8–11.

———. "God's Holiness Demands Justice: I." *The Banner* 125, October 29, 1990, pp. 6–8.

———. "God's Holiness Demands Justice: II." *The Banner* 125, November 5, 1990, pp. 10–13.

———. "Liturgy, Justice, and Holiness." *The Reformed Journal* 39 (December 1989): 12–22.

———. "Liturgy, Justice, and Tears." *Worship* 62 (September 1988): 386–403.

———. "Christianity and Social Justice." *Christian Scholar's Review* 16 (March 1987): 211–28.

———. "The Bible and Economics: The Hermeneutical Issues." *Transformation* 4 (1987): 11–19.

———. "The Wounds of God: Calvin's Theology of Social Justice." *The Reformed Journal* 37 (1987): 14–22.

———. "Why Pursue Justice?" *The Reformed Journal* 36 (August 1986): 9–14.

———. *Until Justice and Peace Embrace.* Grand Rapids, Mich.: Eerdmans, 1983.

———. "Contemporary Christian Views of the State." In *Where Are We Now? The State of Christian Political Reflection.* Edited by William Harper and Theodore Malloch. Washington, D.C.: University Press of America, 1981.

———. "How Does Grand Rapids Reply to Washington?" *The Reformed Journal* 27 (October 1977): 10.

————. *Reason within the Bounds of Religion.* Grand Rapids, Mich.: Eerdmans, 1976.

————. "Religion in the Public Schools." In *Encyclopedia of Education,* vol. 7. Edited by Lee C. Deighton. New York: Macmillan Company, 1971.

————. "Neutrality and Impartiality." In *Religion and Public Education.* Edited by Theodore Sizer. Boston: Houghton Mifflin, 1967.

Wong, David. "On Flourishing and Finding One's Identity in Community." In *Ethical Theory: Character and Virtue.* Edited by Peter French, Theodore Uehling, and Howard Wettstein. Midwest Studies in Philosophy 13. Notre Dame, Ind.: University of Notre Dame Press, 1988.

Woolcock, Peter G. "The Case against Evolutionary Ethics Today." In *Biology and the Foundations of Ethics.* Edited by Jane Maienschein and Michael Ruse. Cambridge: Cambridge University Press, 1999.

Yoder, John Howard. *The Politics of Jesus.* Grand Rapids, Mich.: Eerdmans 1972.

INDEX OF NAMES

I wish to thank Benjamin Fradette for his help creating the indexes.

INDEX OF SUBJECTS